...ical Acclaim for Isabel Losada

...attersea Park Road to Enlightenment

... delight ... Isabel Losada navigates her way through the
...c highways and byways of the new age and human
... movement with scepticism, humour and
...ive open-mindedness. Candid, thought-provoking,
... very very funny.

Mick Brown, The Daily Telegraph

...ll of a crazy joy ... made me laugh out loud.

Impact Cultural Magazine

...umorous and refreshing.

The Canberra Times

...rt-warming and extraordinary ... Losada writes
...eptively and with humour.

Wanderlust Magazine

...t, With Love: A Beginner's Guide to
...g the World

...d must be changed ... Isabel's story brings this truism
... a vivid, funny, heart-warming, delightful way. It is a
..., a live teaching! I enjoyed it, laughed and learned

...or Robert Thurman, Tibetologist and Buddhist Scholar,
Columbia University, New York

About the Author

Isabel Losada has worked as an actress, singer, broadcaster and full-time single parent. She is the author of *New Habits* (which investigates why a woman would want to become a nun), *The Battersea Park Road to Enlightenment* (an exploration of happiness that has now sold over 100,000 copies), *For Tibet, With Love: A Beginner's Guide to Changing the World* (about how one person can make a difference), *Men!* (which explores the sociological phenomenon of the surplus of single women in major cities), *100 Reasons to Be Glad* (a gift book about gratitude) and this book in your hand. Isabel remains firmly committed to narrative nonfiction and swimming against the tide. She really does live on the Battersea Park Road.

The
Battersea Park
Road to Paradise

Five adventures in doing and being

Isabel Losada

WATKINS PUBLISHING
LONDON

This edition published in the UK 2011 by
Watkins Publishing, Sixth Floor, Castle House,
75–76 Wells Street, London W1T 3QH

1 3 5 7 9 10 8 6 4 2

Designed and typeset by Jerry Goldie

Printed and bound by Imago in China

British Library Cataloguing-in-Publication Data Available

ISBN: 978-1-907486-39-5

www.watkinspublishing.co.uk

ACKNOWLEDGEMENTS

All the people in this book are real. In rare cases I have changed someone's name to protect his or her identity, but most appear as themselves, so I would like to thank everyone who is mentioned in these pages and has played a part.

Special thanks are due to Sylvia Bennett, Eddie Lui, Simon Brown, the consultant whose name I don't mention here whose intention I assume was positive, and the Feng Shui Society. From the Anthony Robbins course I'd like to thank again everyone mentioned and Anthony for being so inspirational.

For sending me to Vipassana and warning me what I was letting myself in for, I'd like to thank Thomas, Dale and Alison Key. Thank you to Jo for being sane, Frances Barnes for your patience, Christine for your good nature and Star for enjoying the sparrows. Also Helen, wherever you are – thank you.

I am honoured to thank Mooji for his love and tolerance of my foolishness, and to thank all those who attend his Satsangs for their warm and loving welcome and for mistakenly thinking I had always been there. Thank you especially to Hannah for the invitation.

I would not have found the Ashaninka without the help of Amanda Shakespeare, Hylton and Noo Murray-Philipson. Thank you especially to Dilwyn for being my friend. Please stop smoking.

I could not have gone to Peru or to New York to meet my editor without my guardian angels JJM and CM.

In the publishing world, I am very grateful to Jon Elek, who made this possible by believing in me at a moment when it seemed that no-one else did, and to Michael Mann, my publisher, because I loved him from our first phone call. My editor (and now friend) Anne Barthel made editing this book a joy and every edit a pleasure to receive. She it was who knew that Jesus was not recorded as saying 'Know thyself' anywhere in the canonical Gospels and that we ought instead to attribute the quote to the temple at Delphi. I have to tell this story here as I'm still gasping with awe. Vicky Hartley, Anna Randall, Penny Stopa and Roger Walton have shown me what a pleasure it can be to be well published. Thank you, Watkins, for all your enthusiasm and hard work.

Closer to home I'd like to thank Emily Lucienne and Gala Riani who support me every day and who know how to love without conditions and with eternal patience.

Finally, I'd like to thank that that core bunch of loyal readers; CK and Julie, whose kindness in inexplicable; and every single reader, especially those on my Facebook page who offer words of encouragement, write reviews and buy copies of my books for everyone they know. Your loyalty, wisdom and generous friend-liness make my job a joy. You are too many to list by name – but if you are reading this then you are undoubtedly one of them. Thank you.

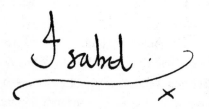

CONTENTS

The Preamble – Stuck Again

Feeling stuck? Yes, me too. I'm in a pothole on the road to enlightenment. You wouldn't have thought a pothole would be deep enough to get stuck in, would you? But I've managed to get totally wedged in. I'm battered, befuddled and too bruised to budge myself. And I get run over on a regular basis.

It would be lovely, I reflect as I sit in my hole, if I thought that anyone was going to come and pull me out; if any human or angelic being was going to find me, direct the traffic around me and lead me home for scones and raspberry jam. But no – no-one is preparing tea. I'm in London, you know how it is in our cities, everyone is too busy dodging the traffic themselves.

It's a strange thing, life, innit? I mean, in theory I'm in one piece and some people even think I'm clever. But in practice I'm just a rather messy pile of flesh and bones, and as another ten-ton steamroller goes over me, attempting to flatten me out permanently, life certainly isn't how I'd planned it.

I suppose I should tell you a little bit about myself and the particular disasters that surround me and then you can look at your own life and decide that you're doing fabulously. By profession I make TV programmes. Except I make them the month before the channel closes or something – so nothing gets aired. And, as you know, I write books, but confused book-sellers say, 'It's about what?' and they don't know where to put them in the bookshop. It's not good. I'm all over the shop. Literally.

And men? Well, I've written a book about men – but still I mess up. I don't lack romantic courage: I'll risk everything for an affair of the heart – cross the world – and then the man will say something like, 'Actually, I'm gay,' or, 'I'm married; I know I should have mentioned it.' I have a spectacular ability to get it wrong. So much so that you have to admire the aplomb of my foolishness.

I've messed up having a family. I've no mother, father, brothers or sisters. Is this not an impressive lack of relatives? I've a daughter, but then no husband – haven't had a husband for years – but somehow, the daughter, Emily, is totally sorted. It's just her mother who is a walking disaster. I set out to be happy and successful with an exciting and sensual relationship and a worthwhile job that makes a genuine contribution to the world and it's all gone wrong.

So why would you want to buy a book written by someone who is a disaster? Good question. Well, I put my case in the important decision of whether to part with the cover price as follows: I'm not alone. We have an international recession; many people's pay has been cut in half, if we have jobs at all. And I recently heard that the divorce rate is no longer one in three; now it's 50 per cent. So I'm hoping it may be OK that everything has gone horribly wrong because it forces me to strip life down to the bare essentials and start again.

The ancient Chinese are known to have had lots of clever theories about life and one of them is of particular interest to me down here in my hole. When they broke life down into its basic elements, they found metal, fire, wood, water and earth. This seems like a pleasing place to start. Why the five elements, you ask? Well, they appeal to my senses, and they are part of the natural world. They are the elements of life itself rather than the made-up, artificial experience of living in our cities. They are beautiful and intuitive and I'm not sure if they stand up to intellectual and academic scrutiny. And I kinda like that.

Using these elements, I invite you to join me on my journey to re-create. I want to consider where I would like to live, how I would like to live, what matters and what doesn't matter, what I can sort out and what I can't. I'd like to discover when we need 'to do' and when we desperately need to stop doing and just 'to be' and how we can get the balance right between those two. I need to decide what beliefs I'd like to throw out of this hole that I find myself in and what I'd like to keep.

In order to save us some time, I'm going to admit to knowing nothing at all. Everything I've learned so far can go. The brain of your narrator is filled with ideas and beliefs that are mostly philosophically dubious, logically questionable and theologically unsound. I know too little about too much and too much about too little – all at the same time. I suspect that everything I've ever learnt should be composted. So I'm throwing it all out. Except one idea I'd like to keep.

His Holiness the XIV Dalai Lama of Tibet has been thoughtful enough, on our behalf, to have spent his entire lifetime studying 2,500 years of Buddhist teachings. I think it is reasonable to assume that he has given the subject of life some thought. Anyway – bothered by a world of people who were having trouble grasping one of the most obscure belief systems in the world, he woke up one morning and invented a catchy little soundbite. I'm sure you know the one.

'My religion ... ' he announced with his usual grin to the assembled world press, 'is kindness.' No questions followed. No questions need to follow. Can't argue with it, can you? So there it is ... I'll throw away everything else I know. I'll keep that teaching, but apart from that I shall adopt what is known as a 'Beginner's Mind'. To get out of this hole whole, this is the only possibility – let's start again.

So please join me. Breathe deeply. And I hope you enjoy the journey.

The First Element –
Metal

*The exterior – guardianship –
boundaries – skin – the nose*

Three Feng Shui Consultations
and Much Confusion

Ah! You're here. Welcome. I'm very glad that you've decided to join me. The journey is twice as much fun with you along.

So, I've decided to start with the hole itself. And I am excited because I've already taken an action and made a phone call. On Friday of this week a Feng Shui man is coming round to examine my environment. Wise people point out to me that environment is a major influence, one I'm hoping he will be able to help. He has asked for the date and place of my birth, although what this has to do with my house I have no idea, and he's going to come over to sort out my life for me. Isn't the idea utterly irresistible? Unemployed? Sick? Divorced and without a lover? No money in the bank? Children rowing? Well, maybe it's your house that's causing these problems.

What I so love about this discipline is the possibility that things can get better in my life with no effort of mine. Someone will come to my house and, by moving a mirror three inches to the left, reflect a new and valuable friendship into my life. Through the placing of a small wooden toad with a coin in his mouth in a corner of my house (which in some mystical way relates to wealth), money will start to appear, effortlessly, in my bank account. By altering the angle of my bed I will be healthier; no need to go running in Battersea Park. It's just become the year of the rat, apparently: an auspicious time to start a whole new life.

Do I sound a tiny bit sceptical? Do I sound like a member of the Royal College of Surgeons giving his thoughts on homeopathy? Or like the Chinese Government? According to them, Feng Shui, like Tibetan Buddhism, is a 'dangerous medieval superstition'. This endears it to me immediately. Many intellectuals would agree with the official Chinese stance; they argue that Feng Shui's mere existence is something that holds back the progress of mankind by denying the supreme importance of logical and scientific deduction. I'm not sure I could even admit to one friend in New York, a paid-up member of The Sceptics Society, about my Friday visitor without endangering our friendship. She would think me so mentally flaky that the respect she has for me would drain away. The thing is, I'm perfectly aware that I'm not being intellectually rigorous – and I'm still excited.

If I am really to be without beliefs, apart from that one simple belief in kindness, then it figures that I should also be without prejudices. It's exciting to be starting anew.

❖

The words *Feng* and *Shui* mean, respectively, 'wind' and 'water'. This may seem academic, but you and I are pretty well air and water ourselves. The energetic magnetism of the moon influences the tides and has been said to have an influence on animal behaviour and women's menstrual cycles. Admissions to casualty, the crime rate, and incidents of distress in mental health wards all rise significantly at the full moon. We are an energy field in which air and water play a vital role, and the theory is, in some subtle way that the Feng Shui books are unable to get too precise about, the energy in our homes, called ch'i, also interacts with us either positively or negatively. Is there really a subtle energy called ch'i moving around my house? If there is, whatever it is, what are the various factors that may influence it?

Different types of ch'i energy are analogous to metal, fire, wood, water and earth. And I'll be considering them all in different ways as I attempt to get out of the hole. If you like, you can use them as a way of looking at your own life. Whether these elements are any more than metaphors I'm not sure. The energy around a fountain or in a bathroom has a quality more like water than the energy around plants or in a fireplace. Plants, according to Feng Shui, produce a wood-like energy because they grow. It figures that to have a growing and flourishing type of energy around your office is a good idea, but how pots, pans and filing cabinets produce a 'metal energy' in the room I really have no idea. Metal, apparently, relates to our environment – the place where we live and what it does or does not do for us. Think of gold, silver, bronze, lead and tin. Ponder (in a sensuous kind of way) the qualities of metal objects. What do you love about them? Shiny and strong? It represents the exterior, protection and boundaries, so that is why we are starting here.

Would you like an exclusive guided tour of the home in question? Please consider your own home as you tour mine and then we can both benefit. I suppose there is no such thing as a 'typical' place of residence unless you live in a building that is the shape of a child's drawing, with one father, one mother, two children and preferably a dog, a cat and some fish. Very few people I know live like this and it's certainly not the setup here.

Visualize a row of Victorian terraced houses. Some clever dude bought a street, knocked the houses into upstairs and downstairs flats, which have two floors each, put the doors at the back, and knocked down the garden fences so there is one large garden. It's horribly noisy on the north road side and unusually pretty on the south garden side. At the end of the row is a gate to the back garden, so that you walk through the garden to reach the properties.

My flat is one of the lower ones, on the ground floor and the 'lower ground floor' (not as low as a basement, according to estate agents, ha ha). So we're a flat on two floors. You step into a hall with the kitchen immediately on your left and a little corridor to the main working and living area on your right. The 'lower ground floor' has the bathroom and three bedrooms. I may not explain to the Feng Shui man that out of the three bedrooms, the largest, which in theory should be mine, is inhabited by Simon the lodger, who, when he's in the house, is constantly studying. The other double room, which has a single bed, a desk and usually a cat asleep somewhere, is my daughter's room. The third bedroom is so small that the double bed almost touches the walls on both sides. This is my room.

The windows in my room and Simon's can't be opened because a miasma of toxic, metallic-smelling fumes would blow in to poison us. My daughter, Emily, has the south-facing room with opening window and view of the garden. She has been given this luxury because it doubles as an office for her. Emily is just starting a career as an actress; may all the angels protect her. This week she is away in Estonia making a film, so she will return to find a list of suggested changes to the décor of her room to assist her career, relationships and income. I shall watch with interest to see whether she will change anything. The final room downstairs at the end of the corridor is a bathroom that also has the loo in it. The Feng Shui books tell me that you should keep the bathroom door closed and the lid to the loo down to stop all the good energy gathered in the house from going down the plug. Really.

So now we go back upstairs and I offer you some posh tea, grind some coffee beans or find you some weird herbal concoction, as you prefer. You are shown into the main upstairs area that is my living and writing room. It's a large space that goes from the front to the back of the house, with wooden floors and windows at each end. The first thing you may notice is a nine-foot-high weeping fig; it's very healthy-looking and takes up most of the bay window on the north side of the room. There is a small, old-fashioned suite, ripped on the arms by generations of cats, and a pretty Russian upright piano on the eastern wall.

'What on earth is Feng Shui anyway?' you may well ask as we consider the impact of our surroundings upon us and you try to sit down among the sundry Feng Shui books that are taking up all the space on the sofa.

I shall answer your question obligingly and knowledgeably based on my extensive one week of research. I hope you are easily impressed.

The books seem to be partly nonsense, partly common sense and partly mystical in ways that I am keen not to dismiss before exploring them. I know I said that I'd start from knowing nothing at all, but I'm not about to hang a picture of my late grandfather, whom I never met, in my 'ancestor's corner', believing that this will please him and he'll pull some career strings for me. If he is up there somewhere, I'm sure he may have better things to occupy him – like reincarnating or something – rather than staying dead to worry about his descendants. So, no ancestor worship for me.

But the common-sense bits I love. If you have broken objects in your home, they use up your physical energy every time you use them and your emotional energy every time you see them. Eventually you may not even be aware of them, but they are still jobs that need doing, nagging away at you when you glance at them; seeing lots of objects like that on a regular basis tires you out. That much is logical, right? So don't have jobs around you that constantly need doing. Do them and then live in an environment that doesn't subtly use up your energy every day. I can understand that. But it's the third, intangible aspect – neither the highly dubious nor the common-sense – that I'm fascinated by and can't pin down.

While I'm chatting with you I feel suddenly conscious of the room. One window ledge has a collection of brightly coloured wooden toys left over from my daughter's first five years and fun for visiting toddlers. But now that I look at them again and ask myself what they make me feel, the answer is, rather sad. They are remnants of a time passed, slowly fading in the sunshine. The little old sofa you are sat on, the armchair and nursing chair: I inherited them from loved ones now dead. I have a large fireplace but no fire. Recently I stayed with friends in Devon who have a real fireplace – it was like living in a home with a heart. Whereas a fireplace without a fire? Not very comforting, is it? I've tried to get rid of things rather than acquire them, but now I look around me I wonder why I couldn't at least have a real fire and chairs that don't remind me of dead people.

There are lots of different types of energy in my home. I can understand that much. There is one form of energy here that allows me to connect my laptop to the www without a wire – it's here even though I can't see it or touch it. I could also argue that love, a different type of energy, is here in some sense. This love has created, on a table, courtesy of my friend Helen, two seemingly energetic vases of red tulips. The tulips themselves have a vibrant colour and celebratory impact on the room; just don't ask me to define it or ask whether the tulips have their own energy or whether the celebration is just in my head. And so it is that we are influenced every day by what is around us. Some of this we are aware of and some of the vibes we just don't notice.

What else to point out to you? At the southern end of the room where my desk is, there is a view of the garden. This must surely be good? But you may well point out that when I look up from my computer I don't look at the garden; I see a notice-board full of demanding pieces of paper: 'Pay me', 'Post me', 'I'm a jobs list. Read me'. There's even a cryptic message that I've written myself that reads 'A+B=C'. I have no idea what it means. Smiling at you, I take them all down and put up a range of bright, colourful images that I love – cards from friends and a rather lovely postcard of a monk on a bicycle whizzing past a traffic jam of businessmen in BMWs. No delays for him on the road to enlightenment. I think you'd approve.

The books are all on the floor-to-ceiling shelves on the left of the fireplace – I make regular trips to my local charity shop with books. The TV? That's that tiny thing in the corner. It's one of the things that don't work properly. I switch it on about twice a year. That huge oil painting above the fireplace of a woman embracing the world? Emily painted it and the figure has so much tenderness she has been given the central hanging place. Of course this is what Emily and I both try to do; look after the world and everyone in it. Tenderness is a strange job, I know. A bit like kindness, only with more affection, but isn't that what the world needs? I digress. Speaking of kindness, you may also notice the photo of your narrator shaking hands with the Dalai

Lama on another wall ... well, I interviewed him once and I'm allowed to be proud, right? Who wouldn't be?

Anyway – I hope you are now not only fully aware of where I am but also a bit more conscious of where you are. And that's it. That's the tour and this is the place from which I'm now writing to you.

As far as I know, the health of the three occupants of the house is good. We live in peace and harmony 98 per cent of the time but we're not the company that any of us would choose if we started from scratch. I'd like to be living with a man I fell in love with, but I'm not going to mention him or readers of my last book will start sending e-mails. (And if you didn't read *Men!*, let's just say that it was a real-life true love story.) Emily would like to be living in Paris, but her career is here, and I'm sure Simon must wonder why on earth he chose to live with us. We are all nice to each other. It's just a bit stuck. Think I'll go and open the window.

I suppose that I could say a bit more about myself too ... but, well, I'm not going to. After all, if we met walking along the road, I'm sure you wouldn't interrogate me – you'd be happy, would you not, to get to know me as we walked along? It's more fun like that, I think. And anyway, spare a thought for those readers who have read my previous books and already know far more about me than is necessary to explore the places we are visiting. All will become clear. I promise. So let's skip any more introduction and just get on with the narrative, shall we?

First Feng Shui Man (Dubious)

I can't tell you who he is or what he looks like – for reasons that will become apparent. He may be in his 60s, some may consider him stocky, and one may surmise that he doesn't spend huge amounts of money at a hairdresser. On the other hand, one may be wrong – I really couldn't say. He gets out his very posh Chinese Feng Shui compass, called a lopan, and confirms that my front door is east-facing. And that I am an 8:6, 'shorthand for a combination of stem and branch' – whatever that means.

Then he sits down and starts to explain my Ba Zi, my life according to his interpretation of the significance of my birth dates. The 'Book of Changes', he informs me, divides time into 60-year cycles with 60 pairs of characters, with a pair for each year and a pair for each stem of the compass. We are in the Eighth Fate, apparently, this fate having started in 1996 and ending in 2016. Am I losing you? Yes, me too. He speaks with lots of jargon that I don't stand a rat's chance of understanding, and I say so. His explanation: 'This is information that you can be humble enough to get that you don't understand.' Fair enough. I understand so little of anything – that's not hard.

Having established that I know nothing, he pronounces, 'I know what your big fate is, that is, the moment when your fate is decided. Yours came early, at about two years eight months – maybe the birth of a sibling?' Having no siblings, I shut up. 'This meeting is a year late; I should have been here a year ago. Last year can't have been an easy year for you?'

I keep quiet and listen – not because I want to test him but because I want to find out what the Ba Zi can tell him about me that may be accurate, if anything. 'Last year,' he goes on, 'you had everything given and everything taken away – the blessings of heaven.'

This much is true – I had been given my heart's greatest desire (man that I'm not mentioning) and my dream job and then I lost them both through circumstances over which I had no control. But then haven't we all lost people, jobs and projects we dearly wanted?

'How can I have everything taken away and the blessings of heaven at the same time?'

'Don't ask me, I'm just reading the zodiac.'

I smile at him. No-one ever said that interpretation of the movements of the stars is a precise science. But I don't believe in making assumptions about people based on when they were born. I'd asked for Feng Shui on the house, not on me.

'Fu Gong' – he points at something in the Ba Zi – 'makes you a risk-taker who could be a millionaire or go to jail. You are someone who pushes the boat out. Ma Yuk means that your parents probably didn't stay together. Your father was probably a bit of an adventurer and felt justified in that.'

Did you ever meet a man who was 'an adventurer' who didn't feel justified in his actions? As for me being a risk-taker? Well, yes ...

'The Ma Yuk pattern of your father repeats in this pillar, so you have probably had difficulties with wandering men.' If you are a female reader who has not at any time in your life had difficulty with a wandering man, please write to me. I would be reassured to hear your story.

'Do you have a sister?'

'You tell me.'

'There is something here that speaks of a competitive aspect between women.'

I think I'm supposed to be saying, 'Oh, yes.' But I don't want to tell him my stories prompted by generalizations, so I keep quiet. I could tell him that I have a sisterly relationship with my daughter; it's not that I don't want to help, just that I don't see what this has to do with my house.

There's a pause, then he says, 'It helps if you can feed back if any of this is accurate.'

Gently I try to re-focus him. 'I was really hoping that you'd look around the flat. I'm interested in knowing your impressions of the energy here.'

He looks up at the main work room. 'This tells me that you have father issues. A piece of the room missing in the northeast speaks of issues with learning, authority and discipline. I see an uneasy combination of spiritual and intellectual, which I think describes you.'

'Really? Uneasy?' I'm pretty sure I'm aware what my 'issues' are, or were before I threw them out of the hole, but this was never one of them. 'I wouldn't say it was uneasy. My intellect has always had a peaceful interest in spiritual matters.'

'An uneasy relationship between intellect and feelings, then. I'm just giving my impressions.'

As I often write about my feelings and I was an actress for ten years, I'm also confident that I know how to express them. Sometimes I surprise people because if they ask, 'How are you?'

instead of saying 'finethanksow'reyou?' I'll say, 'Sad. How are you?' On the other hand, I'm presenting him with my intellect and not asking him for help with my feelings because I'm really interested to hear what he has to say about the house.

'You scare the hell out of me,' he says suddenly.

This is not my intention. 'Really? I'm sorry.'

'You don't need to be sorry – I'm telling you how I feel.'

'Can I reassure you that I really want to learn about Feng Shui and you have no need to feel nervous?'

'No. I'm telling you how I feel. You don't need to heal me, correct me or make me better, that's the bloke's job.'

What would you say to this? I don't know what to say. He goes on. 'If you receive how I feel, we'd be a little bit closer. I'm just telling you that I feel threatened.'

'But I'm not allowed to respond or do anything about it?'

'You can do what you like. I'm just telling you.'

But before I have time to respond in any way, he says, 'That tree would be better in that corner. You are missing wood in the southeast. A ying tree there would bring healing, thoroughness.'

'OK, then let's move it.' I smile. I'm willing to try new things. Maybe he's thrown because during the Ba Zi reading I didn't tell him my life story, I just listened, so he still doesn't know anything about me. We move the tree, which is far too big for that end of the room. He moves the sofa into the northern bay window and the armchair into the northeast 'father corner', leaving the centre of the room empty apart from the small nursing chair, which is now lost in the middle of the space. I quite like the arrangement for a yoga class, as my floor is now totally clear, but ten feet between the chairs isn't exactly likely to encourage intimate conversation when friends come over. He walks off into the kitchen. I follow him.

'The kitchen in this position suggests that you are not keen to be a traditional woman and mother but that you feel constrained to do so. Some people would call this the relationships area, but I wouldn't. Having metal in an earth position speaks of a protective relationship with men. This kitchen is in a very poor position. I could do all the calculations but then I'd disappear for about two and a half hours and I don't have time for that today.'

Metal in an earth position? A traditional woman? What is he talking about?

'So are you saying that the kitchen causes the issues or that the issues cause the kitchen?'

'I'd give up on the idea of causality all together.'

Instead, I give up on the idea of understanding him and I pick out something that could easily be changed. 'I'm interested to know your thoughts on the placement of the mirror at the top of the stairs. I've never been quite sure what it does there.'

'A mirror in the northeast is about a woman going through emotional pain.'

Oh, really? Hands up all women readers who haven't been through emotional pain of some kind. This man is very aggressive in his manner and I don't feel inclined to tell him about any emotional pain, recent or even long-gone. I say nothing.

'In the Eighth Fate, if you get the position right it's about money, but I'm not clever enough to get it right every time.'

'I thought you were going to talk to me about the subtle movement of ch'i and the way that the mirror may or may not influence the movement of energy up and down the stairs?'

'I'm saying the same thing in a different way. You have water-type ch'i in an earth-type area.'

'So the mirror is in the wrong place?' I ask, perhaps a little desperately.

'I'd have to look at it with the compass to be precise, but part of it at least will be, yes. It's about a woman soul-searching.'

Maybe I'm supposed to say, 'That's accurate – I'm soul-searching,' but I'm feeling unusually and increasingly defensive, so I ask, 'Aren't all women soul-searching?'

'You may as well say aren't all people soul-searching?'

'No. I think some men are not soul-searching,' I reply honestly. 'They are just enjoying their lives, not questioning them. My ex-husband wasn't even comfortable with the metaphor of life as a journey.'

'I think it's true that more women are soul-searching than men. Most men never grow up and basically some women don't.'

'Are you happy to be quoted on that?'

'Yes. The tape recorder is on. But I mean intensive, uncomfortable soul-searching.'

I'm unclear exactly how this relates to the mirror.

'Can I just show you the mirror we are talking about?'

But he wanders past the mirror down the stairs. 'The ch'i above the stairs there is quite nasty. I would hang something up there. A seven-pipe wind chime.'

He walks into Simon's room. 'There is stuck energy here. A certain trappedness. Unorthodox types of relationships.'

I begin to feel guilty for not telling him who is where. 'This is my lodger's room,' I admit. 'I have no relationship with him. He comes in, he studies and he leaves. He likes it here and keeps himself much to himself.'

He walks out again and goes into the large room, which I guess he must assume is mine. 'This is a blokey room.' It's Emily's room and one wall is covered with photos and necklaces on a pinboard -- really not too blokey. He's strident when he speaks: 'This is about subterranean submerged stuff, unconscious sort of behaviour. It's the undergroundness of it. Long-term habits tend to stick in places like this.'

'This is my daughter's room.'

'What's the upset?'

'What?'

'I heard upset in your voice.'

Yes, he's misrepresenting my daughter.

'In that case it's upset on my daughter's behalf. I'm not really all that happy about us coming into her space. And any upset she feels is because she'd rather be living in Paris with her boyfriend but her career is doing well in London, so she's stuck here with her mother for now.' I'd thought he was going to talk about the energy of the house, not make pronouncements on people who weren't even here. If my daughter had been in the house, she would almost certainly have shown him out of the east-facing front door by now. 'Anyway, she's away making a film. So let's go into my room, shall we?'

'This is the room of a virgin,' he says, going into my room. 'And there is certainly upset in you.' He certainly seems determined to make it so. I take a breath and talk about the room.

'I was reading in the Feng Shui books that the colours we choose often indicate unconscious choices. I have painted this room white and picked out pictures with water and sky and little bits of light blue, which I see as peaceful. What would you say about this room?'

'This room is in the father position and all the water in this room is draining the father, so this room is about a battle with the father. This room says, "Up yours, Daddy."'

I haven't told him that I never met my father, who left my mother before I was born after a passionate romance that resulted in me. He didn't marry my mother, but I don't hold it against him: he was young and stupid and I have done stupid things too. He gave me life and I was brought up by my mother and grandmother, who both adored me. I count myself very blessed.

I tell my frustrated Feng Shui man that I really don't think I'm battling with my late father. (I learned in my 30s of his death, but as I'd never met him I found it hard to be very upset.) 'So should I take the pictures of the sea down, then?'

'I can't make recommendations unless you tell me what you want.'

'Well, I'd rather not be in this room, but Simon gives me rent and we pay the bills with it.'

'So earn more money and then you won't have to have a lodger.'

Why wasn't this man advising the city banks? 'I was aiming at earning more money but then my TV series fell through.'

'That was a choice. It's all your choice.'

'Not a staff change at Channel Five, then?'

'No. Self-sabotage. It's all based on your choices.'

'Oh, so you're saying that I didn't really want something I worked for six months to create?'

'No, you've chosen not to have it or you'd have it. It's all our choices.'

'But Channel Five abandoned their arts policy and they removed the editor who had commissioned our series. Everything she commissioned was dropped, not just my series. It was nothing to do with me.'

'If you didn't get it, then it was self-sabotage.'

'Maybe Channel Five really believed that my funky series wouldn't get high enough viewing figures?' I venture to suggest.

But he's adamant. 'On some level it was choice.'

'And I chose not to be with the man that I wanted to spend the rest of my life with, too?'

'If he's not here, yes.'

'What about his choice? His constraints? His reality?'

'It's not about him.'

Sigh. I am familiar with this as a belief system. I'm sure you are too. The belief is that we choose everything. That we are responsible for everything. If we get cancer, we choose it. If I get run over, I choose it. There are many who would have me believe that I want the illness, the accident. This viewpoint may sometimes hold true on some level. I'm aware that if I get a broken heart, then I break it: I am responsible. But I also think it is more complex than that. There are other factors and other people involved. This man tells his clients that they have chosen all the misfortune in their lives? I am willing to discuss whether there are or are not limits to our personal responsibility – with friends, late at night, over great food and a bottle of wine. But what I really want now is not to be told that my belief systems are limiting my income. I want to have a Feng Shui consultation about my home.

'So what do you suggest for this room?'

'Pillar-box red. I want to see a lot of red here – on the door, the shelves maybe, and the walls. I don't do interior design. Where you put it is up to you.'

'I thought these bits of light blue were peaceful?'

'It's the bedroom of a virgin and it's draining the father.'

He keeps saying that. Is he being aggressive, dim or just plain rude? It's true that my life right now is fairly virginal, but why I would want to 'drain' a long-dead father I've never met? He seems to be trying to provoke me to anger, but I really don't feel angry with my father. I'm fairly certain that I haven't suppressed any such emotion – and I'm reasonably certain that I'm not a virgin either. I sigh and focus on the positive.

'OK – I think I'll have fun bringing in some red paint.'

'And you don't want to be facing due south.'

'But I have no choice in a room this size unless I sleep in a single bed, and I don't want to because that does make me feel like a virgin. At least with a double bed, when I meet a man I'd like to share it with, I'll have the option.'

'You have to work with what's here and you don't want to be facing south. That direction speaks of difficulties in projects. What you are describing about having things fall away relates to that position in this year. You need to change the position in which you are sleeping.'

'What about moving the bed upstairs?'

'No. You don't want to do that. You need to work from where you are. Sleep the way that I say and wait for the next move. You have to accept this. What you resist persists. In order to be redeemed, you have to admit that you have done the killing. Like in the film *Dead Man Walking*. Don't move out of the northwest. Integrate it. This is mathematical stuff.'

But he hasn't done the maths – and I still have this crazy idea from the books that we could be talking about the house. I'm starting to manifest the upset he's seeking.

'You haven't looked in the bathroom.'

'I don't do bathrooms.'

Walking back upstairs, he tells me that I need to 'work in the bedroom'. He advises me, 'The more deeply you go, the longer it will take. What you can do is take this year to do this work.'

'A year?'

'You take the months of this year. It's an earth rat year, which relates to 1973, and you need to look at the lessons that you didn't learn in 1973. Feel into it and learn what you needed to learn.'

'I can't even remember where I was in 1973.'

'It doesn't matter. You feel into it. You see, you have this lack of integration between mind and heart.'

'So if I go and get my diaries and look up where I was in 1973 in order to "feel into it", then I'm demonstrating that I'm not integrated?'

'You just sit in the father corner and say "1973" and let it happen. The real process is healing you.'

I know I'd said I'd keep an open mind, but this is just crap. 'That may be so – but this isn't Feng Shui. This feels like a form of unsolicited confrontational therapy. If I'd wanted therapy, I'd have called a qualified therapist.'

'This is very much Feng Shui. You have a 4:3 and a 3:4, which means men that won't commit and projects that don't complete.' Perfect. The only things that I have confided are now being combined with figures I can't possibly understand to prove that he's right. Presumably, if I'd told him which of his Ba Zi interpretations were closer to accurate, he'd now be using that information against me too to prove that I need his help. It's weird; because I haven't bared my soul to him, he's bullying me to do so.

He tells me again that I'm out of touch with my feelings. I want to prove I'm not. So I end up telling him of the sadness and even desolation I've been feeling as a result of the sad ending of the love story that I'm not mentioning to you. 'I met a man I wanted to spend the rest of my life with and I can't even see his face or hear his voice. And I miss him. I miss his laughter. I miss his smile.'

Tears fill my eyes. At least, I think, he can see that I have emotions and know how to communicate them. But no – he's still not happy. He tells me that the desolation is just covering a different feeling that I don't want to look at. Desolation, it seems, isn't enough for him. Question marks start to fly out of my head. Amazement between the tears.

'It's all about choice,' he tells me yet again.

I struggle to defend myself from this prolonged attack. If your husband was killed because he worked in the Twin Towers, or you lost your factory job in a worldwide recession, is this your choice? Did my friend who carried a healthy baby for nine months choose that he should be born but never breathe and be placed dead into her arms? Was this her choice? God help me I'm going to kill him and use his blood to paint my bedroom red.

'I'm dealing with this stuff every day of the week and what I'm saying to you is that you can have it differently and the process that I'm describing will take you there.'

It's about 5pm by now. He's been in my home for hours. I'm exhausted and I suspect that he is too. I'm obviously not going to be told about the subtle energies that may or may not be passing around my house and how they may be influencing a working day. He isn't going to get me to express whatever emotion he wants me to express that is deeper than desolation. I'm being bullied and I've had enough. If the 'breakthrough' that he wants is for me to admit that I'm responsible for everything, then he can stick his breakthrough somewhere unpublishable. I say good-bye very gladly and wish him well like the good Buddhist I now am (with my one belief in kindness). I wish him well but without any clients. Ever. Don't think those wishes are incompatible in any way. Do you? And that is the story of my first visit from a Feng Shui man. I really hadn't been expecting to be run over again. Dammit.

So I go out and enjoy the film *Juno* with one of my oldest friends, who listens to the story and says some not very kind things about him. Two days later I ring the Feng Shui Society. In all my years in what are generically called 'New Age' disciplines, this is the first time I have ever experienced anything that I consider, on reflection, to be malpractice. This man is no doubt genuine in his desire to make a difference for people, yet he talks lots of jargon, setting himself up as someone who under-stands more about his clients than they do, using 'proofs' from incomprehensible facets of Chinese astrology. Then – in my case – wants me to paint a tiny room bright red and spend a year sleeping in a single bed, despite the fact that I specifically said that I don't want to be in one. He wants me to work through father issues that have never troubled me, and presumably consult him when I don't find myself in touch with whatever I was doing in 1973. I am angry when I consider that he must be telling his clients, some of whom will have been through major life tragedies, that it is all their choice – and that he has the solutions.

I know that there are a lot of well-meaning people out there with some very dubious ideas, but this one turns his under-standing of Feng Shui into a kind of bullying. Logically, there are limits to our personal responsibility. People get hit by cars when they are standing on the pavement. Are they responsible for the accident? Only because they left the house that day. Was Al Gore responsible for losing his hard-fought election? Only because he had decided to stand for president. I think the American electoral system had something to do with his loss as well. So to make us 100 per cent responsible for what happens to us is to take a good principle and push it to the point of nonsensical.

I ring the Feng Shui Society and tell them all this and they listen, but he is still on their recommended list. So with this, as with doctors or teachers of any kind, be careful who you choose. However, there is a second reason I want to speak with them. I would still like a Feng Shui consultation. From a consultant who concentrates on the house. They have just the man. He's Chinese and will do a traditional Chinese consultation. I'm now looking forward to meeting him because, between what I'm reading in the books and what I didn't get from Consultant Number One, I have developed a real interest in Feng Shui.

Second Feng Shui Man (Chinese)

Eddie, from Hong Kong, is a surprise. At first he hardly speaks at all. When he does it's in that rather charming clipped manner sometimes used by Chinese speakers of English.

'Lovely,' he looks at the garden. 'I'll need to walk around the house.' He walks around without comment and then takes out a lopan compass to check the degree that I'm on.

'You are 350 degrees. Almost north.' I'm not sure what this signifies. 'There are many different schools of Feng Shui. No two consultants will agree. Terraced housing bad, as you only have energy coming in from two sides.'

'I see.'

'Detached house always better so that you can bring in energy from all sides then easy to achieve balanced life.'

'I see.'

'Fire energy comes from the south, water from the north, metal from the west and wood from east. In your case fire and water energies dominant as you having no energy entering house from east or west. This isn't good or bad. Depends on who is living there. Different energies can be manipulated. I will need fifteen minutes.'

'I see.' Why do I keep saying 'I see'?

I make him some green tea and he sits and writes on a rough sketch of a floor plan with lots of Chinese script. Apparently he's putting my birth date and my daughter's in place and working out what is best to be done. He's pulling a very serious face.

'Your element is metal. You're a weak metal. So you need more metal or something that supports metal. Earth supports metal. Earth and metal are your friends. Water and wood – you don't want. Fire is fifty-fifty for you. It depends on whether you can use it or not.' He makes a note on the floor plan and frowns. 'Your bedroom is in the north. This is not ideal for you. You like sleeping on the floor?'

Following the visit of Feng Shui Man One, I have removed the bed base and put the mattress on the floor so that I can sleep in any direction.

'You are sleeping in the best position in a no-good room. You should put a small table lamp between your bed and the northern door. Keep the lamp on as much as possible. If you want to not use too much energy, choose a low-voltage lamp.

This will strengthen your chance in relationship area because fire is your man.'

Fire is my man? 'What? Why?'

'Because you are metal.' Of course. What? 'Fire is one of the criteria for you. By making use of fire energy it will increase your chance to meet someone good for you.'

'So why does putting a lamp there help?'

'You see better. Lamp echoes fire that comes from south, so it brings fire energy through into your bedroom.'

'Of course.' Do lamp manufacturers know this stuff? 'Er, well, a bedside lamp will be lovely there anyway.' Don't know why I haven't ever bought myself one.

'Your daughter is weak earth. She has a lot of water from the day of her birth. She is in the best room for her. For the rest of her life she should always choose a south-facing bedroom and she should have a suntan. No north-facing rooms for her.'

'I see. What about the position of her bed?'

'Yes. It is good. You need to be able to see the door, and head to the south for her is good. When she moves out you should move back into that room.'

'I see.'

'Normally we don't recommend the kitchen in the south. It's not a good place for a kitchen. But nothing that you can do about it. Put five stones on ceramic bowl in the south side of kitchen. Stones drain fire.'

I've been gathering stones about me for many years. Stealing them from beaches and carrying them home. Didn't know they were draining fire. He goes on, 'In the twenty-four-mountain system your home is an earth mountain. This energy is weak, so not good for a business growth, but OK for sleeping.'

'But my daughter, my lodger and I all work from home.'

'Never mind. Nothing you can do about it.'

'You don't have any Feng Shui cures, then?'

'No. The direction of your home better for retirement home or for temple. For growth you want to face north, south, east or west directly.'

'I see. Not at 350 degrees?'

'No. Also you have toilet and bathroom in the south, and fire and water don't mix, so not ideal place for a bathroom either.'

So my problems could be blamed on the house after all?

'Anything I can do about the bathroom then?'

'You can put more plants in there. Also Emily should have earth energy on her window sill. Something in yellow, terracotta, brown or beige. Bright curtain in purple, pink, lilac or orange to attract the fire energy. Also your doormat should be a fire colour.'

I struggle not to say *I see*. 'OK. Yes. A fire colour.'

'You want to support and reinforce earth and metal.'

'I notice that I have light blue in my bedroom.' I've already taken a lot out in case my father's ghost was feeling inexplicably drained. 'Do you have any comments on that?'

'Light blue is water. You don't want water in there at all.'

'I have been told that my choice of light blue means that I'm trying to drain the father.'

'I would not interpret it that way. I may say looking at your Ba Zi that you don't get much help from your father.'

I laugh. 'That would be one hundred per cent accurate. What

about the business of putting two mandarin ducks or a pair of whatevers in the relationship corner? Do you have any comment on that sort of practice, Eddie?'

'Difficult as no Feng Shui perfect. Change every year. So depend on whether you choose based on Ba Zi, the direction of the house, the animal sign or energy of year. If all four come together you lucky but more often you have to choose. Personally I wouldn't use anything that would upset relationship element of your Ba Zi.'

'So what can I do to support it?'

'I told you. Buy a lamp.'

'Of course ... buy a lamp.' He had told me. 'Can you explain, Eddie, how the different things in the house that are actually made of wood, or metal, relate to the different elements that you are trying to attract? For example, Emily and I actually bought a sheet of metal art as decoration and hung it on the kitchen wall.'

'A piece of metal definitely increases metal, but compared to energy coming in through door it's minimal. So not something you worry about a lot. If you don't like wood, can you choose to get rid of all wood in your house? No.'

'You could, I suppose . . .'

'But compared to what is coming through window and door from universe, influence very small. If you are asking do they have any significance? Of course they have. But minimal. Be careful when moving furniture to change environment. May not be significant. Only a small portion. Not significant enough to worry about.'

'This house not bad for you. You have fire coming in. Fire will support your earth; earth will support your metal. If you want to redecorate your room, earth and metal colours are good for you.'

Earth colours? Not red?

'Remind me again – earth colours?'

'Brown, beige, terracotta, yellow are all earthy colours. Metal colours silver and copper – colours of metal.'

'I thought white was a metal colour?'

'White not strong metal; in between.'

'So I should take out of my room the image of the sea?'

'You don't want water there.'

Well – at least he and Feng Shui Man One agree on something.

'You aren't going to say anything about the direction any of my furniture is in?'

'Don't need to. More important – energy coming in.'

Really? He really thinks this?

'So you are telling me, Eddie, that the energy coming into my house is of a different quality because my windows open to the south? If I had west-facing windows they would bring in different energy?'

I have asked a question so absurdly naïve it's almost laughable. He's being polite and tolerating me, as one would a flat-earther.

'If you face there – east. If you face there – west.' He stands up to demonstrate. 'This north. This south. Of course different.'

Subtext: isn't this obvious?

'Well, Eddie, you are laughing at me, but you must appreciate that many people would say that it's just air whichever way you are facing?'

'That's very true.'

Subtext: many people are ignorant.

'These four directions basis of Feng Shui, so what I've said to you based on four directions.'

Mmmm. 'The last practitioner seemed to base everything on the Ba Zi.'

'I used your Ba Zi. That's how I worked out all this. But maybe his Ba Zi different to my Ba Zi. I'd like to know what he said.'

'He seemed to be interested mainly in my relationship with my father and, er – well, he told me that the reason I had chosen water-type colours in my bedroom was because I wanted to say, "Fuck you, Daddy."'

Eddie laughs. 'Based on Ba Zi your father element not your favourable element. I would interpret differently. I would say maybe you don't get help from father. Two people can look at same Ba Zi and interpret differently. Not supported by father. Whether you hate him another matter.'

So I'm not supported by my father partly because of my birth date and partly because of the shape of my house? Is it any wonder I'm confused?

'I suggested a table lamp next to bed. That is suggested solution.'

'Is there anything else I need to know, then?'

'I don't think so.'

'OK. Thank you, Eddie.'

And off he potters.

Eddie has been pleasant and polite but ... put five stones in a ceramic dish in the south side of the kitchen, put earth colours in my bedroom and on Emily's window ledge, and buy a lamp? There is so much more to Feng Shui. This is just dusting. Where is the fresh understanding that I'm seeking? I'm in a slough of disappointment about it all until Helen, the girlfriend who sent the energetic red tulips, calls.

'You sound unusually glum.'

'I'm trying to learn about Feng Shui. I've had two men in and I'm more confused than I was when I was just reading the books myself. Now I know exactly where my house is in relation to north and where I should hang wind chimes, but the two consultants only agree that I shouldn't have blue in my bedroom. What kind of a discipline is this?'

'What's the point of hanging wind chimes indoors where they never get blown by the wind?'

'I've often wondered that.'

'I tell you what you've done wrong.'

'Mmm?'

'Try calling a woman.'

Third Feng Shui Man (Female)

This piece of experiential research is not intending to express a preference for a female practitioner. This is just how it worked out. I ring back the Feng Shui Society and this time I speak to a lady called Sylvia Bennett: the boss. I relay my tale of woe and mirrors hung to be indicative of emotional pain, light blues pissing off my long-dead father, and the cryptic assertion that, although I obviously need a lamp, fire is my man. 'The worst part of it is,' I tell her, 'I want my enthusiasm back.' I'm developing a genuine interest in the principles of Feng Shui. She offers to come herself to redeem both my house and my faith in her discipline.

So a week later I am once again tidying up in anticipation of a Feng Shui consultation. This will be the last time. I have been asked to make a scale floor plan of the property and spent last night pacing around with rulers, working out where my walls and doors were. She'd asked for my birth date and time, Emily's birth date and time, the date when the house was originally built, when it was converted, and when I'd moved in. My beginner's mind is rebelling. It feels like hocus-pocus.

Sylvia arrives at 10.30 in the morning and starts with a careful look around the garden outside the house. While she looks at the garden, I look at her. She's wearing trousers with a loose-fitting jacket, with a no-nonsense 'there-ain't-no-flies-on-me' manner; in her 40s, a long-haired brunette with attentive eyes, she looks at the environment as if she can see more than most of us can. I look at the garden she's looking at so carefully. As it's communal, I have no control over the layout, so I'm happy to hear how the ch'i apparently gathers well in the centre and flows around.

'Imagine the energy like invisible smoke,' Sylvia explains. 'If there was smoke in this garden it would be prevented from coming into your house by this hedge. You can see that it would hit this hedge and splay out sideways, not entering your house or this neighbour's.'

'Yes, I see that.'

'The ch'i that does enter is from the south and the east – your door faces east but the general aspect is south.'

She holds up her lopan – at least all three of them used one of these. She peers in all the directions and back at the compass and then instead of saying something incomprehensible she looks at the plants. 'It would help you a lot to consider the energy coming in. Plants can provide vitality but this one's blocking the ch'i and the light.'

I look at the huge, rather mangy shrub that she is referring to and realize that I've never actually liked it. I just tolerate it because it's there.

'I could take it out altogether,' I suggest, surprised to hear myself pronouncing a death sentence while standing within earshot of the plant.

'I think that would be a good idea. Then you could put up a trellis and have some flowering jasmine growing up this corner. It would look beautiful and the perfume would be lovely every time you come in and out. You could do with some more colour. Just buy something very cheap in little pots to provide energy and vitality.' I look at the neglected entrance – there's an ugly red bucket that I use for composting and a watering can with a broken spout. Yes, some vitality seems called for.

'When was the last time you bought a new doormat?' Ah – the doormat that should be red.

Sylvia looks at everything as she steps into the house.

'The entrance is important. I'd like you to see if you can make this entrance much more inviting. Maybe pictures of some bright flowers? The light doesn't work, Isabel. It's very important to have hallways well lit.'

'Yes, that's logical. I'll fix it.' No need to tell her how many visitors have nearly killed themselves manoeuvring the lightless stairs at night.

She comes into the living area, spreads the floor plan on the table, draws lines on it and checks her work by making some sort of calculation. 'Different masters would take a different stance on the east-south double aspect. I've trained with four masters, so I use what works, having tried their different approaches for fifteen years.'

'I read that if someone has a neighbour who is sending bad vibes, you can put up a mirror to send whatever energy they give out straight back?'

'Yes, but what we usually advise is that you tilt the mirror upwards so that any bad energy is bounced straight off the mirror and up into the heavens, where it dissipates. I had a client with a neighbour who was always coming round with problems, to the point where she felt under siege, so she took a normal handbag mirror and placed it inside her porch to reflect that neighbour's house but also tilted it towards the sky. The neighbour never visited again.'

Mmmm. Sceptical? However, I do have a neighbour ... I wish this person no harm, but the energy coming from his house to mine is not always entirely positive. It's nonsense, I'm sure, but I like the idea of bouncing vibes back at him and sending those skywards so they dissipate like so much hot air. I like the idea even if it's nonsense.

'You can get different results again with concave and convex mirrors – the physics is quite complex ... But for the problems that most people describe, a normal hand mirror will do the job. You can also protect yourself from energy coming through walls from unhappy neighbours by putting pocket-sized mirrors on the backs of pictures. Of course, this isn't aggressive, because if the energy that is coming towards you is positive, you reflect that back – so it's an example of instant karma. You are sending back to others exactly what they are wishing for you.'

I remind myself, I have a beginner's mind.

'You could put some begonias in there with the geraniums. White would be good there.'

'Plants are so expensive.' Am I making excuses?

'You can spend five pounds on some cheap begonias. You want the cascading type: they'll fill up those pots beautifully; they don't mind the droughts or the downpours either. You can afford five pounds. The outside of the house is important.'

Just as I'm thinking how marvellously practical she is, she starts to talk inexplicable Feng Shui language. 'Time is in cycles of twenty years. Different masters work in different ways, but this is the time period of eight.'

Ye-es? And?

'Every twenty years is a new time cycle and there are nine of those in a one-hundred-eighty-year cycle. In 2004 we moved into a new cycle.'

I listen patiently for the punch line. There isn't one. She

smiles and says, 'The potential of the house is good. The incoming and most propitious ch'i is coming into the career area. You need water inside the house, and you need the ch'i worked on, as it's all a bit old. It's do-able.'

She opens a notebook. 'Now, I'd like to ask you some questions, OK?'

Is she about to ask about my earliest memories based on a Chinese reading of my stars? I so hope not.

'I'd like to ask you four questions. One: what do you want from this consultation? How would you like Feng Shui to help you?'

What an excellent question.

'Two: what are your problems living here? If any?'

I'm very grateful for the 'if any.' She isn't assuming that I and the house are utterly broken – a hopeless space or a hopeless person.

'OK.'

'Three: what are your desires for yourself in this place? Four: how do you feel in your living space?'

I'm very happy with these questions.

'So you're not going to be consulting the stars?'

'No. I don't do a lot on the Ba Zi – I just check the basic elemental information. I let the client lead.'

How refreshing.

'A client once said, "I want my daughter to pass her exams." I told her that Feng Shui isn't magic but then she went on that the daughter hadn't been sleeping very well and found it difficult to concentrate at her desk. These are all things that I can do something about by looking at changes to a bedroom or study area.'

Drat. If only it was magic. If only we lived in that world where she could weave spells. But maybe that's what this is about – learning how spaces cast subtle spells on our mood.

'Well, Sylvia, I'm interested in how the environment influences us even on an unconscious level and in your observations on this living space. The main problem is the fumes and the bedrooms with non-opening windows. How do I feel in this space? Basically I like it but, as I said, it has felt stuck for a while.'

We go outside and walk round to the roadside. She peers down at the basement.

'Take out all the crap that people throw down and clean the windows.'

'I do, but they throw it down regularly.'

'How often do you clean it out?'

'Probably twice a year.'

'I recommend cleaning this once a month.'

'I see.'

'You could consider painting the brickwork that faces the window white. It would reflect more light in.'

This is an absolutely brilliant suggestion. It's so obvious – why have I never thought of painting a grubby old basement wall white?

There's one thing I can't wait to ask her. (I know I need to get a life.) 'What colour should I paint the front door?'

'East-facing? Green. A lively natural plant green.' Good – green it will go, then. The thought of painting my front door is absurdly, irrationally exciting. I think this is probably crazy – but later I discover that other people who have front doors can get excited about what colour they are too.

We step back through the not-yet-green door.

'Feng Shui is about protection, support and strengthening,' Sylvia tells me. 'Each year there is one area that we want to protect. This year it's the south, so I'm going to show you how to make some salt cures.'

I am keeping an open mind. I am keeping an open mind. 'Salt cures?'

'You need a small container like a glass, some good-quality salt, six copper coins – one-penny pieces will do – and one silver coin. Do you have some five-pence pieces?'

I produce all the required odds and ends. 'Now you put the salt in the bottom like this, lay the five pence in the middle and surround it with the six copper coins. Now we'll cover it with water. Have you got some cling film?'

I have. She covers the glass with it and makes some small holes.

'What's this for?'

'To stop the water evaporating.'

I didn't mean the cling film. Never mind. Ha ha. Eye of newt and toe of frog, anyone?

'Put one of these in the south part of your kitchen, one in the south area of your living room, and you need another one in the northwest corner to sort out the energy there.'

This really does seem like weaving spells. What exactly can salt and copper coins protect me from? Maybe this is what the

Chinese Government mean by 'superstition': mutts like me that don't really believe in all this doing it anyway.

'How's the kitchen?'

'In strict Feng Shui terms, nothing in your kitchen is clashing. You don't have the sink or the fridge opposite the stove. So it's fine.' I don't hear any psychobabble about me being in resistance to the traditional woman's role.

'I was told that I need to sit in the northeast corner to address my father issues. Apparently I'm angry, and if I say I'm not I'm in denial,' I smile. I'd have liked to know my father, but I honestly don't think I'm angry with a dead man I never met.

Sylvia sighs wearily. 'That's not my style of practice. Even if you had raised such an issue, which you haven't, my first concern would be to create peace in that space, which heals any conflicts metaphorically.'

'I don't have to sit in the northeast corner and think of 1973, then?'

'What happened in 1973?'

'I've no idea.'

'So why would you want to sit there?'

I laugh. 'Well, I wouldn't. Let's move on.'

Sylvia walks over to the weeping fig. 'Put your hand over this plant. What do you feel? The temperature of the air?'

'Warm, I'd say.'

'Now put your hand over these dried flowers. What do you feel?'

'Feels cold.'

'It does, doesn't it? Do you know why that is? It's because they

43

want to be alive, so they are trying to draw ch'i from the atmosphere.'

'I don't believe it.'

'You just felt it yourself.'

'I know. But –'

'Try again.'

I definitely have the impression that the air is warm over the plant and cooler over the dried flowers.

'Anyway, you don't have to believe it if you don't want to. Just take my recommendation. No dried flowers, please. Only healthy living ones.'

'OK.'

'Fix the broken leg on that horse, please. Make sure he's not broken. Does that clock work?'

'Yes, but it's old and I tend not to wind it.'

'Clocks that are not moving add to the feeling of stopped time.'

Obvious enough, I suppose.

She glances at the empty fireplace. I answer the question before she asks. 'The gas point is there but I've never had a fire put in. Too expensive.'

'Mmmm. If you want that space to look less bleak, you could at least fill it with logs or candles. Have you actually looked into the price of gas fires?'

I have not. Strange how little attention I've given this place in which I spend so much of my time.

Downstairs, Emily is in for once. I knock on the door tentatively. 'Feng Shui consultation for your room now available. Not compulsory and no obligation. The mother will not be offended if you say, "Get your crazy ideas out of my space."'

She's in an obliging mood. 'No, I'm interested, come in.'

Fantastic. Now I don't have to say anything. All advice will be coming from a third party.

Sylvia looks around. 'You'd benefit from a headboard behind your bed. It will give you more support, not to mention something to lean against if you want to sit up in bed and read, warmer than leaning on the outside wall.'

'What happened to the old bed backs, mother?'

'We threw them away.'

Funny that it takes strangers to point things out that you would have thought were obvious. Maybe anyone can have one simple version of a Feng Shui consultation by asking everyone who comes to visit you, 'How would you improve this environment?' and then implementing suggestions that please you.

Sylvia peers at the photos on Emily's notice board. 'Are these images current?'

'No, they're mainly of Paris and South America, where I used to live.'

'So it's mainly stuff that you miss and friends you don't see much of now?'

'Yup.'

'You need to bring your images into the present. Things that are meaningful now and in the future.'

'So these should come down, then?' She looks at them sadly.

'Only into albums – you can still open the albums but you won't be looking, every day, at what you don't have anymore. Try some images that are strong and positive about who you are and what you want now. Is the boyfriend current?'

'Yes – in a long-distance-Paris kind of way.'

'As long as he's current, that's fine. Keeping up pictures of old boyfriends is never a good idea.'

Oh dear – I have pictures of lots of men I love and I know love me – but whom I rarely see – upstairs in the lounge. I wonder if Sylvia is being clever and commenting on those too.

Next I follow her into my little room. 'If you took those shelves down, the room would feel twice as wide.'

The previous owners put shelves up. I've left them there even though they are ridiculously placed. 'It's true. I'll take them down. So much of what you are saying is common sense that I seemingly lack.'

'If you want to attract a relationship, you could put a rose quartz crystal in the southwest corner and a pair of figures of some kind, for example, an embracing couple. You may think, "This is so superficial. Surely real practitioners wouldn't use stuff like this?" But masters use this stuff and I've seen some very happy outcomes.'

I repeat 'I have a beginner's mind' to myself one more time. Placement of objects in my room may increase my chances of meeting someone I want to share the space with? Maybe it will influence my focus? Make me more open? Or have I opened my mind so far my brain is oozing out? Back to looking at the room. 'Do you have any comments about the colours in here?'

'No, the white is obviously good for the light. I'd take the mirror outside; it will make the room less noisy and you'll sleep better.'

'You don't think anything about this room is to do with my relationship with my father? Even unconsciously?'

'Why, do you think it has?'

'No.'

'Then I don't either.'

What astounding logic.

We go back upstairs. 'That's it for today,' she says. 'There is another bit that I call the Sylvia Bennett extra – it's not really part of Feng Shui, but space cleansing is something else that I do to renew the ch'i. I'd have to come back to do that.'

'Are you talking about spiritual entities? Dead people? Have you ever done that?'

'Very, very occasionally I've been able to assist where that has been necessary, but as far as I'm concerned that is not Feng Shui. It's a very helpful associated practice that enhances a Feng Shui consultation when it is appropriate. For example, someone was living in a converted old children's home where it was known that many children had died. The client was experiencing cold spots and I could feel them too. I may have to call in another specialist, but it's very rare and I'm led by the clients. Why – are you having any problems or sensing any energies?'

'Nope. There may be hundreds of dead people living in the house for all I'm aware, but they don't trouble me and I don't trouble them.'

'Good. Anyway, what I do is that I remove residual ch'i: residues from previous occupants and, in your case, previous lodgers, especially any who may have been troubled.'

'I've had a few of those. Many lost souls still living in their mortal bodies rent rooms in other people's houses.'

She's gathering her odds and ends to leave. 'In general, it would be good to bring the house up to date as much as possible. There are lots of things about to remind you of times gone by. Put those toys on the windowsill in a box away somewhere.'

It's good advice, I think. Put the past away. Bring flowers to perfume the present.

I'm still not sure what ch'i is, but I have a jobs list for the rest of the month.

'I've got to leave now to get my train,' Sylvia says on her way out the soon-to-be-green door. 'Please call me if you have any questions, OK?'

So now I'm working subtle magic on the house and I'm beginning to like Feng Shui again. I've taken out the high hedge and it has completely opened up the light and increased the view – it may even have brought in a bit of ch'i, if there is such a thing. Today I spent an hour outside moving pots around and repainting the railings. Tomorrow I'm going to get up absurdly early and go to the flower market and buy lots of cheap flowers for very little money. As soon as I start to make improvements outside, my neighbour is forced to join in so that his entrance doesn't look tatty compared to mine.

Every object in the house has to make a case for being allowed to stay. I'm feeling surprisingly ruthless with innocent objects I've kept for years. Even dolls from my childhood are starting to get jittery. I've always been a great thrower away of things, but even so there are some things that I've held on to quite illogically. Do those dolls make me happy? Not really, and all I'm doing by keeping them is passing on a job to Emily. If I die before her, then she will one day have to decide what to do with them. And they are my childhood toys, not hers. She will have a hard enough time getting rid of her own dolls and bears without having to send mine out into the wide world too.

I should know this. My mother was a great hoarder and my grandmother too, so I've spent a lifetime taking things to the charity shop. Often when I visit friends' houses that are cluttered I think to myself, 'Oh please spare your children the job of getting rid of all this stuff.' Why do we have so many objects? For some people it becomes obsessive. I recently spent 12 hours helping a young friend of mine (male, 28) remove eight sackloads of rubbish from his room. He had become so overwhelmed by the task that he simply didn't know where to begin. Not a single piece of paper had been thrown away for ten years.

Another friend had two family bereavements in two years. After an agonizing time going through the houses of first her mother and then her brother, all their remaining possessions were brought into her flat so that their homes could be sold. It took *more* than a day to help her free herself from that sad inheritance.

So I'm very aware of this one: any day we may die and someone will have the task of deciding what is to be done with every object we own, every piece of paper, and every item of clothing. And if that thought isn't enough to get you rushing to your filing cabinet to do some clearing out, I'm not sure what will get you there.

Now, that old Chinese clock I bought at Portobello market, perhaps I should just take it back there?

A month on, I have made every single change that Sylvia suggested and some more besides. All the light blue is gone from my bedroom and the colour red is moving in. It feels strangely like a complete character change, or at least an emphasis on a different aspect of me. I've managed to keep the bed turned sideways – which will be fine as long as I don't find a lover who is an inch taller than I am or his head will press one wall and his feet the other. We'll have to move the mattress around every night before we go to sleep. But the bedroom doesn't look as if it's designed for just sleeping in any more.

Upstairs the toys on the window ledge are gone, the piano is being played and I've even acquired a 'water feature', which Sylvia recommended. The daughter complained. 'I'm not sitting anywhere near that. It makes me want to pee and it's not ecologically excusable to use up energy just so that you can enjoy the sound of running water.'

She's right but, dammit, it's not much energy and it is working as a humidifier for a stuffy room and I don't have it on much and I love it. The front door is the brightest green you could imagine, the man at the charity shop is almost in love with me because I've taken him so much great stuff to sell, and the house feels new, more spacious and full of possibility.

So, the home is sorted. The hole looks very nice. Now I have to get myself out of it.

The Second Element – Fire

*The heart – energy – impetuousness –
vitality – the mind and the blood –
the tongue*

Playing with Fire

If you ever want to overhaul your life and challenge your attitudes, there is one man who holds the record as the best international superhero to help you. He branded the process of sorting out your life, wrote the book, invented the seminar and is the most hated by those who loathe motivational gurus: Mr 'Awaken the Giant Within', Anthony Robbins, is in town. These huge American seminar-type events are very good at shattering any excuses we have for everything that we've never done. Luckily for you, you can come with me. If you pay attention you can pick up tips and all without the slightest inconvenience to yourself.

The morning of day one of the Anthony Robbins workshop 'Unleash the Power Within!' finds me curled up on the sofa, in the northern corner of my happily well-balanced living space, reading *Norwegian Wood* by the Japanese writer Haruki Murakami. Murakami writes in a deeply sensual, velvety, almost existential style – his characters are eternally trapped by their destiny or, most often, by unrequited or hopeless love. They are all isolated and usually comforted only by literature or classical music. I can imagine that they would all rather commit hara-kiri than go and get motivated. We can relate to them, can't we?

The greater part of my soul loathes the idea of going to a place with 8,000 people, none of whom I know or have any desire to meet, to get talked at by some large-headed Californian. I really don't feel like moving and I make the mistake of admitting as much to Emily, who, having been encouraged by me to attend motivational seminars herself in the past, is enjoying the irony.

'So the great Isabel – proponent of all things nauseating and positive – wants to stay on the sofa in her slippers? Are you choosing a negative state and not taking responsibility for yourself?' She grins widely.

'Oh, fuck off,' her mother replies eloquently. She and I have never had the traditional mother–daughter relationship.

She loves the fact that I don't really want to go. I explain pathetically, 'Apparently they shout out, "Are you having fun?" and you are encouraged to punch the air and shout, "Aye!"'

'Oh, my God. I'm so glad that I'm not going.'

It's all very well for her: while I'm off being seminared she has her Parisian lover flying in to spend the weekend with her.

'They will turn you into one of those people with a fixed Cheshire-cat grin like your friend Stacey.'

'Don't remind me. I couldn't bear to be in the same room as her for about a month.'

'Oh, this is hysterical.' She sits at her stylish new Apple laptop and opens www.tonyrobbins.com. 'He says, "It's going to be such damn fun you're not going to believe it." Oh, my God, he's annoying. And you'll be walking over fire?'

I pull a blanket a little further over my head. 'Yes, that's this evening.'

'That's OK, we have burns cream in the cupboard. Ha ha ha.' She acquires his Californian accent. '"Robbins gets results!" Aren't you going to get ready? Surely you're not going to be late and demonstrate your resistance to the process?'

'No – I won't be late.' I may decide to spend the entire weekend in Starbucks with Murakami but, if I'm going, I won't be late.

'I can just see you punching the air.' Ha ha ha. She throws on an irritatingly well-cut jacket. 'I'm off to meet Pierre. Be back as late as you can, won't you, and don't forget to text me to let me know when you're arriving. We may be busy.' She assumes the Californian accent again. 'And have a really great da-ay.'

Step One

I hate the seminar immediately because of the location. The Excel exhibition centre in London is loathed by everyone who ever visits or exhibits. One year the London Book Fair was here but there were so many complaints from agents and publishers that next year it was back at Olympia, within shouting distance of Kensington. Alas, the Anthony Robbins lot obviously don't mind us having to trek down to somewhere that Emily would describe as 'Bumblefuck'. I register my arrival and am given a

'General' wristband, as I've paid only £250, for the cheapest seat possible. The prices are varied according to how far forward you want to sit, and the more expensive seats, in the front rows, are allocated individually. The queue to go in feels like an airport during a plane strike. Eight thousand people all herded together into a huge waiting area and left there for an hour. None of this doing anything to improve my mood.

When the huge metal door finally opens, we all surge forward to find seats. The auditorium is filled with loud music and strobe lighting. It feels like a rock concert, with Robbins on stage and his face projected up onto five huge screens. I am completely ready to dismiss him as a well-hyped phoney, but instead, and to my utter amazement, I find myself listening to what he's saying. He's dynamic and has his audience, and even your bad-tempered narrator, laughing immediately. He fills us in on what will happen that day, interspersing the information with self-deprecating jokes. 'While I'm explaining all this you are probably looking at me and thinking, "Wow! He has amazingly large teeth."'

Which, of course, is exactly what I'm thinking. I'm also distracted by realizing that I'm looking at a Disney character. Have you ever seen the Disney film *Beauty and the Beast*? Do you remember the paragon Gaston? Disney has to have modelled Gaston on Anthony Robbins. Our heroic presenter today is very good-looking, tall and wide in all the right ways – toned, well dressed, stylish, with a smile straight out of a Disney cartoon. Barring the fact that he's 6'8", he's the kind of guy you can see any group of men wanting to take to the pub with them. I think

I can safely guess what the 4,000 women present want to do with him ... well, let's just say that his charm is irresistible.

He introduces himself, telling funny stories about his childhood. 'I was a talker. Hard to imagine, isn't it?'

Five minutes of chatter and 8,000 people have been won over. Billy Connolly has this utterly winning quality – he comes on stage and has everyone laughing in seconds. In Robbins' case, he also has a belief that he has something worthwhile to teach us and knows that everyone is here because they want to learn it. I listen attentively and start to take notes.

'I don't believe in positive thinking.'

Really?

'I believe in intelligence. See things as they are and not as worse than they are. People say "I'm sceptical" – no, you're gutless. It doesn't take any courage to be sceptical and do nothing but make excuses. "I'm big-boned" – no, you're fat because you eat like a pig and don't move your body.'

Oooooh – a risk-taker not afraid of being accused of being fattist. When I speak, I wouldn't dream of using the word 'fat', even in a talk to overweight women who admit that the quality of their lives is ruined by obesity. But he's pulling no punches.

'You are not broken, but you may have some patterns and strategies that don't work for you. So are you willing to try some new stuff this weekend? If you are, put your hand in the air and say "Aye!"' People around me shout, 'Aye!' A whole room of hands in the air. Already.

'This is not about changing yourself. Change is automatic but progress is not automatic. Nothing is going to progress unless you have something compelling that you want to go after, you have energy and a strategy, and you take action.' It's such a relief to hear stuff that makes sense, that is relevant and that I need reminding of that I find myself shouting 'Aye!' before the first hour of the seminar is up. Oh God, did I just admit that?

Having energy, he tells us, is as much about psychology as about food. 'If you are tired, get up off your ass.' He explains that profane language is necessary in order to encourage people, especially the British, to get real. My views exactly – say what you mean, and if you mean something passionately, an expletive often helps. Apologizing for language he will be using, he says, 'If adult language offends you – well, fuck you!' But he delivers the line with style and nobody leaves. His audience is completely in his hands.

He starts to make us laugh with stories of excuses that people make to account for why they haven't achieved what they are capable of. We are too young or too old or don't have enough time or aren't qualified or something went wrong ... we have lots of reasons. Then he tells stories to take away our excuses – a 98-year-old marathon runner, a woman who competed in an 'Iron Man' competition on her 72nd birthday, a walker of 104.

'You think, "If I have that person I'll be happy"?' Mmmm, I think your narrator has been guilty of that one. 'You think that if you have children they are always going to love you? You clearly don't have a sixteen-year-old.'

Lots of play. He asks us, 'What does a beautiful woman look like?' Four thousand men don't know how to answer and then

57

one woman near the front yells out, 'Me!' He grins at her. 'Good for you, ma'am.'

Next he has to deal with the fact that his audience all hate each other. As it's a human-potential seminar, obviously everyone here is a disaster, like your narrator. We're asked to introduce ourselves to others with the assumption that meeting them is a total waste of time. It feels good to shake people's hands and mumble, 'Pleased to meet you,' whilst barely making eye contact. Then he has us go round and meet again as if we are really pleased to meet people. I expect a rather obvious point about assumptions influencing our experience – but no, it turns out that he's teaching about physiology. 'The way you use your body represents the majority of what actually influences people when you communicate.'

He has us stand in the way we feel when we're depressed. People fold in around themselves, put their shoulders forwards, stomachs out, heads down. Then he puts music on and we're asked to follow him in jumping up and down and with our arms in the air.

'Now how do you feel? Do you feel better already?'

It's actually fun shouting 'Aye!' I can do Tigger-like enthusiasm with the rest.

'In order to feel good, your body needs oxygen. When you jump like this, you open up your diaphragm and it works to get some oxygen into your bloodstream. It's that easy to change the state that your body is in and influence how you are feeling. To take control of your life, start by taking control of your body,' he enthuses whilst jumping up and down. 'You don't need an excuse to feel good! You're only here for three days – don't worry – we won't tell anyone that you had a good time.'

In a very short space of time the mere idea of feeling bad seems absurd.

'Why would you need an excuse to feel good? You often don't need an excuse to feel bad, do you? How are you today? I feel like crap. Why? I woke up.'

We laugh.

'How many people came because someone else made you come?'

A large number of hands go up.

'So, in order to avoid their pain, you're here?'

More laughter.

'How many of you have someone not here who didn't want you to come?'

Large number of hands go up.

'Put your hand down if that person hasn't ever done this course themselves.'

As far as I can see, all the hands go down again. It's an interesting phenomenon – what's called 'condemnation before examination'. I'm completely guilty of it. I knew Anthony Robbins's reputation as 'the best in the world', but I'd still declare, 'It's not for me,' and moan on about how commercial it was. Am I so profoundly dim?

He tells us about the 'Science of Achievement' and the 'Art of Fulfilment' and that contributing to other people's lives is the way to feel fulfilled. Hooray. Then we hear about our needs and our drives. Apparently we need 'certainty' in our lives, to know that we have a roof over our heads and enough money to eat – but we also need 'uncertainty' if we want to feel alive. We have a need for 'significance' – to feel special and important in some way. We have a need for 'connection and love', and he has defined two spiritual needs: 'growth' and 'contribution to others'. To understand ourselves we need to understand what drives us to act the way that we do. Some people have achieved a feeling of significance in other's lives by being sicker than anyone else or having more problems. Many have an interest (that they may not be aware of) in being helpless, because in their very helplessness is their power over others. So their need for significance is met but they won't have genuine love and intimacy.

One girl stands up and tells us that her main belief about herself is that it's her soul's destiny to be there for others but never to have her own needs met. 'My soul is here to make others happy,' she proclaims.

Robbins invites her up onto the stage and then tells her this is bullshit and a lie. I'm shocked at the severity with which he speaks to her. A ruthless kindness.

'You are here to make others happy but will never be happy yourself?'

'Yes.'

'That's a lie.'

She looks stunned and furious. 'No, it isn't. That's what I believe about myself. That's my destiny.'

He asks the room what needs she's meeting by having this belief about herself. People shout out various ideas, but the overriding conclusion is significance. 'So everyone else deserves to be happy but not you? Is that right? Are you more special than everyone else?'

'No.' It's interesting watching someone deflate a limiting belief. The scales fall, almost visibly, from her eyes.

'Do you deserve happiness just as much as everyone else?'

'I suppose I do.' She laughs now. By inviting her to look at the need for significance that she has been using against herself, he has just zapped her major limiting belief and invited her to step down and join the rest of the human race. He has also given her the right to be happy.

'Are you in relationship?' he asks.

'Yes – but it's crap.'

'Can everyone see how difficult it would be to be in relationship with someone who believed that it was their job to make everyone else happy but that they couldn't be happy themselves?' Who wants to live with a martyr?

The girl stands on stage looking horrified. 'Oh, my God!' she groans.

'So what do you think now?'

'That I can stop being so bloody special and I have as much right to be happy as everyone else!'

And it seems so obvious – yet she had firmly stated a different belief only five minutes before. Even she looks amazed at the ease and suddenness of the shift.

'Our fears will never leave us,' Robbins declares as she scrambles off the stage. He looks up at his audience. 'Aren't you glad you came to this positive class?'

It's true we are not expecting to be told this. 'Do you know the acronym for fear?' I learnt this years ago, so I shout out along with some others, 'Fantasy Expectation Appearing Real.'

Robbins has a different one: 'Fuck Everything And Run.' He's funny and he isn't patronizing his audience at all. He speaks with the assumption that we all understand these concepts. I keep writing down little snippets that please me. 'All thinking is about asking and answering questions – so don't ask lousy questions'. The question 'Why am I depressed?' puts our focus immediately on all the thinking that makes us miserable. Robbins plays with this concept.

'I want you to think about what you focus on when you are really depressed. Now increase the level – don't forget the posture, shallow breathing. And now snap out of it.'

We know exactly what to do in order to achieve an unhappy and miserable state of mind and body. And of course if we know how to make ourselves unhappy, we have to admit that we know how to make ourselves happy too.

We arrived at Excel at 10am and I've lost all track of time. Every so often they put music on and we stop and dance or give a shoulder massage to the person next to us. It's weird at first, massage from strangers, but you soon get over it. The crowd is many different languages and cultures, headscarves, dreadlocks, suits, all sorts – and an equal number of men and women. I believe that this is because Robbins uses a large amount of Neuro-Linguistic Programming in his work. This discipline, which is about the study of excellence and our understanding of the way that language impacts us, has become popular among men, as it has tangible use. Unlike some of the more mystical ends of personal development, NLP can be applied to make salesmen better salesmen, bosses better bosses, lovers better lovers. It works – so the guys are here. But, it has to be said, they're not a confident-looking bunch. I don't see one I want to flirt with in the breaks. The man on the stage keeps me happy, though. It's a pleasure to be in the same space as him. Just a shame it isn't a considerably smaller space.

And now he's about to begin his major job of the day: persuading 8,000 people to walk over burning coals. As it happens, your happy-footed narrator has already done a fire-walk, so the waves of fear that circulate through the room when the pictures of the flames go up don't scare me, they fascinate me. I'm in my element in every way. According to Eddie, fire is my man.

But the pictures of flames have a different effect on some of my neighbours. One spindly man glances at me with terror in his eyes and says, 'But doesn't it burn?' Before I have time to reassure him, he takes two puffs from an asthma inhaler and bolts – presumably deciding to return tomorrow when the fire-walk is over.

It is arranged so that each of us can walk across 12 feet of red hot coals. On the ground in front of the coals will be grass and after the walk our feet will be hosed down with cold water. I have the pleasure of not being terrified, and so I'm able to enjoy the masterful work between stage and audience.

We are instinctively programmed to run from fire. You walk up to the coals and everything inside you screams, 'Hell, no!' He asks us to think of a time when we 'felt good standing by a warm fire'. Then he has to teach us how to create a state in ourselves in which we will be happy stepping out. He has to get it just right. Fire-walking is quite safe (though the first time I did one, I did get blisters on my feet), but the state that you are in when you walk is important. If you don't walk in the right way, or if you try and run, it can all go horribly wrong. If you run you can fall, and if you fall, well – as he says, focusing on the worst thing that can happen isn't going to help you take that first step. Or as he puts it succinctly, 'If you focus on the fucking fire you're going to freak out.' You can learn to overcome fear in almost all circumstances. If you can dance with your fears and realize that they are much the same as excitement, then you can do anything. It's all about where you put your focus.

He takes us through a couple of lovely exercises asking us to remember a time when we'd felt guided and loved, and that's it – we're off outside to do the seemingly impossible. They have about 20 paths of hot coals so the walk won't take too long. We take our shoes and socks off, revealing vulnerable tender skin, and walk outside chanting, 'Yes!' All we have to do is keep walking, but some people still run away from the flames. Sometimes we allow our fear to dominate us.

I come up to the fire and, oh fuck, it is extremely scary when you see the red-hot coals and feel the heat – but I know that I can walk on fire. Just don't look down. I step firmly and confidently, repeating the words 'cool moss' in a loud voice at each step. Shit, it's hot, it's impossible not to notice the heat, but I don't focus on it – I focus on the positive – I look at the smiling faces ahead of me cheering me on. Another step, another step, hotter and hotter – then six paces later I step onto the cool grass and the cool water of the hose swills over my feet. My heart thumps and the adrenaline flows. I look around and everyone is cheering.

I recommend fire-walking – really. Like jumping out of planes, walking on red-hot coals is something to be done at least once in your lifetime. If anyone ever invites you to do a fire-walk, just say 'Yes' – quickly, before you've had time to hesitate.

I turn around to watch others. In case of panic they have volunteers standing by to provide support and encouragement. It's like anything you are scared of – often the longer you hesitate the harder it is. Most people just step out as Robbins has instructed us, but the occasional person stands and looks at the red coals. Helpers coax and encourage and eventually most just walk. I see one woman frozen in fear. She's young, very overweight and wearing a purple sari. She stares at the coals. 'Head up,' the volunteer says to her, 'Say to yourself, "Cool moss, cool moss," as you take each step.' Still she's frozen. I stand at the other side with her friends, smiling and waving. I love the image: you can get there, to that place of celebration and joy, but you have to trust and step out.

In her case, the volunteers take her hands, so she does walk, but she couldn't have done it without their support. Everything in these seminars becomes a metaphor. She gets by, with a little help from others who have done what she is trying to do. Reaching the other side, she's in a state of pure joy and she shouts and jumps about. I love this work.

I stay to watch for a while: the walking, the celebration, the proud feeling of conquering a fear. It warms my heart with the best kind of joyful fire. I watch and clap as if each one of these people were a child of mine, a sister, brother, mother or father. Then, just when I began to glow with pleasure, one girl bursts into tears. I walk up to her.

'Hey, you just walked over hot coals. You're supposed to be happy.'

'But I've burned my feet.'

'Really?'

I see no shrivelled stumps.

'I've burned my feet!' she wails. I wonder what has gone wrong.

'I'll walk back with you.' I take her arm as she hobbles along. She's the only person out of the hundreds I've watched who has had any kind of negative experience, so I'm interested.

'I thought it was all a joke. I thought it was just to make us scared. I didn't realize that the hot coals would be real.'

She had somehow imagined that Robbins had spent the last two hours preparing people for some kind of trick.

'What did you expect?'

'I don't know. But when I saw they were putting fresh red-hot coals down, I couldn't believe it.'

'Well, yes, that was the exercise.' I smile at her with what I hope is reassurance. I'm concerned that she may indeed have burned her feet. It is a possibility if things go wrong.

But when we get into the conference centre, I sit her on a table and look. Mmmm. No big bubbly blisters, no second-degree melted flesh.

'I have news for you. Your feet are fine. There are no burns.'

'Really?'

I do my best to re-program her.

'You did well, just like everyone else. In fact, you did better, because everyone else was mentally and emotionally prepared. You weren't, but you stepped out anyway. That's pretty impressive work – stepping onto hot coals with no preparation. I think you may have been crying just from the shock. You did a brilliant job. Really. In future you don't have to be frightened of anything you come across – even if it's real. Could be useful if you meet a ghost.'

She smiles. Looks at her unburnt feet and smiles some more. We collect our shoes, wash our happy feet and escape from the Excel in time to get the Docklands Light Railway.

When I get home, Emily and her boyfriend are still up. He's playing love songs to her on a guitar. Not that I'm envious at all. Of course – none of us girls would like a young Frenchman to serenade us, would we? She looks up and grins as I step in to say hello and goodnight.

'So? How was it? Did you say "Aye!"?' She punches the air with vigour. Her boyfriend joins in, punching the air too to show willing. I smile at them.

'I did exactly that.'

'Oh, my God – mother has had her brain removed.'

'Yes. Also he is very, er, charismatic. I've decided I'd quite like to have sex with him, actually.'

'What? Mother has fallen in love with Anthony Robbins?'

'Eight thousand people fell in love with Anthony Robbins

today. But I didn't mention love, did I? I think it was simple lust. Actually.'

'That is just so corny and predictable of you.'

'Well, he is ... er ... very much a man. He's fantastically male, strong, a leader, funny, and the best communicator that I've ever heard. What's not to fall in lust with?'

'I never thought you'd be won over so easily.'

'No – me neither.'

'And how was the course?'

'I danced. Took lots of notes. Walked on fire. You know, as one does on a Friday evening.'

And they offer me red wine and I'm absurdly happy and grateful about everything. Just as I've been programmed to feel. It's 1am. I have to be back at Excel by 8, and I'm ashamed to admit I'm looking forward to it.

Step Two

Many people who come on these courses bring friends, but doing a weekend of this kind with a partner has advantages and disadvantages. It can be harder to do this work with someone you know well. It is always easier to discuss your deepest secrets or your most fragile hopes with a total stranger who will be kind but whom you are unlikely ever to see again. On the other hand, with a partner or best friend, when the course is over you have a dramatically increased level of intimacy and support for whatever it is that you are trying to achieve in your life. Some people buy an entire row and invite everyone they know. Business owners have been known to offer the course to all their staff, as they know that people will return happy, motivated and grateful.

On this occasion I'm alone. I have no support in what I'm trying to do but neither do I have anyone who is critical of my attendance. In a quieter moment earlier in the week, I asked Emily what she really thought of me attending a course of this kind. If it was up to her, would she prefer that I didn't? She said no, that even if a large amount of the course is obvious, if I learn anything at all that's useful and can apply it, then it's worth being here. I don't know about you, but I often need reminding of the bleeding obvious, and often these courses offer far more than the obvious.

Having had a really difficult year, I'm delighted that Tony isn't telling me, as the mad Feng Shui man did, that it was all my choice. On the contrary, he's reassuring.

'There is no human on earth who gets it right the first time,' he says. It's soothing for my soul. Some people are happy in one job all their lives; they're increasingly rare but they do still exist. For the rest of us life has become harder and harder as the competition escalates. When I was a young actress I sometimes felt overwhelmed by the odds, but now those odds are against us in all walks of life. We have more choice but less security, and this means that we have to have a clear idea of what we want or we can be sure of not getting it. This is what morning two is about – the vital subject of our goals and dreams.

Did you know that apparently only 7 per cent of the population have goals and dreams they have clarified sufficiently to have written them down? We are about to be given 'The

Ultimate Success Formula', which may sound like hype, except success is defined as achieving 'things that you desire for yourself and for the people that you love'. We fill in sheets of paper and Robbins tells us, 'You guys just joined the seven per cent.'

I'm sure Tony (see, he's become Tony in my mind) will be happy for me to share this with you as he wants everyone to live happier lives. So – are you paying attention now?

1. *Clarity is power.* Obviously the clearer you are about what you are aiming at, the more likely you are to get there.

    For example, the goal of Tiger Woods is apparently to be not only the best golf player in the world but the best golf player who has ever lived. So if you are feeling that your goals may be a little difficult to accomplish, be glad you haven't set that one for yourself.

2. *Know why it's MUST.* In other words, before you even start to work out *how* to achieve what you want, you have to be really clear about *why* you want it.

    He asks us to imagine a house that we want to get into, only it's surrounded by electrified barbed wire, guard dogs, security men, watchtowers, the lot.

    'Do you think you could get into the house?' he asks. People think not. Most wouldn't even bother to try. 'In the house is one of the people you love most in life.' We imagine them in the house in danger of some kind. 'Now do you think you could get into the house?' Yes – everyone could or some might die trying.

    We are more likely to achieve something if we really

know why we want it. It's not enough to want to have more money. But if we know what we are going to do with the money – buy a yacht and take our family to sail the open seas or open a children's home in Asia – either way we'll be far more likely to make the money.

Logical, huh?

3. *Take massive action.* 'Were you ever told that knowledge is power?' We all say 'Aye!' and raise hands. He says, 'Knowledge is not power. *Action* is power.' Thank you, Anthony. The people who succeed are not necessarily those who are the brightest or the cleverest, but those who take the most actions. This can't be said often enough. You don't have to be the most talented, but if you are the most determined you'll take more actions and because you do – you'll succeed. Feel free to underline.

In my own life I've rarely succeeded in any area without joyful perseverance and when I'm told that I am "lucky" I usually want to throttle the speaker. My first book was turned down by 18 publishing companies – but I just kept on knocking on more doors.

'The amount of people who succeed is directly proportionate to the number of people who keep going,' he says. But of course it's no good just keeping on doing the same thing if it's not working. We know that, as Einstein put it, madness is doing the same thing and expecting a different result. But it seems that we all do our own version of this. I've been repeating that phrase for years and I'm still doing the same things. So you have to pay very particular attention to the results you are achieving.

'You have to change your approach again and again until you get what you want. Success is the result of good judgement,' Robbins tells us reassuringly.

I want to shout, 'Aye!' all on my own. I love this. It gives us all back our power. If someone else has succeeded where I have failed, it's because they were wiser than I was and took better decisions. Innit?

Tony tells us stories of his own potholes, times when he'd lost everything. 'I remember I went back to a rented flat that I was about to be evicted from and lit a candle.'

They put a spiritual-looking picture of a candle on the projector screens.

'No, it wasn't because I was spiritual; it was because I hadn't paid the electricity bill.'

It's easy to learn from him. He doesn't for a moment set himself up as someone better than us – just as someone who has applied different strategies. He tells us how to achieve immediate change: by looking at the consequences of not changing and the massive pain that will result. Not too hard to do that. If I don't get out of my pothole, I'm going to die a mad old lady – why do I find that very easy to visualize? Another tip he gives us is to interrupt and annihilate any existing pattern that doesn't work for us. He suggests, for example, that if you overeat you may like to leap up from your table as soon as you find yourself tempted to do so and shout 'PIG!' at the chair.

He talks to us about passion, which is one of my favourite

subjects. You can join in if you like. I know this isn't a workbook, but I wouldn't want to deny you the pleasure. So stop reading for a bit – turn the corner of the page over – you're allowed to – and write a list of all the things you love, all the things you hate, what you are passionate about and what you really want.

Cool exercise, huh?

Now, how much of that good stuff do you do on a regular basis? It's so weird the way we treat our lives as if they will last for ever. Tony is telling us again in his charming and smiling way, 'Hesitation when it comes to your life and your dreams won't help. You have to have COURAGE and take MASSIVE ACTION!' Even putting it all in capitals isn't enough.

I'm doing well and shouting 'Aye!' with passion. But it's all about to go pear-shaped.

Tony asked us to write down answers to these questions: *What do you most want? What are you passionate about? What makes you feel happy and glad to be alive? What do you most love? What inspires you?* In my case a certain man's name came up for me more times than is logical. Now Tony is talking about the power of decision. Anything that is going to change our lives requires a decision because there is no action without a decision. 'Think,' he asks us, 'of the little decisions that you've made that have led to a different life. How a relatively small decision can lead to a huge change.'

Then he talks about major decisions – of how they often lead first to a feeling of struggle, then to commitment, then to resolution, which finally becomes peaceful. A large number of people may have come on the course because they want to make a decision but can't summon the courage. He invites us to think of a decision that we want to make. Then he says, 'You know in your heart that it's the right decision.' I am horribly trapped by this process. One simple instruction, 'make a decision', and I'm in pieces. I want to get out of my hole – but even all this fire isn't helping me. What decision can I make? That I should never see or speak to this man again? Yet there he is, the answer to all the questions about what makes me glad to be alive. I can make no such decision – I don't want to cut off that which I most love, even if it's the 'right decision' – and who knows what is right and what isn't? Certainly I don't.

Maybe I can make a different decision? Maybe I can decide to take a new lover this year? That's all very well, but with no particular man in mind, surely that only counts as a wish? What else – to move house? But I'm not sure if it's the right time. Maybe I should go back to casting a man I love from my mind and heart? I'm sure everyone would tell me that this is the 'right' decision. Fuck making the right decision. I start to cry – why should I give up that which I most love because of a stupid exercise? This is supposed to be an upbeat part of the seminar and everyone around me is enthused. Behind me is a man who told me earlier that his three greatest passions are 'helping people', 'exercise' and 'nutrition' and that he hates his job. I said, 'Have you thought of becoming a personal fitness trainer?' and he decided that I was some kind of genius. Now he is looking at me with huge concern and handing me tissues. 'I'm

OK,' I explain, 'I just don't want to reach a decision.' Then it's a break for food.

The girl standing next to me is called Tish. I know this as I can read her name label. She takes me out on her arm. 'I'm OK.' I smile at her. 'Just having a little difficulty with that process. I know how powerful it is, you see. I'm quite good. If I make a decision I stick to it. So I'm very careful what decisions I make.'

'I did this course first in 1994,' she tells me quite openly. 'In this exercise he projected us forwards and as a result I decided to leave my first husband. I knew that I'd be lonelier in that marriage than I would be on my own.'

'But don't you think this process is pushed? Isn't there a danger that people may make decisions that they're not ready to make?'

'I suppose so. But he's not telling you what decision to make, is he? And I think a lot of people are here because they are ready to make huge decisions. I was suicidal in my first marriage and had been clinically depressed. The only thing that was stopping me killing myself was the fear of killing myself.'

'That's very funny. Woody Allen could have said that.'

'Yes, I can see the funny side of it now. Thank God. Or thank What-the-fuck?'

'I can see you thinking *tablets and whiskey?* No.

'I was so doing that.'

'What else did you consider?'

'Gun.'

'Where would you get one?'

'Fuck knows. And I couldn't hang myself.'

'Why not?'

'It would have hurt.'

'Yes, there is that.'

'You have to be pretty committed to the idea. Anyway, I didn't have the guts, and I was even depressed about the fact that I was too spineless to kill myself. A friend dragged me on this course and I decided to leave my husband, even though I was terrified. Slowly but surely I turned my life around. I met my second husband, to whom I'm now married, and we have a little boy of four.'

'Gosh – you sound like an Anthony Robbins commercial.'

'Yes, the course saved my life. So what about you? Did you make a decision? I saw that it was a hard one.'

'No, I didn't make a decision. I just felt everything crumbling away beneath me just being invited to make a decision. It's a long story. What about you? Did you make another decision?'

'Yes. I decided to have another baby.' Wow. A conception pre-conception. She had certainly got value from that process.

After the food break we are promised the secret of wealth and happiness. Having had such a bad two hours, I am back to my sceptical, resistant self. But as soon as Tony starts talking I'm agreeing with him again.

'The problem is that most people in the world are focused on themselves.'

Well, what d'ya know? California meets Tibet. His Holiness the Dalai Lama teaches that all the unhappiness in the world comes from looking after ourselves and all the happiness comes from looking after others. And here's Tony saying the same. (Or course, even this one takes good judgement. You can't look after others in a martyred way like the girl on the first day.)

'The real test of consciousness is who do you care about? The more people you care about – the more you grow.' I love him again now.

Some people do seminars but then disappear into themselves. They apply the teaching to 'love themselves' in the wrong way and end up not loving anyone else. As ever, Tony is direct and simple with his solutions. 'If you think you've got problems, go and sign up to feed the homeless once a month – you'll soon learn how many problems you have.'

You'd think that this stuff is obvious – unless of course it isn't. Many people don't help others who are not part of their own nuclear family. In my talks I have often defended people who do nothing for others, saying that it's not necessarily self-ishness, it's just that everyone works so hard just to pay the mortgage and keep a roof over their own heads that they are too exhausted to reach out to support strangers. But think of the happiest people that you know in your own life and I'd be willing to bet that they do the most for others. And by that I mean people they have no reason to help. An elderly woman used to live near me and now lives in an old people's home. She has no family and very few visitors. I'm the only one of her old neighbours who visits, and I only visit myself every two weeks. Why are we all so busy? Where is it getting us?

Anthony is reading my mind. 'In the next 48 hours go do something for a total stranger who can do nothing back for you.

If you go to an elderly persons' residential home and ask what someone remembers that they never want to forget, and put them into a state of gratitude for that memory, do you think they will remember and appreciate your visit?'

Well, obviously everyone would agree with that.

'Don't just agree – Do it. So many of us are so busy doing shit that we forget to give and then we wonder why we aren't happy.'

While I think about the excuses we make for ourselves, Anthony starts to talk about love. One of my favourite subjects.

'There are different types of love. There is a level where you demand it from others. Then there is horse trading – giving love and measuring what you get back. Then there is a third level where you love because it's who you are and a fourth where you love even when you experience pain.' (Although a fellow American of Tony's with a daft name, a Mr Chuck Spezzano, wrote a book called *If It Hurts, It Isn't Love*.)

Tony gives us his version of the Golden Rule: 'Treat people well even when they treat you poorly.' I have always done this simply because being good to people who aren't good to you is fun; they don't expect it and it confuses them.

'Create magic moments with people.' Whispering into the mike, he tells us about a woman who cooked him a simple birthday meal in her own home and served it while he sat on a rug by candlelight. He said that he remembered it more than any meal he had ever had in an expensive restaurant. These teachings may seem obvious, but can we be reminded of this enough times?

Have you discovered the joy of being lovely to petty authoritarians who give you a hard time for no reason? Tony asks, 'When someone is really unpleasant to you, is he or she necessarily a horrible person?'

We shout 'No!'

'Of course not – he is just in a horrible state.' There are a million ways in NLP to interrupt people's horrible states and make them laugh or just feel happy again.

I'd done some state changing on a total stranger myself only a few days ago. A woman had forced herself onto a train in what we could call 'a bad state'. The train was very crowded and she had too many shopping bags. I smiled at her sympathetically. 'I've been to Top Shop,' she said. 'In the rush hour. I'm never ever doing that again. Now I've got to go and change for a party but I'm in such a bad mood after Oxford Street I don't know that I even want to go to the party now. Of course there are no seats on this train either.'

'Would you like to change your mood?' I asked.

'I suppose so.' We were standing in that strange absurdly close proximity that you have with total strangers on tube trains.

'Tell me what you are grateful for.'

She smiled at me. 'My family.'

I felt happy for her. 'Are your parents still alive?'

'Yes.'

'Both of them?'

'Yes, and they are both in good health too.'

'You're very blessed.' I didn't have to make up my feelings of envy one tiny bit. 'I never had a father and my mother died when I was 18.'

'I'm sorry.'

'That's OK. It was a long time ago now. But it's an amazing blessing to have two parents alive.'

'Yes.'

'Do you have siblings too?'

'Yes.'

'Goodness – I have no brothers or sisters. You have the best kind of wealth.'

'Yes. I get on with them as well.' Thinking about them, she warmed up with a huge grateful smile.

Her stop came. She really had shifted her focus very quickly from Top Shop.

'Thank you.' She smiled, realizing the 'trick' that I'd played on her.

I smiled back as she disappeared in the crowd.

Back at Excel Tony says I did something sensible.

'You have to decide what to focus on as this determines how you feel. What's wrong is always available to us, and we know the consequences of focusing on that, don't we?'

We all shout 'Aye!' with a passion.

The right question to ask when something happens to us, he says, is, 'What does it mean?' The answer being just the meaning that we give it. Whatever 'it' may be. And the next question is, 'What are we going to do about it?' He goes with the energy of a dynamo. 'Do something for strangers. And do something for yourself that you've always wanted to do but you haven't done.' To keep the energy up, dance music comes on and we all leap about like Ecstasy-filled teenagers.

He's about to give us his next most important strategy for living a great life. When someone fabulous is talking about strategies for success and happiness, he is guaranteed 100 per cent of my attention.

'If you have considered your goals and dreams and why you want them, you also need to consider who will be your expert mentors, coaches and guides.' Then he puts it more plainly. 'If you lie down with dogs you will wake up with fleas.' Wow. 'You can love your family but you should choose your peer group.'

Now I'm feeling like a double disaster. Not only do I not have family, but also I don't have a peer group.

'You need people who are playing the game of life at a higher level than you are. You need a team that is going to challenge you – not a team that is going to support you.'

This is all great, but writing is notoriously isolating. I don't have anyone encouraging me, egging me on, providing feedback or advice. I have consistently failed to find people like this. Friends, yes; mentors, coaches, career guides, no. Do people really have these people in their lives? I have an agent whose only piece of advice has always been, 'Go and write your next book.' Then when I say, 'Finished it!' he says, 'Have you edited it so that it's the best that it can be?' And if I say, 'I think so, yes,' he says, 'Then go and write your next book.' Don't think this is quite what Anthony has in mind.

He talks about creating rapport. 'People like people who are like them and will want to help people who are like them.' It's all very well dividing people into family, friends, peer group and mentors – but all I have is friends and most of those live all over the country. This is the nature of the modern world. More and more of us are working from home with most of our relationships online. Here I am looking for solutions and I feel as though I'm just being reminded how bad the problem is.

They play music again. Oh well. May as well dance. Everyone else seems to be having fun. I dance. Anthony's wonderful – but this hasn't been a good day.

I sit on the train on the way home doing just what he has told us not to do. I apply my mind to the negative and eliminate the positive. I have made no decisions and have no peer group or mentors. A stupid day, I think, and forget all the good bits. All very well for Tish to decide to have a baby – but has she consulted her husband on this decision? And if I decide to move house – shouldn't I discuss this with my daughter first and see how she feels? I'm a bad student. I've had enough of the jumping up and down like a demented Zebedee.

When I get home there's a note from Emily and Pierre: 'Gone clubbing – probably back sometime tomorrow morning after you've already left. Thanks for being out all weekend – most thoughtful of you. Enjoy waking up at 6 again.'

I make some tea, open Facebook and inform my 1,000 virtual friends and readers, most of whom I haven't met, that 'on Anthony Robbins courses you jump up and down a lot'. And go to bed. Sod it all. Where's my Murakami?

Step Three

I'm still in a bad mood the following morning when, on the train, I strike up a conversation with a girl reading through the course manual. 'I'm a laughologist,' she says. Typical of the kind of nutcases that you meet on cranky American courses like this, I think. Sometimes I am the most judgemental person on the planet. 'You are studying laughter?' I ask rather dismissively.

'Yes, I'm doing an MA in the psychology of humour. I work at Alderhay Children's Hospital, and we are looking at distraction techniques and how humour can lower high anxiety and depression. When I've done my Phil I'll be a doctor of laughter.'

'Which is rather funny in itself.'

'I think so.'

'So does it make you depressed?' (Excellent focus on the positive, Isabel.) 'You know, in a Spike Milligan kind of way? Do you end up with the shadow side of the clown experience?'

'No, because I choose to have a good day every day. How can you have a bad day when you laugh for a living, I give so much to other people, and it's infectious?' She's lovely. I am a sceptical fool sometimes.

'Is this after the work of Patch Adams?'

'Yes. I'm a great admirer of his work.' Amazing, I find myself thinking – the interesting people you meet on courses like this.

The first session of the day is a talk from Anthony about being outstanding. And it was. And he is. And we can be.

I wonder whether to write in my notebook, 'He is one of the best communicators I've ever heard,' or 'He is the best communicator I've ever heard.' It's an excellent competition. Others that have been outstanding are the theologian Matthew Fox, the NLP genius and madman Richard Bandler, and His Holiness the Dalai Lama. These are all speakers who do far more than just communicate their subjects with clarity and precision – they communicate with who they are. Matthew Fox inspires the soul, Bandler made me laugh until my sides ached, and His Holiness somehow short-circuits the brain and touches the heart before he has even opened his mouth. What Anthony Robbins is doing is teaching us with humour, provocation and all the tricks in the book. I can't even work out exactly how he is so good, but he's fantastically compelling. There's something about his very presence that's inspiring.

'What is the difference that makes the difference in people's lives?' He is talking about effective strategies. 'Ignorance isn't bliss – ignorance is pain. There are people who want to lose weight and they've gone on the Atkins diet. It's the wrong strategy because Atkins will take the weight off but for the wrong reason and it will destroy your health. Sometimes you may have tried everything but be only a couple of millimetres from a breakthrough and a strategy that works.

'Or people want to sustain passion in their relationships but have adopted a set of beliefs that say that no-one can sustain passion in a relationship for thirty years. This belief isn't going to help them get what they are looking for. If we want to sustain our relationships, we need to find people who are still passionate thirty years later. I met a couple in their sixties who could hardly keep their hands off each other and I asked them how they kept the relationship so fresh. The woman smiled at me coyly and said, "We'll try anything once and if we like it we do it again." The ladies will tell you, guys – another millimetre one way or another can make a huge difference.'

He is funny and charming ... did I mention that?

Then he gives us a long talk on some details of NLP and the study of people's buttons. We have visual, kinaesthetic, olfactory, gustatory and auditory buttons. Do you happen to know if your partner is more turned on if you whisper your desires in his or her right ear or left ear? Because he or she, like you, will have a preference. Is the sound of your voice more important to your partner than the visual, and if so, does he or she like you to speak louder or quieter, at a higher pitch or a lower one? Do you use the timbre of your voice in a way that makes people purr or grates on the nerves?

'These are what are called the submodalities – the little things that control the emotions in your life. Don't you think that you could have a lot of fun just figuring these out?' You bet! I would so love to spend the rest of my life learning all the ways to please someone most ... Mmmmmm.

Returning to the subject of passion, he says, 'Couples come to me when the passion has gone from their relationships and ask me to work with them, but I just don't have time to work with everyone. So I give them this one primary tip ...'

PAY ATTENTION NOW!

'Breathe together. Breathing at the same time creates

connection like nothing else does. And when you want to make love, make sure you are breathing together for an hour and a half first. I ask them to try that for a couple of weeks and, if they are still having difficulty, to get back in touch. Only one couple has ever come back.'

I remember when I was learning about Tantric sex they said that the woman should lead the breathing and the man should follow her. But I guess if you are just starting, the woman could try following the man. Either way you could have a good time experimenting. Now aren't you glad that you bought this book? Dammit – it's worth the full cover price for that tip alone.

Imagine a man giving you the best tip ever on how to achieve greater intimacy. Why don't more men acquire techniques and skills to fill the lives of the women they love with joy? Not because they 'should', but just for the joy of it? And why don't more women do the same? He tells a great story about a man who comes and complains that his wife is leaving him. He confides in Anthony, 'I did nothing to her,' but doesn't understand why she is leaving. Ha ha.

He's now in full swing, encouraging us to raise the standards in every area of our lives.

'It's no good doing well in your life. I guess that most of you who are parents are "good" parents. If you are a good parent it's almost guaranteed that your children will be doing lots of drugs by the time they are teenagers. If you are a poor parent they will be in trouble with the law. I'm guessing that most of you are aiming at "excellent", but have you noticed even that isn't good enough any more? Someone out there raised the stakes – so now excellent won't do. It's necessary to be outstanding.'

Oh, goodness, how true this is.

'But I'm exhausted,' you say.

He is mind-reading again.

'You need to give more energy when you thought there was no more to give. You are knocked down? You just have to get up again. Don't settle. Raise the standard. From this moment on we're doing "outstanding".'

I look at the 8,000 strangers around me, people being inspired to be outstanding in every area of their lives. And I see them with a new admiration. Then – jumping sideways into the negative – I suddenly hate the status quo in the UK. The people here this weekend are those who are humble enough to admit that they could do with some inspiration. Many of the people I know in the media in London wouldn't be seen dead in a place like this. Those who are already the best achievers would never come to learn more. Yet many of those very same cynical people aren't happy. Very few people aim at being outstanding, very few have happiness or passion in their relationships or (bizarrely) even aim at creating it.

Emily and I had a conversation a couple of weeks ago about happy families in which she casually announced that there was no such thing.

'Don't be absurd,' I said. 'Of course there are happy families out there. Millions of them.'

'No, there aren't.'

'There are – I promise you.'

'Name one.'

I flicked frantically through my mental Rolodex of everyone she and I know well. Everyone I thought of – the families were broken, divorced, struggling. Even some families that are together have teenagers on drugs or mothers on antidepressants. We know families where the man has constant affairs and everyone knows except the wife. Emily has friends who hate their own parents, friends who have alcoholic parents and friends whose parents live what I call 'charading marriages' from which any real joy and passion has gone – homes where people tolerate each other rather than cherish their loved ones. We don't personally know any examples of real abuse, but we don't know much real cherishing either. The pause got longer and longer.

'So?'

'I can't think of a good example of a happy family among people we know well, but that doesn't mean ...'

'Then I rest my case.'

I have often thought of that conversation. I've found examples since. I have a friend, Anna, a mother of two young boys aged nine and eleven who does about six jobs and still gives up one evening a week to volunteer for Childline. She and her husband and two boys have a unique (in my experience) level of respect and love for each other. What is so noticeable when I'm with them is the respectful way that the parents speak to the boys and, of course, the respect that the sons offer their parents in return. No teasing, bitching or shouting, just each of them very busy and loving and supporting the others. An occasional temper tantrum by one of the boys is dealt with gently and firmly by the parents and, with humour thrown in, soon blows over. Most of the time the family seem to bask in the pleasure of one another's presence. Really.

And I know a family in Bristol – my friend Lela and her husband, both married for the second time, who, having had hard times before, cherish each other very much. With two teenagers, a five-year-old, a one-year-old and a three-legged dog, it really is a house filled with joy. The eldest teenage daughter said of her two tiny sisters last time I visited, 'They make me so happy.' Of course they still have as many problems as any family, but they are problems with the outside world, not problems within the family. So I've thought of two – but I know hundreds of families. And funnily enough, all four of those parents I can see in a seminar of this kind – open to considering new information from any source. But the parents in most of the unhappy families and passionless, stuck marriages – those people wouldn't be here. They think that they know better. Or they're determined that there are no solutions and that we are victims of circumstance.

So – are you with them or with Tony and me? Anyone interested in being outstanding?

We had a break and I'm back on track again. Good thing, as he tells us that we're about to go into the most demanding exercise of the seminar. Robbins has devised a process that he calls the

Dickens Process, based on the story of Ebenezer Scrooge in Dickens' *A Christmas Carol*. It would be safe to say that Scrooge was a little stuck. He believed that he had to work very hard in order to acquire money, and he was always in at the office before anyone and working later than anyone. He had no friends and just looked after himself. This was until – to use Anthony's phrase – 'three neuro-associative conditioning specialists show up in his house'.

What the ghosts do is show Scrooge the consequences of holding on to his beliefs and then what will happen if he changes them. They create what Robbins calls 'leverage'. They go beyond showing him what he 'could' change or 'should' change and demonstrate what he 'must' change. If you remember, when he wakes up from his dreams he can't wait to be different – to help others, to spread all the joy that he can in the world. To catch up.

Robbins is about to take our lives and create a little leverage – ouch. Looking at our most entrenched limiting beliefs isn't fun. Apparently huge numbers of us believe crap such as that we are not good enough, we are not loveable, love only leads to pain or we'll never have anything that we really want. Attractive people believe that they are not attractive, talented people believe that they are not talented ... it goes on and on. This is what the Buddhists call *Namtok* and what Robbins calls Bullshit. Are you enjoying thinking about what bad things you believe about yourself?

Just to raise the stakes a little he says, 'This process takes a level of courage that many people don't show up with.' Now we all want to do the process because we want to show we have courage.

'Your thoughts are controlled by your values and beliefs. But who picked out your beliefs? How did they get there?' There are many sources for acquiring bullshit beliefs. It doesn't really matter how they got there – the point is to challenge them and preferably to remove them.

We are invited to consider our most limiting beliefs, and, though it hurts me to admit it, I don't have to think very long for mine. Based on all that has happened to me in the last couple of years, I have come to fear that I may always be alone. That I met my 'soul mate' (whatever that means) but that it was not my 'destiny' (whatever that means) to be with him. Remember we are dealing with bullshit here. So all this leaves me with a wonderful little limiting belief: 'I may always be alone.' Now, aren't you glad you don't have that one? And if you do – pay attention!

'All beliefs carry with them consequences. When you have a limiting belief, you automatically think of the WORST possible result of that belief.'

So now we have to close our eyes and focus on the consequences of the most limiting belief we have chosen for ourselves. Not nice. He's laying it on for us. 'Carry yourself forward in time for five years and look at the consequences for your life of really holding on to this belief. What does it do to you?' There I am, lonely, sad, no-one around me, Emily and other friends off living somewhere with fun, happy people and me at home cooking dinner for one.

'What are the consequences of holding on to this belief for those who love you?' Oh, God, this is painful. I see friends pitying me and Emily feeling guilty when she thinks about me. Instead of the inspiring mother I could have been, I am a miserable creature that she never wants to see and visits home are duty rather than pleasure. Friends don't want to invite me to visit and people don't want to spend time with me. Who wants to spend time with people who are miserable and feeling sorry for themselves? This is what holding on to a belief like this will get me.

He goes on. 'What are the consequences for your health and vitality?' Cancer – obviously. So many people teach that if we are unhappy all the time we compromise our immune systems and invite illness to develop in our bodies.

He isn't done with us yet. Now we're asked to carry this bullshit belief forward ten years. I think, 'I may always be alone,' and see myself walking to the cinema aged 50, 60, 70; alone and coming back to an empty, joyless house every night. I take every possible source of happiness away from the images.

'Put yourself in this place and feel the results of this belief on your body now.' God – it's agony. My body stiffens up, lacks all flow and flexibility, my shoulders are raised and tense, my neck aches, I feel pinched, dry, cracked, locked in. I'm in a worse state than Ebenezer Scrooge ever was. 'Now turn up the intensity of this experience,' he insists. 'See where this bullshit belief will take you. Turn up the intensity 100 per cent now.' Around the room people start to cry, to moan and to scream. I make some strange noise that I can't quite identify. It's a sound like despair. 'Now carry this belief with you further still. Now increase the intensity ...' He goes on without mercy. For how long? I've no idea. Maybe 20 or 30 minutes. It's painful, but I will do this exercise. I will force myself not to cop out and to realize the consequences of believing bullshit.

Then, eventually, when he's pushed us all as far as we can possibly go and a little more for some, he finally brings us out of it. He asks us to shake out our bodies, drink water, and come back into the present. Then he coaches us with a sublime ease.

'The truth is the exact opposite of what you believe. Think about it.'

The first thing I notice is that I'm certainly not alone. There are 8,000 people around me. Alone I'm not. This makes me smile; perhaps I am missing the obvious here.

Also – are we ever really alone? Isn't it all in our heads? Even if we're physically alone, don't we carry all those we love and all those who love us? (This is aside from the more spiritual perspective in which we are told that we are all one anyway.) Aren't there always many people ready to love us and many we can love if we choose to? Just as even Scrooge discovered? Is it not equally possible that, even if I'm never with the man that I would have chosen, I may have many more lovers or meet someone I'll be happier with than I would have been with him? Might I not choose to live with friends? Might I not meet someone, as so many have done, who has a family and brings a mother and father, brothers, sisters and children with him? The truth, as Robbins points out, is that I am deeply loved and admired by many and the chances of me being alone are really very small.

It's all in my head, in what I choose to believe and create.

'Choose a new belief. You can be sure it's the exact opposite to the bullshit belief that you had before and you can know that this one is the truth.'

I choose 'I am never alone' and smile looking around the room. Then he takes us on the second journey.

'Close your eyes and see how you are with this belief.' I close my eyes and think of all the people who I know love me. I think of all those who tell me that they love me on a regular basis; rows of friends' and loved ones' faces lined up in my mind's eye for consideration. I smile at them and thank them for the love I have for them and the love they have for me.

Like Scrooge, I look at those who have loved me in the past, those who love me now and those who I know, without a shadow of a doubt, will love me as long as they have breath and longer if it's possible.

'Think of how your life will be ten years from now with this belief.' I see many people around me, maybe a new partner, maybe new family as well as my daughter, maybe family for her too. Maybe holidays where we all choose to be together.

'Think of the consequences for those you love of you having this belief.' They will have a friend who is grateful. I will be permanently focused on how blessed I am – gratitude and joy will permeate my life and spill over to others. I will be someone I would want to spend time with.

'Think of the consequences for your health and your body of holding this belief.' I see myself dancing, enjoying yoga, riding my bike, swimming, scuba diving, being fitter than I am now. I feel tension draining from each muscle.

'So from this place,' he asks, 'do you want to keep your bullshit belief? Do you want to fight for it? You have choice!' He is shouting. 'Look where you are now. If you could put back the card that life dealt you and take another one – would you take a different one?' I would not.

'Remember who you are!'

This one always calls me to attention. Even with doubts, fears and hesitations I have an absolute knowledge that I love humanity and a conviction that I can make a difference for the better in people's lives. That we all can make a difference.

'Are you ready to step up?'

We shout, 'Aye!'

He has a powerful series of one-liners for us to repeat like a chant. The first is 'Now I am the voice.' As in, 'I am the creator of my life.' But also useful for anyone who has internalized any of the negative voices that are sometimes louder than our own.

'Now I am the voice.'

Eight thousand people – 'Now I am the voice.'

'I will lead, not follow.' It's not about following Anthony Robbins – he'll be gone by Tuesday.

'I will lead, not follow.'

'I will believe, not doubt.'

'I will believe, not doubt.'

'I will create, not destroy.' Amen to that.

'I will create, not destroy.'

'I am a force for good.' Eight thousand people being programmed to be a force for good – isn't that an excellent thought? Unsolicited acts of kindness spreading out from Excel.

'I am a force for good.'

'I am a leader.' He means for ourselves, of course. We'll soon notice if others want to follow.

'I am a leader.'

Am I doing this scene justice? Imagine 8,000 people shouting – hands in the air – promising to take responsibility for their lives. Now if you are cynical you'll be thinking this is all hype – nonsense or worse, dangerous, like Hitler, just beating up enthusiasm and manipulating crowds. Well, may I ask you, can crowds be led to good decisions as well as bad ones? Can crowds be inspired as well as 'brainwashed'? Or is this kind of work done with large numbers inherently suspect? Well, you'll have to trust me on this one. I think not. I'm not in the least hysterical and very aware of crowd dynamics, and I'm having fun.

'Defy the odds!'

I shout with joy along with everyone else. 'Defy the odds!'

'Set a new standard.' I particularly like this one. Standards of happiness, health, love, cherishing, honesty, connection, joy and all things good are SO often SO low. A new standard is required. Even if it means me having to set my alarm an hour earlier.

'Set a new standard.'

'Step up!'

'Step up!'

'Step Up!'

'Step Up!'

'STEP UP!' It's as if he's saying, 'Will you step up?' We will. You can even shout it out yourself right now if you feel inclined to surprise all those in earshot.

'STEP UP!'

There's a break, more dancing, and then he blows me away all over again. It's as if this fire is going to burn through every aspect of my life. Now the past is to be purified.

We're standing with our eyes closed. He invites us to imagine ourselves standing on a time line. That's a line where your past stretches away from you in one direction and your future in the other. Most people visualize this with their futures in front and their past behind them. For some reason I seem to have the future diagonally off to the right in front and the past diagonally off to the left behind. We have to imagine ourselves in a little flying bubble that we can operate with various levers. Playful music comes on and we are invited to take the bubble for a spin. I have never flown a heli-bubble before, so it's fun taking the driving sticks and making the bubble go up and down, right and left, round in circles. What fun a little imagination can create. Then when we've finished playing we're invited to take the bubble back down the time line into the past.

'As you travel back you'll notice that some of the memories are bright and in full colour, some of them are blurred and some of them are a sort of black colour. There's probably stuff there that you don't much want to look at, so don't bother looking at those. In fact, while you are there, notice that you have a special suction section whereby you can suck up all those old black videos into the bubble. So do that now. Right – now you have them but you don't have to play any of them. Just feed them through a special machine that you have in the bubble so you can retrieve all that you learned from these experiences, all the positive lessons that have made you wise and strong.'

I obediently put the videos through a machine – click, clunk, click, clunk.

'Now you have a chute where you can post all those old black tapes that you don't like the look of right out of the bubble. And now you're going to step out of the bubble and torch them.'

My brain steps in momentarily with an objection – 'Hold on a minute, I don't want to torch my unpleasant and forgotten memories. I'd rather just embrace them, accept them and integrate them.' But we've saved the lessons learned, so I play along with the instructions and pick up a blowtorch and torch the whole lot. It's rather fun. The playful music goes on.

'Done that? Right, now back in the bubble. I want you to keep going back down the time line till you are very young – perhaps even before you were born – and I want you to look for a memory that isn't there but you would like to have there in bold colours. Make some stuff up.'

Mmm. OK, something that isn't here but I'd like to be. Let's have my mother and father kissing when they met in Paris 12 or so months before I was born. Yes – that looks fun.

'Now another one that you don't see there but would like to have. You notice that there is lots of space where you took out the old black ones, so make another to go into the space.' I'm making up memories? How weird is this? OK, me as a toddler being shooed out of the master bedroom.

'And another.' Er ... Mother and Father at home in the evening, not doing anything much, just being there. And we'd have my grandmother too – having not lost her husband – so a grandfather there as well.

'And another.' How about a father looking after my mother? A father who helped her paint the house, mow the lawn, wash the car. Just like the old Ladybird books. I slot these made-up memories into place.

The playful music goes on. 'Now just add loads more – you have lots of space.'

I look at the new memories I've created so far and realize that they are all memories for my late mother. All to do with looking after her. While I'm creating new memories I may as well create some for myself too. So here is one of my father taking me to the zoo, a Tuesday and he's driving me to school in his funny car, here he is giving me a shoulder-back ride, here he is listening carefully because I've had a horrid day at school, here he is helping me fix my bike, that's him coming to see a school show and applauding loudly because I've danced well in my new point shoes. How cool is this? If I'm allowed to make up whatever I like I'll have him waking me one birthday when he and my mother (still cherishing each other, of course) have bought a boxer puppy with a daft face. Yes, this is a good game.

'Now I want you to glance at all these new memories, all well slotted into place, and cover them with a golden sheen. Sprinkle them with gold dust.' I can do that. Wheeee. My inner six-year-old is still playing when he says, 'Now I want you to bring your bubble back to the present and, looking back at all those memories, ask yourself – how would you feel now if that had been your past?'

Staring at this invisible version of my past, my jaw falls, literally. If this had been my past, I would feel measurably different. I can't quite believe it. Something inside me would be noticeably, subtly but profoundly different. Can we shift the way that we feel now by re-programming our pasts? Or even by realizing exactly how certain events have impacted on us, by imagining different versions of ourselves that have had different experiences? Here I am experiencing the difference it would have made to me to have had someone to take care of my mother so that I could relax. My whole body feels different, as if I can let go of some invisible burden. Suddenly there is no feeling of lack in the past. I've been doing personal awareness work for over ten years and I haven't ever understood this much.

Somewhere in the Excel centre Anthony says, 'Now take your bubble forward ...' but I'm still standing there, eyes open, spun round to my diagonal left looking back at invisible tapes. Why haven't I understood this? Why haven't I seen what I'd lacked and what it has done to me? If this had been my past, I wouldn't have developed the bullshit belief I've had that I may always be alone. I developed it because the lack was there – in the past. If this had been my past, I wouldn't have to try so hard. I become a cartoon with exclamation marks flying out of my head. What staggeringly obvious things do we miss about ourselves until we are forced to consider our lives?

Robbins is busy taking people around in the future, but I can't join them – I'm too busy catching up with the present and trying to pinpoint the change this makes in my body. I had not been expecting this from a seminar with Anthony Robbins. Motivation I had known I would receive. I had guessed that he would get me off my backside, start me running again, all the stuff about goals and strategies – yes, I had expected all that. But new information, something that I hadn't realized before, profound but subtle change? From a seminar at Excel?

He brings the others back from the future in their bubbles. And as the bubbles come in to land, he smiles. 'Did you enjoy that? Remember the old saying – it's never too late to have a happy childhood.'

We have one more day. I wondered what they could possibly be teaching us on Monday.

At home, Emily and Pierre are curled up sleeping like little bunnies with all the doors open so that I can see them and say *Ahhhh* to myself. To complete the picture, Smudge, the neighbour's cat, is curled up on their bed too.

I'm exhausted but feeling happy. I find my room and am soon curled up happily myself, contemplating all things that are beautiful, wise and true. And the faces of boxer-dog puppies.

Step Four

The element of fire is about energy, which is what you'll need if you are going to pursue your goals. So Monday is a full day on health, diet, exercise – less extraordinary but intensely practical and easy to apply. Anthony's approach is based on loads of common sense backed up by personal experience of what works. He also has his own research organization, which is constantly researching which foods lead to maximum vitality and why. When he thinks he has been wrong, he says so. In one of his books he recommended that you eat nothing but fruit until midday. Turns out that he no longer thinks that.

He says if you read one book by a very well qualified doctor and nutritionist with all the facts 'scientifically proven', you can then read another by an equally prestigious doctor with contra-dictory conclusions. So what do you do? You learn by experimenting and seeing what works for you. He is inviting us to try out his suggestions for a period of ten days. 'Or thirty days if you are really keen.' Of course I instantly make a commitment to myself to try his recommendations for 30 days before I know what they are.

Tony and his helpers walk their talk. They look fantastically healthy and Tony is on stage for ten hours at a time. The energy levels are certainly not coming from anything artificial, so whatever vegetables he is on, I want some of them.

As usual, everything is taught with humour – with videos, with stories. His premise is that we all deserve to be healthy and that if we keep our bodies at maximum health and our immune systems strong then disease isn't going to zap us. When do we all get colds and flu? When we've been sitting around like couch potatoes filling our bodies with stuff that isn't good for us between Christmas and New Year and feeling stressed because Christmas is never quite as it 'should' be and we've drunk too much and eaten too much and not done any exercise for weeks. He tells us that the USA likes to label flu 'Shanghai strain A' or 'Hong Kong B' as if it is the Communists who are to blame rather than the fact that Americans are stuck on their sofas.

He is a great believer in oxygen. If you smoke, you are ruining your health and energy levels and committing slow suicide – just thought I'd mention that in case you don't read what's written on the packets. Oxygen is vital for your health and you have to get enough of it to your blood cells every day. Aerobic exercise, not anaerobic – in other words, if you are running so fast that you can't talk to the person that you are running with, then your cells may be ending up with less oxygen when what you need is more. He says that 'no pain, no gain' is a fallacy. Pain, he tells us, is usually a sign that we are doing something wrong and he recommends that we exercise in a totally enjoyable way. Hooray.

Do I have to remind you of the consequences of not exercising? I don't think so. But obviously decreased energy levels, insomnia and a diminished sex drive – well, those three should be enough to get any of us out of the door, really. I have one friend who has been an insomniac for many years, never exercises at all and insists that there is no connection between the two. Funny – she may be right but I don't see her training for a triathlon to test her theory.

He's a great believer in drinking water, in the right essential fatty acids, in drinking wheatgrass (yeuk) and, basically, in an alkaline diet. I love all this – I'll try anything to increase my energy levels. The curious thing about keeping the foods in your body alkaline instead of acid is that it's often counterintu-itive. Water with lemon juice, for example, which you would expect to be acid, actually becomes alkaline in your body. Bread – a food that we'd think would be alkaline – becomes acid.

He gave us simple lists of things that he has found to work: eating loads of greens, taking digestive enzymes to assist us in assimilating the nutrients in our food, taking acidophilus (the good 'germs' that we need in our gut), taking antioxidants and a good multivitamin once a day as well as any supplements we need for specific conditions. He recommends a complete dietary cleanse (generally known as a 'detox' programme) at least twice a year. I sit feeling a little guilty, as I've never done a detox programme in my life. This, in his terms, is a bit like confessing to never having cleaned my house.

They have a way of dealing with all the moans, complaints and sceptics. Anthony has us all cross our arms in front of us, shake our heads and say, 'I don't think so,' a couple of times. Then again, but saying, 'I don't think – wait a minute, perhaps I could learn something new here?'

He's giving us this lecture along with his work-mate, Joe McClendon, a dynamic, good-looking black guy who has made various appearances over the weekend and will soon be running these courses on his own in the UK and Europe. Once they have finished telling us what they recommend, they start on what they don't recommend. Sigh.

'You don't want to eat meat.' We hear stories of what is put into meat that made us cringe, groan, laugh and feel sick. Do you know what gives meat the flavour? It's the uric acid. Piss, in other words. How do we know that? Because kosher meat, in which religious laws insist that all the urine be drained out along with the blood, is tasteless. Do you know what makes meat tender? It has started to decompose. He adds, 'If you must eat meat, at least make sure that you know the source, and that the meat is free-range, organic, antibiotic-free and kosher, that it's local and that the animals are treated humanely.'

'What about chicken?' someone asks. He shows us a video about how chickens are killed and prepared for sale – images that everyone will remember if they are ever tempted to eat chicken again.

Fish? Well, Anthony says, 'All my life I've never eaten anything with a face, but recently I've been advised to be a little flexible. If you must eat fish, eat the smaller fish because of the pollution and mercury levels in larger fish like tuna. Again, check the source and that it is sustainable. Some fish can be OK.'

The not-recommended list grows: no milk or milk products. 'Why on earth do we drink this substance that is designed for baby cows? I mean, if you stand in the common-sense corner it really makes none. For the protein? Do you know what percentage of human breast milk is protein?'

Bear in mind that breast milk is designed for the time when we surely need maximum protein. So play along with him and have a guess. Answer is at the end of this chapter so you can see if you were right.

Anyway, the gist of it is that I have just agreed to 30 days with no milk products. He goes on. Of course, no nicotine, but as I'm not a smoker that doesn't trouble me. No drugs is also OK, as I don't take even the over-the-counter kind. I'm vegetarian anyway. But still the list goes on. No 'whites' – sigh – that is white bread, white rice, pizza, sugar, even potatoes. Why not? Well, obviously all these foods are high in carbohydrates, so they 'spike' our blood sugar levels, which messes most of us up. And still he goes on – no vinegar. Vinegar contains acetic acid, which affects the liver in much the same bad way that alcohol does; it also thickens the blood and interferes with the digestion of starch. Then no sugar, and finally the one I've been dreading – no coffee.

'Oh, shit!' I exclaim in a very loud voice.

'It's only for ten or thirty days,' says my neighbour. Mmm, that's true – but he's obviously hoping we'll try these things out, find that we feel better and keep going. This, though, is radical. Can I really eat 70–80 per cent alkali-forming foods? Well, for 30 days I can try anything.

And that's it – just health tips and energy tips for the rest of the day and a 152-page book on Vital Life Energy to take home. The bizarre thing – no, the extraordinary thing – is that I'm actually looking forward to getting home and beginning. Find the climbing equipment – I'm up out of that hole.

I know what all you sceptics are thinking. You're thinking, *But did it work? How long did you keep going? Isn't it boring?* Well, as I write this it is nine days after the seminar. I am blessed with a daughter who, when I say to her, 'I'm having steamed broccoli with lemon juice and olive oil for breakfast – would you like some?' says, 'Yes, please' enthusiastically. It's not normal. I know. We have always been partial in this house to 'rabbit food' – lots of greens, lettuce, spinach, kale, cabbage, all that. So I didn't inflict a batty new diet on anyone else, I just started buying loads more green vegetables and having them for breakfast, lunch and dinner.

There is loads of avocado in Robbins' recommended recipes, which I love. I never used to eat much of that, as I thought that the fat content was too high, but according to this particular health regime, the fat in avocado is good. He allows hummus, tabbouleh, falafels and fantastic soups, and much to my amazement I'm actually enjoying it. The other day I had a unique experience. Travelling to Bristol, I arrived a little early for the train. For ten years I've been getting on trains with coffee and a croissant, but I actually found a little stall in Paddington Station where they sell fresh soup! Radical, huh? What's more, I was totally amazed to find that it tasted better than the coffee. I'd already had a huge green salad for breakfast – so the result of this is that, with all those things taken away, I'm eating better than I have done for years.

I don't like drinking wheat grass (Robbins recommends two ounces a day) but if you just take it like a shot followed by a fresh orange juice chaser you can actually consume the stuff without feeling sick. Have you tried it? It is the most repulsive drink. Really, really horrible. Apparently it's a wonder drink: of the 102 minerals in the earth, 92 of them are absorbed by wheatgrass. Not to mention the amino acids, vitamins, enzymes and chlorophyll it contains. I still hate it but I'm drinking it as often as I can. I'm taking the acidophilus and that really is a wonder. You want to experience 'regular'? Well, I won't explain – just try taking this. It needs to be fresh and kept in the fridge. If it's not in a fridge, it's not the real thing – so go to a health-food shop, not a chemist. I haven't bought essential fatty acids yet, but I'm getting there. Now, are you taking a good quality multivitamin tablet every day, and if not, why not? Do you really think that your diet is perfect? Go buy your multivitamins and get with the programme.

It's easier to get up earlier, easier to go running. I've started to play the piano every day and do some yoga. One morning I even got up at 7.30 and went rollerblading in Battersea Park. This is not normal behaviour for me. I've rung friends I've not spoken to in ages. I've driven my daughter crazy by dancing a lot and singing in the shower.

'I'm sorry – I warned you that I might be unbearable for a couple of weeks after the course.'

'Yes, but do we have to have singing in the shower at 7am? Can't the piano only be played after 8.30?' she groans as I chop up some more spinach. But, although she rips the piss out of me, I've a sneaky suspicion that she likes me like this. When I got back from Bristol, seeing her missing her boyfriend and looking glum, I said, 'Do you want to go out?'

'What?'

'It's only 8.30 – we could make a 9pm film. Anything you'd like to see?'

'Well, yes – but you only just got in. Aren't you tired?'

And the truth was that I really wasn't tired at all, although I'd been on the go nonstop for over 12 hours. So we went out. The following morning I went to a friend's house to help him do some space clearing in his home and we worked for 12 hours with a 30-minute break for lunch. He was flagging and I wasn't, even when I got in at 1 am. So – so far – it's all going well. It may wear off, but I'm not sure. Robbins said so many times, 'Life will never be the same again.'

So now what? You may well ask. Out of the hole and full of wheatgrass juice, with just a belief in kindness to guide me, it is tempting to go bounding off down the road Tigger-like to 'help' the first lost person who comes along and may not need or want my help anyway. No, now a little fresh wisdom needs to be acquired. And there are old-fashioned ways to acquire this. I have been taught about the importance of moving the body and jumping up and down. Now I have to learn how to be still.

* FYI – Human breast milk is only 2 per cent protein.

The Third Element – Wood

Houses the soul • controls judgement •
the dawn • new growth • strategy • gives
direction in life • eyes

Be Still – Ten-Day Silent Retreat

The day before I leave, they send the programme. It's the same for every day.

4:00am	Morning wake-up bell
4:30–6:30am	Meditate in the hall or in your room
6:30–8:00am	Breakfast break
8:00–9:00am	Group meditation in the hall
9:00–11:00am	Meditate in the hall or in your room, according to the teacher's instructions
11:00–12 noon	Lunch break
12 noon–1:00pm	Rest and interviews with the teacher
1:00–2:30pm	Meditate in the hall or in your room
2:30–3:30pm	Group meditation in the hall
3:30–5:00pm	Meditate in the hall or in your room, according to the teacher's instructions
5:00–6:00pm	Tea break

6:00–7:00pm	Group meditation in the hall
7:00–8:15pm	Teacher's discourse in the hall
8:15–9:00pm	Group meditation in the hall
9:00–9:30pm	Question time in the hall
9:30pm	Retire to your own room; lights out

There was a reason I'd thought this would be a good idea – but now that I'm looking at the programme it slips my mind.

Movement, I'm told, is discouraged. This is the Vipassana technique, and I chose it initially because a friend who had taken the course said, 'They don't mess about.' He tells me he was nearly sick from the physical pain of sitting still for so long. Another friend informs me that, on this course, she had her first 'out of body' experience, which she attributed to her frantic desire to escape the pain. I'm not even there yet and I can feel myself rebelling. 'What's wrong with movement anyway?' That very same movement that Anthony Robbins says is so important to keep our minds and bodies healthy. Right now I love Anthony Robbins ... and would like to have sex with him. Lots of movement.

Sex, of course, is another thing that they don't allow. But they take it further than that: there should be 'no physical contact whatsoever between persons of the same or opposite sex'. Just how erotic or distracting can shaking hands be? I was hoping to seek inspiration from the gentle, flexible growing-ness of wood, not turning myself into a dried-out block of it.

And it goes further – you must make every effort not to distract others in any way, or be distracted by others. This means that I have to go ten days without making anyone laugh. There are a million ways to make people laugh without speech; a tilt of the head, raising an eyebrow, a positioning of a fork can do it. I am going to have to refrain from all such antics. The instructions say, 'Students should cultivate the feeling that they are working in isolation.' Oh, great. Isolation. For a writer. Just what I need more of.

Speaking of being a writer, the list of things that you are not allowed on the course, which includes intoxicants, drugs, sleeping pills, tranquilizers, tobacco, computers, TV, radio, music, cameras, mobile phones or pagers, personal food, religious or spiritual items of any kind, and books, also includes writing materials. They are attempting to deprive me of the one piece of wood that I am really dependent on ... a pencil. As a writer, attempting to share my experience of this course with you, how will I able to remember ten days' worth of experience? I often don't even remember what day of the week it is, let alone what I was doing eight days ago. I shall have to break the rules. They are not making this easy for me.

The sitting-still-and-not-moving malarkey has to have been dreamt up by a man. No woman with half a brain and periods is going to make up any spiritual discipline that involves sitting completely still for that long. Surely we suffer enough with our bodies? No – this has to have been some crazy male idea. Some man who is concerned that his dick seems to be ruling him has dreamt this up as a means to suppress his troubling organ. Makes sense, doesn't it? Women have pain every month anyway – do they need more pain? No, they know that suffering has dubious benefits. It makes you feel rotten and prevents you from being able to do all the jobs that need doing.

According to the course blurb, 'Vipassana is one of India's most ancient meditation techniques. Long lost to humanity, it was rediscovered by Gautama the Buddha more than twenty-five hundred years ago. The word *Vipassana* means "seeing things as they really are". It's the process of self-purification by self-obser-vation.' There you are – 'self-purification'? I told you that it's about men not being happy with their dicks. What I'd like to know is – what did Buddha's mother have to say about all this? I mean, while he was sat under a tree purifying himself, I bet she had a shelf that needed fixing and firewood that needed collecting.

Why are nearly all the great spiritual teachers celibate, anyway? Monks and nuns of all traditions have been doing this 'avoid the pleasure' nonsense for far too long (in my not-so-humble opinion). There is enough suffering in life naturally – why can't we enjoy the pleasures that life has to offer? Surely it's about balance?

And listen to this: anyone crazy enough to return for a second time isn't allowed a 'high or luxurious bed' (rather a generous description of the quite ordinary beds they give first-timers) and is asked to refrain from 'sensual entertainment'. Do they just mean masturbation or would picking your toenails and scratching your back be included? Now I suddenly want to roll up my futon that is on the floor and go out and buy a 'high and luxurious bed'. I feel thoroughly irritated by it all. What the hell is wrong with a wooden base for support and a mattress on top of it? I have a young friend who is a member of the Hare Krishna movement. As a result of this he not only has no sex, but has also removed the mattress from his bed and sleeps on a board. In my observation, the result of this, far from him accruing any spiritual benefit, is that he delays going to bed for as long as possible, sleeps badly and goes around shouting at his family. Now I may not be very enlightened, but it strikes me that a spring mattress and a good shag would do him and those he lives with a whole load of good.

As for not making eye contact with anyone – what kind of a life principle is this? I don't mind giving my eyes a week off and only looking inwards, but even on a strict Anglican convent retreat I wasn't forbidden to smile at the nuns. Doesn't everything that is important in life have to do with our relationship with others? Isn't placing too much value on our own selves going down the wrong path?

A friend from California called yesterday and I confided rather glumly, 'I'd rather be going away for ten days with someone I love.'

'But you are going away with someone you love, aren't you?'

Silly sod was trying to remind me that I'm supposed to love myself. I should have expected that reply. Perhaps I don't love myself to the lengths demanded in California, but I think I'm just fine.

Another thing, the people going, 40 men and 40 women, apparently – I mean, who ARE these people? On this retreat I have to practise the elimination of craving and aversion. This means that I may not think, 'Mmm, he's got a lovely vibe, I'd like to sit near him,' or, 'That woman looks anxious about everything – I'll keep away from her.' Nope, no making friends. Would you have believed that there are 80 people in the UK who want to subject themselves to this? This course is booked up months in advance and happens regularly all year round, all over the world.

The whole objective of the course seems dubious. 'To eradicate suffering.' What's wrong with suffering anyway? I can embrace suffering as a part of life. Maybe that's a particularly feminine thought? Physical suffering we are obliged to accept as part of life on a monthly basis, and personally, as love and suffering seem so often to go together, I'd rather have both than neither. There is that wonderful line in the song *Didn't We Almost Have It All?* that goes, 'The ride with you was worth the fall.' And that's how I feel about painful experiences. The last man – I wouldn't trade a single moment that I had with him to take away the suffering. I feel no need to eradicate suffering.

I know what you are thinking. You are wondering, if I don't agree with the ethos of the course, don't want what that they offering, think it's going to be painful and am going to break the rules – why am I going? Good question. That's what I've been asking myself all morning. Well, the answer is that, in spite of all the above, I think I may learn something. I think ten days sitting still would be good for anyone and everyone. We can all learn something. I just have no idea what it is.

First Breath (Days 1–2)

I am woken by a bell at 4am and unless I'm in the shower at 4.03 I know that all the showers will be taken. I have 40 women around me and no men. But this is not the joyful experience that the company of the female sex would normally be because they're silent and they keep their eyes fixed firmly to the ground. The trees around us exude a subtle and gentle energy. The people less so.

At 4.30, I will sit down on the floor with my legs crossed for two hours. I even have instructions about where my thoughts may or may not go. I may not visualize anything of a spiritual nature; if I am a devout Roman Catholic I may not visualize Mary or Jesus, if I am Muslim I may not consider the goodness of the Prophet, I may not even repeat the word *Om* to myself to assist my mind in becoming still. I may not visualize the trees outside with their roots in the earth and their leaves turned to the sky. I may not even reflect on why I am here or where I'm going. I am allowed one sole focus: the feeling of the air passing in and out of my nostrils. That's it.

The mind and the body rebel. I sit for ten minutes focusing on the breath, then, still sitting up with my legs crossed and my back straight, my mind checks out and I fall asleep. A short time later, I have no idea how short, I wake with my body screaming at me – 'Move!' But I'm encouraged by the pre-recorded instructions just to keep my focus on the air passing in and out of my nostrils. Another eight hours of this today. Total silence of mind and body must be maintained for the next nine days. Wish you were here?

Depending on your point of view, I have either entered some strange cultish group, controlling in the extreme, and signed away all pleasure along with my humanity, or I am on a rigorous meditation course that, for many, produces life-changing results.

I have no chance to decide that this is madness and make a dash for the door. I had a lift here from one of the men but they are on the other side of the meditation hall and we have no interaction with them. I can't call anyone because I had to give my phone to them when I arrived and no-one is giving it back for the next ten days. The only way out would be to kick up a fuss and say that I'd changed my mind. So I'm observing my breath. Which is going in and out.

Coming here was fun. I met Tom, a young art student (20 years old and doing a course like this?), and Justin, in his 40s, who owns his own business, and we had a good laugh on the drive up here. Justin, a carnivore and self-confessed junk-food addict, knowing that he was going to eat nothing but light vegetarian food for the next ten days, decided to stop at a super-market. He bought sliced dead pig, chocolate éclairs, cakes, caramels and brightly coloured candies so artificial that you could get a sugar high just looking at them.

'I expect I'll lose weight on this course,' he said, happily stuffing all this in his mouth.

Tom and I laughed at him and helped him out with the éclairs. I asked Tom how on earth a fantastically sensible-looking person like him came to be doing a course like this. 'A friend recommended it.'

'You, Justin?'

'Yes, me too.' Weird friends people have.

I've seen a film about this course and the results that it achieves in Indian prisoners. They take an entire high-security prison, both the prisoners and the warders, and they put them all through the process. The results are extraordinary. In only ten days, the prisoners learn that the source of all animosity is within themselves, and they all come out ready to take vows never to harm another living creature and to speak only words that will bring peace and harmony to others. I decided that I could tolerate a little pain to learn whatever they were teaching.

The rules are sacrosanct. But, as you see, I am breaking one of them. I have smuggled in writing materials. I am not supposed to write because, although you're not here, I'm still talking to you. Even if it's a bit of a one-sided conversation, I'm not solely within myself. Well, maybe – but I've thought about it a great deal. My challenges are to be free from distraction, to concentrate on the course and to share it all with you. If I don't allow myself a Lamy pen and some paper, I'll spend the course feeling more anxious about recall than I would be if I wrote some quick notes. But it's a tough decision that has required telling a lie, and this is not something that I ever do lightly. When I got here I was asked to agree to the rules and I said that I would keep them all, but I had smuggled in my forbidden notebook in my wash bag.

This course is different from others of its kind because it is being led by a Mr Goenka, an elderly Burmese man, who isn't here. Each evening we have an hour of his recorded discourses on video. They have been using the same tapes for years. Since these same tapes are played to the inmates of the aforementioned Indian prisons, we are soon hearing, as if it is a radical concept, that stealing or lying isn't a good idea and committing murder or rape is right out.

All audio instruction on how to meditate is also pre-recorded Goenka. There are two assistant teachers in the hall, but they don't actually teach. Twice a day they answer questions. Between 12 noon and 1pm you may book yourself a ten-minute session, or after the final meditation before bed at 9pm you may ask your question but it will delay your chance to sleep.

On day one, I love the focus on the breath, but I seem to be the only one who has trouble standing at the end because my legs have gone to sleep. I know we are supposed to be learning not to become attached to things, but I am already attached to the idea of keeping still. It's not enough for my ego just to learn how to meditate – I want to meditate well. How absurd is that?

By evening I am despairing. I keep falling asleep after having been aware of about three breaths. You are not encouraged to breathe in any particular way, but just to 'observe what is'. As a special dispensation, you are permitted to take a few slightly deeper breaths than normal as needed to avoid falling asleep. This doesn't really work, as the deeper breaths just make me more relaxed and it's only the pain that's keeping me awake. We have been meditating for seven and a half hours; I must have been asleep for about seven of them, maybe notched up about 15 minutes of the required state of mind and body, and spent the remaining 15 minutes rubbing aching legs.

On the morning of day two a girl near the front of the

meditation hall starts to cry hysterically. She must have brought some negative experience with her; the meditation, according to the teachings, will have 'brought it to the surface'. The volunteer helpers gather round and gently persuade her to leave the hall. I almost envy her – I have no such strong emotions surfacing.

I try to imagine that I am here forever. I have become a nun and it is my body's job to adjust to sitting calmly like this without providing shooting pains or sending me to sleep. All I have to do is sit and be aware of my breath. I mean, how hard can it be? Realize at 2pm that all I get for the rest of today is an apple and a pear and start to think about digestive biscuits. This is not where my focus is supposed to be. Focus on the breath. The breath.

I discover that you can have pain shouting at you and still fall asleep. How is this possible? And I have no idea what the pain is. What is in that bit of our bodies? The liver? A kidney? Is it the spleen? What does a spleen do anyway? I know practically nothing about the inside of my own body.

At the end of day two it all seems stupid. How can I concentrate on my breath when I'm worried about why a kidney is hurting? Why not just move? Why not just sit in a chair? Is it just an endurance test? But I'm glad I can't share my negativity with others. Like the process or hate it, you have to keep your thoughts to yourself. And focus on the breath.

They are intent on the course being serious, which means excluding all possible levity from every interaction, but I'm still managing to amuse others. A man I love taught me to wear odd socks as it always raises a smile. This trick works well here, as everyone is always looking down. And this morning I heard stifled laughter from behind me when I sat down at a weird angle and actually managed to fall off my own meditation cushion. But I am focusing on the breath. Really. The breath. The breath. The breath.

Second Breath (Days 3–4)

On day three, I decide that the 'lifts' page on the organization's website is a scam. It appears to be a generous, well-organized system in which all participants are encouraged to either give or receive a lift to get here, but it is actually one more thing that prevents us from leaving. Or that is how it appears to me at 5.03am this morning. The 4.30–6.30am meditation is a killer – the body is used to sleep at that time, but here you put it into the torture of the meditation position and it's agony for mind and body.

But, oh joy, today we are led from just thinking about the breath to thinking about 'sensation' in the nostril area. So, without moving, you ask, 'Is it itchy? Does it feel dry, moist, pulsating, perspiring or what?' This is strangely fascinating. I find that, suddenly and inexplicably, one nostril feels larger than the other, or there is a curious feeling of warmth on the upper lip between the nostrils, or, yes, an itch that you are encouraged not to scratch but to observe neutrally until it goes away.

All this would be enjoyable were it not for the screaming pain from my kidneys. Can kidneys suffer from coffee withdrawal? When we finally have a chance to ask questions,

I moan about the pain and not understanding what it is or why it's there.

The assistant teacher – one Frances Barnes, a practitioner of this meditation method for many years, who receives no pay for helping out this week – speaks to me very quietly. 'Just ignore the pain. It will pass. Concentrate on the sensation in the nose area.'

I see the slightest suggestion of a twinkle in her eyes. Already I had guessed that this would be her answer, and she seems to know that. Then it's back to the meditation again. Mr Goenka's voice comes over the speakers:

'Start again. Start again. Start with a calm and quiet mind. Alert and attentive mind. Pay complete attention to the triangle of the nostrils and the area of the upper lip. Be patiently persevering and you are bound to succeed. Bound to succeed.'

I imagine mass murderers in jails across India listening to this and being bound to succeed in experiencing sensation in their upper lip. In my case, I succeed for five minutes of a two-hour session, then either my kidneys demand my attention or I'm asleep.

On day three at teatime I radically catch the eye of one of the other participants. When we arrived, we had a couple of hours when we girls could talk before the 'Noble Silence' was introduced. As girls often tend to chat about boys, I told one, called Jo, that I was likely to be distracted this week by a date that I'd been on the day before.

I haven't told you, have I? About my hot date? Well, last year I was a speaker at a conference. There was another speaker, over six foot, Jamaican, and drop-dead gorgeous, with a passionate concern for the underprivileged, a job fighting street crime and a charisma to die for. After the conference I approached him and asked him if he would be happy to receive some feedback on his presentation. He modestly said that he would be, and I leaned over and gave him a kiss on the cheek. I'm such a shrinking violet – I know.

Nine months, maybe a year, went by and I forgot all about him. I had assumed anyway that a charismatic man like this would be married with six children. But he went away and read one of my books, and, about a month ago, I received an e-mail. 'Remember me? I knew when we met that we would meet again because I would make it so.'

Wow! An alpha male taking proactive action. Can you imagine such a thing, girls? And asking me if I'd meet him for dinner. I replied asking him what his marital status was. No single woman wants dinner with an attractive and interesting married man. He was separated, he told me. I was tempted to reply, 'Does your wife know this?' but thought better of it. Still, I checked: 'And there is no other woman who is going to be sending a paid killer after me if she hears that I've met with you?' Apparently not. So he got his dinner.

And he was interesting. He knew both how to talk and how to listen. Women will be thinking that I have strayed into the land of literary fiction now – but no, I assure you, it was so. And we seemed to have chemistry between us that made people look at us when we walked down the street together.

'Why are people looking at us?'

'Because I'm black and you're white.'

'That's it?'

'I'd say so.' Pity. My ego had imagined it was because he was drop-dead gorgeous and I was glowing as I walked along with him.

'This doesn't happen to you all the time, then?'

'Not if I'm walking with a black girl, no. It's not that people are necessarily for or against, it's just that they are trying to figure it out.'

Yes, well, I was trying to figure it out myself.

Anyway, I'm digressing on this digression. What I confided in Jo was that at the end of the evening, when we had reached the parting of ways, he had given me two little pecks on the lips, and, well, the man has lips. Viv's lips, I knew instantly, were in danger of becoming the major distraction of my retreat. The 'I am not supposed to be thinking about Viv's lips' retreat. Even though, I considered, they are worthy of contemplation, meditation and visualization.

So now I catch Jo's eye, she smiles and I remember this conversation. I have to lower my eyes quickly. Leaving the canteen later, she glances back at me, stifling giggles. This is dangerous stuff. One spontaneous piece of levity and the entire atmosphere of focused concentration that they have worked so hard to create will unravel. Now I will have to avoid her for fear of smiling. I seem to have made a friend.

During the evening video discourse on day three, Mr Goenka has a knock at all the major religions. He likens most religious observance to a sick person going to the doctor, then raving about how good the doctor is and reading out the prescription every day but never taking the medicine. All spiritual practice, he teaches, should make us better people. It is no good following the God of love, he says, if we aren't loving in our everyday behaviour. This may seem obvious, but according to him it isn't. So what is he teaching? I should be loving in my behaviour? Mmm, think we have that one covered in 'My religion is kindness'. Nothing else I need to learn, then? Excellent.

I'm summoned by calm Frances to ask if I'm OK because I have occasionally moved my spot in the meditation hall to be able to lean against the wall. I tell her that the pain is really quite intense and she suggests that there may be something spiritual going on, 'the body releasing old sankharas'. A sankhara, apparently, is a mind/body trauma, what we might call an 'issue', that is stored in the body. As the course works with the unconscious mind, the pain is said to suggest some kind of progress; it isn't just pointless suffering. Well, that's good to know. Have to stop writing now and go to bed. It's 10pm and I'm sitting in the loos as my roommate went to sleep at 9.30pm. Nothing like getting up before 4am every day to inspire early nights.

Day four is Vipassana day. Later today we will be taught what all this is about. I am still in agony and am forced to be entirely engaged by the sundry pains that my body is providing for my enhancement. We are only sitting cross-legged on cushions. Why should anyone experience such torment doing that? Some of my fellow sufferers have provided themselves with an amusing collection of extra cushions. We are given one each, but they don't seem to mind how many you use as long as you sit on the floor and keep still. Only those people over 70 and one heavily pregnant woman have been given chairs. Everyone else is endeavouring to make themselves as comfortable as possible. Some of the men, I see on the other side of the hall, have allowed themselves as many as four cushions on top of each other. Not too flexible, the guys.

I manage to stay awake for the entire 4.30–6.30am meditation. It's amazing what the body can get used to. One of the men breaks down in the 8.30 session. Jolly decent of him to show some solidarity with the woman who broke down on day two.

Had a wondrous experience in one of the meditation sessions this morning: a brief moment of no pain. To not be in pain is indeed a wonderful thing much underappreciated. The Vietnamese Buddhist monk Thich Nhat Hanh has a lovely way of getting us to remember this. He reminds us that if we ever have toothache, the only thing that we want is for the toothache to go away. Yet when we don't have toothache we forget to appreciate it. So in his tradition they have a greeting: 'How is your non-toothache day?' So I hope, as you read this, you are enjoying a non-kidney-ache day, a non-knee-ache day and a non-leg-ache day. In fact, I hope that your day is and will remain totally free from any of the agonies that I will be inflicting on myself this afternoon.

Meanwhile, I have discovered that it is possible to cheat in the attempt to focus only on upper-lip sensations. I have been attempting not to think about a certain man. If I flip this around and connect thoughts of him to sensation in my upper lip, and, furthermore, tell myself that if I stop thinking of my upper lip then I must stop thinking of him too, then it becomes far easier, worryingly easy in fact, not only to focus on my upper lip but to enjoy doing so. But of course this is not the exercise.

And there is a second way that I have found to cheat. When my body is in a lot of pain, I think of Viv's lips and the pain seems to dissipate. Naughty Isabel. We have been told not to use such tricks. I must not think of a man whose name I'm not mentioning and I must not remember the touch of Viv's mouth on mine. Even though it seems that on my own behalf I don't have the strength to maintain my concentration, as soon as I bring in the strength of an old love or a little texture, I appear to make instant progress. How pathetic is that? On the other hand, I think to myself, we have only been forbidden to visualize religious imagery or recite mantras. I don't recall that lips were specifically singled out. I could ask, 'Er, Frances – when Mr Goenka said that we shouldn't use visualization, do you think he meant Viv's lips?' She would say, 'No visualization of any kind.' Without even cracking a smile. Sigh.

The mind does strange things during this process. We are told that memories long forgotten may surface. This morning, coming round from daydreams of my hot date, I found myself remembering a scene from my childhood – my mother on her deathbed. This is not an image I've dwelt on much, guessing that she would prefer me to remember her in happier times. But this morning there she was, weak, unconscious, about to breathe her last. I looked at the image and observed it with 'equanimity', as we had been advised to do, and then pulled my monkey mind back to focusing on the sensation just below my nostrils.

After lunch the absent Mr Goenka teaches us the Vipassana technique. He takes our point of focused concentration, which he has been helping us to hone with attention on our upper lips, and has us move it to the crown of the head. From there, the technique requires you to move your attention downwards slowly, observing, with as much equanimity as you can muster, every sensation in every part of your body. When you reach the tips of your toes, you start again. It's that simple and that complex.

It takes him two hours to lead us through this in a guided meditation while we sit totally still. I concentrate completely for the first hour as he re-frames all the pain in our bodies as different types of sensation – throbbing, pulsing, pushing, perspiration, dry, heavy, pulling and so on. But after two hours I'm ready to kill him. Or unplug him at least. I can see that this technique would be very useful for people planning to put themselves through prolonged periods of torture. Planning to work as a spy? Danger of being caught? Find your local Vipassana course. I know I shouldn't joke about torture, but the levels of pain they are teaching us with are very generous. I know I'm not the only one appreciating them because I've seen the agonized faces. But of course no-one can complain or comfort anyone else, even with a sceptical glance.

I do notice that as I move my focus to one area of the body I tend not to notice the pain in other areas. But this is supposed to be about body awareness, not the lack thereof. Anyway, I have no desire to torture myself. All that Anthony Robbins says about the importance of moving our bodies makes this self-punishing stillness seem even more ridiculous. I'm a million miles from any serenity.

I know that they have our best interests at heart. They are certainly not after our money – there is no charge for the food and lodging, payment for the course is voluntary, and even that is not accepted unless you complete the ten days. It's generous and impressive. But there is another way to see all this discipline. We have all given up our individuality in the name of some kind of spiritual gain. I'm reminded of the words of Richard Dawkins: 'The flip side of trusting obedience is slavish gullibility.'

It's like being part of some kind of social-science experiment like the famous Stanford Prison research in 1971. A group of college students were selected at random and asked to become either 'prisoners' or 'guards' in an experiment that was intended to last for two weeks. The students had no history of psychological problems, medical disability, crime or drug abuse; they were just 24 college students who wanted to earn the small amount of money on offer for participating in what they all knew was an experiment. They were put into a simulated prison. Those who were the prisoners started to become depressed and show signs of extreme stress, while those who had been designated guards became genuinely sadistic. The experiment had to be cut short after only six days.

I'm not suggesting that anyone is experimenting on us, but the way that we give up our freedom and power is very scary. My roommate is looking utterly miserable and I can't even pass her a note, because firstly it would be interference in her process and secondly I'm not supposed to have pen and paper. If she were sobbing in the middle of the night I might not comfort her, as it could be a 'sankhara releasing'. It feels Orwellian. This may be the most interesting course that I have ever taken but if I have to torture myself to discover, experientially, the benefits of not craving or being attached, then it seems I'm just not craving the experience of nonattachment enough. I want to go and dance in the woods. Naked. Preferably.

Third Breath (Days 5–6)

Then, just as quickly as I wanted to leave, I want to stay. I manage, somehow, a one-hour meditation in my room between 4.30 and 5.30am and then 50 minutes in the meditation hall, without even leaning against the wall. This has to count as progress. In one of the early discourses Mr Goenka quoted the famous imperative from the temple at Delphi – 'Know thyself' – and I'm sure this must have been part of what Apollo meant; it is certainly one aspect of knowing yourself to sit and give your full attention to all the different sensations inside your own body. It is a high demand to do this with neither any aversion to the feelings of pain or craving for the feelings he calls 'bliss'. Personally, I have yet to experience any of the latter; my body obviously thinks the former is the better teacher. Damnation. The closest that I get to bliss is ending the meditation and going outside to listen to the birds. But, slowly and surely, the body does seem to give up the struggle against the pain. I have a strange new twinge under my arm, which of course I have decided must be a lymph gland and so, naturally, a sign of the onset of cancer. But what to do about these aches and pains that we all have? Here, at least, the answer is simple: just observe.

Compared to many, I don't have that much stress. Being a writer, I don't have to commute and my time is my own. But here, I can now see how stressed I've actually been. The kidney pain seems to be linked to worry in some way, as it sometimes disappears completely if my mind is focused on other things. It's all weirdly compelling – especially as they say in the literature that many 'dis-eases' are psychosomatic. Pain certainly feels real enough, which is why the focus here is on the body. The constant exercise of observing your body and scanning it again and again from head to toes and from toes to head is all about reality. We have been constantly told to look for the sensations that are there, not for those that we wish were there. Look for the subtlest sensation and don't use the mind to invent anything. Shucks.

I have to confess to having cheated again in one of the meditation sessions. (Please try not to condemn me; remember we have ten of these a day.) Instead of looking for any discernable sensation on the crown of my head, I imagined Viv's lips kissing the crown of my head, then moving down to my forehead, and so on down to the tips of my toes, and then back up. And so on. This kind of disobedience is self-defeating, I know – but it sure makes an hour of meditation more fun.

Lunchtime on day five and a notice has gone up. We are now exhorted to demand four 'hours of strong determination' of ourselves every day. This sounds good in Pali but ridiculous in

English. We must be 'strongly determined' not to open our hands, eyes or legs, not even for a second's break. It's hard. This morning I did open my eyes and what I saw was magical. Eighty figures, 40 men on one side of the hall and 40 women on the other, all sat wrapped in blankets, their backs straight, as still as statues, the discipline impeccable. If we had been a community of monks, which is what we resemble during these ten days, we could not have been more still. I'm impressed with the way the fantastically controlling nature of the course has brought this about. There is certainly a heavy price to pay, but anyone who came here wanting to learn how to sit still has succeeded already – and this is only day five.

A friend of mine, the American author Pamela Bloom, once had the privilege of discussing meditation with His Holiness Gyalwa Karmapa, the head of the Kagyu lineage of Tibetan Buddhism, in the early '80s. Pamela complained that she just couldn't sit still and that, although she had a sense of the value and importance of doing so, she just hated it. She said that he looked at her for a very long time with deep compassion and then said, very slowly, 'I think – if you continue to practise – in 10 or 15 years – it is – going to get – easier.' When Pamela tells this story today, she adds that he was right. It is now over 15 years later and, with daily practice, it has become easier for her. Sigh. So – back to sitting still.

Occasionally strange things happen. In a moment when I'm actually doing what I am supposed to, a white light seems to flicker inside my mind's eye. It is bright and pouring onto me and into me. I instantly put this strange experience down to a lack of oxygen (have I been holding my breath?) or too much oxygen (have I been breathing too deeply?) or something. At least here there is no chance of me giving it any religious significance or seeing it as any kind of blessing. On this course the teaching is clear – there is nothing external impacting on us. There is only the mind.

More bad behaviour. I drink a cup of coffee after lunch. Also wink at Jo. Very bad. But then I do the meditation after lunch in my room. Manage 55 minutes and crack just before the hour is up. More flashing white light. Wonder if it may be my subconscious trying to signal to me, 'Have you gone crazy? Move your legs!' Feel strangely confident that I may make the 60 minutes in the 2.30 session. It's weird the things that can give a sense of accomplishment here.

But at 2.30 I manage only 45 minutes before I open my eyes and glance up at the clock. Before I came here, friends teased me about how I would manage ten days without speaking, as I'm so gregarious. That, it turns out, is the easiest part. Getting the mouth not to move is painless compared to insisting that the body and the mind not move.

Unless I allow myself to fly away completely. In one session today I give my mind wings and soar off to bestow 100 kisses upon the unsuspecting body of a man I love. I wonder if thought does travel and if, as he is working at his desk, he becomes aware of a strange tingle on his fingers or the back of his neck. One hundred kisses later, I leave him to his work and fly off to check up on Viv's lips. I wonder if they are feeling kissed today, because they have been.

This is only a brief escape. The work of the course goes on. What sensation do I feel in my scalp? (Ignore pain in the back.) Ah, there is some sensation on the scalp – an itch – hooray. Next, what sensation do I feel from my face? Yes, good, I can feel some tension. (I said, ignore the back.) What sensation do I feel in my nose? Dryness. And I can feel my hair falling on my ear and – Ow! My back hurts. Decide more firmly to ignore the pain in my back. What sensation do I feel in my neck? And so on. And so on. We have been told not to miss a single part of the body in our search for sensation and, of course, not to label any sensation as good or bad. Just observe. Just observe. As our old Burmese teacher has told us 1,000 times. We are not to prefer the warm tingle of a nipple on a T-shirt to the hot tightness of a tense thigh muscle.

Find myself alone in my room and make up another way that thinking of Viv's lips can help me release all the tension in my body. Ha ha. I wonder if I have broken the rules again. Can't remember whether the rules say no sexual contact or no sexual activity. Ah well. Body is much more relaxed anyway.

This leads to another weird hour of the inexplicable white light flickering in my head. This time it just keeps coming, so I am able to try out my theory that it may be based on a lack of oxygen. I try breathing harder but the flickers keep coming anyway. Only manage to get the light, or whatever it is, to flow down as far as my shoulders before it dissipates. Also I seem to be experiencing huge amounts of heat in my body during the meditations. Who turned the heat up?

Day six. The mind is so undisciplined. I say 'the' mind rather than 'my' mind as I am encouraged to place little importance on the idea of 'I'. In joyful obedience to this concept, I decide that i will enjoy writing 'i' with a small letter, but it proves to be impossible. In the West we are so full of 'I' that when I type this up my computer won't allow me this small symbolic piece of humility. It corrects my attempts to use a small letter. It's hopeless. On top of that, my editor looks at the writing and says, 'I'd like more of your opinions here.'

'Oh, for heaven's sake. I'm supposed to have no ego but still have opinions?'

So, to step back into the course again: as I understand it, we are attempting, in a serious and committed way, to liberate ourselves from the suffering caused to us by our reaction to pleasure and pain. Of course, we react with craving to pleasure – we want more of it. We react with aversion to suffering – we want none of it. We perceive the causes of suffering as outside and beyond ourselves: a relationship that we can't have, a job that doesn't happen, the loss of a loved one.

Of course – enlightened as I know you are – you know, in theory, that it is not the events themselves but our reaction to them that causes our grief or our joy. This course is not, as the first Feng Shui man claimed, saying that we cause the external events. It is just raising our awareness of how we respond to every single stimulus, whether it is an internal thought or pain from an external source. And we are being taught to understand this on an experiential body level. As you learn to be objective, viewing pain as merely one set of stimuli and pleasure as another, you can step back, or step inside, and see everything as it really is – which is just more changing phenomena. An itch will pass quickly, a pain will not take much longer. Yesterday, Mr Goenka made everyone laugh by describing how an experienced Vipassana meditator will approach dying. He will look at the body in complete consciousness, thinking, 'Ah, this is an interesting sensation.' We all know that the very stuff that we are made of will eventually pass away. Everyone we love we will eventually lose. I'm not meaning to depress you – but this is so. The more equanimity we can acquire in the face of these realities, the more we will see any craving and aversion as a bit daft. All attachment is futile. And what's my opinion about all this? Well, it makes sense, innit?

And where does that leave Viv's lips? They are not less attractive, but perhaps if this course really does the job I can approach them with a little more of what our venerable teacher calls 'a calm and balanced mind'. Maybe I will still be happy to get up in the morning if I decide, or Viv decides, that those lips are not for me to kiss or be kissed by.

I do understand they need to guard against every possible distraction. In moments when it is too hard and too painful, you go on concentrating anyway because there is just nothing else to do. Even exercise like yoga is forbidden. You may walk in the fields nearby in the few brief breaks, and that's it. So it does become easier to focus on watching the body. In my case, the pain moves a bit but refuses to go away. So what is that about? According to the teachings, it is some deep-rooted attachment to something, and when I see the sensation with objectivity it may simply pass away.

So we all go on. The people here are amazingly dedicated. At 4.30 this morning almost 80 people sat, like statues, dedicated to learning. I wonder if any of them are dealing with sensations that out in the world would be called 'cancer'. Here we have been specifically told not to attribute causes to the sensations or apply labels such as 'old sports injury' – they are all just sensations. So for a cancer sufferer, the sensation of what he or she may know to be a tumour growing is as unimportant as a cramp in the foot: just another changing phenomenon to be observed and to remind you to be 'equanimous'. Goenka uses this word about 100 times every day. We don't use the word like this, but tend to only speak of 'equanimity'. I listen to him and I long for a dictionary – but I let it pass like an itch. He's hard not to be fond of, this old man whose 20-year-old course is putting us through all this pain.

I skip a one-hour session this afternoon to lie in the sunshine and listen to the birds. Jo sees me and seems unsure whether to smile or look disapproving. Her face, which I'm not supposed to be glancing up at, betrays her indecision. But then I feel guilty about the time off so vow to work extra hard tonight. When you concentrate hard on all the sensations, moving your mind up and down your body, a kind of mind current is created that you can actually feel. After doing this for an hour, I feel so hot that I'd pull all my clothes off if I hadn't a sneaky suspicion that this would be against the rules.

Later I see Jo walking on the grass barefoot. This is not against the rules, as she is obviously using the grass to help her focus on sensation, but it still seems outrageous. I feel like a strict elderly nun – shocked at the sight of someone's feet.

Fourth Breath (Day 7)

Day seven and I do the entire 4.30–6.30am meditation in the hall in strong determination to keep alert. I hope that I will achieve many things in my life but I don't expect that getting up at 4 on a regular basis will be one of them.

It's starting to feel like the home stretch, especially as day ten will include smiling, talking and free time – all radical concepts difficult to imagine on day seven. It's fascinating how much you can tell about people without having spoken to them. One returning student has a look of such superiority on her face that it is almost comical. One girl has looked scarily angry all week. A third is now regularly returning my smiles and even initiating them. Today I made someone laugh out loud by attempting to walk through a door with an umbrella up. Yesterday someone signalled me with a sound to look at some sparrows that were happily taking a dust bath. It's easy to see who is ministered to by the prolific bird life and who is oblivious to it. I know that this is supposed to be about looking inwards and not looking outwards – but wouldn't many of the wisest saints tell us that ultimately it's all the same? Surely the sparrows are part of the process too? Are we not also the sparrows?

The looking inwards sometimes seems obsessive. It may be harder for me than for others; my roommate has observed every rule with such fanaticism that I worry about how far she would go. In observing her I've been reminded of another fascinating study about our tendency to obey.

In the early 1960s, Stanley Milgram conducted some

research in which random individuals were shown into a room with one other person and asked to draw cards that appeared to designate them as either 'teacher' or 'learner'. In fact, the volunteers were always designated 'teacher' – the learner was an actor – but they thought the selection was random. The 'learner' went into another room and was asked a series of questions. For each incorrect answer, the 'teacher' was required to administer an electric shock to the 'learner' in the next room. Are you following?

As more wrong answers were given, the intensity of the shocks increased. The 'teacher' heard the 'learner' crying out in apparent pain (the shouts and screams coming from a tape recorder) and, understandably, started to express discomfort.

In order to get the 'teacher' to keep administering the shocks, the people conducting the experiment (dressed in white coats and looking like important scientists) could say these four sentences, in this order, and nothing else:

1. 'Please continue.'
2. 'The experiment requires that you continue.'
3. 'You must continue.'
4. 'You have no other choice, you must go on.'

Two more points. The actor playing the 'learner' had been told to mention that he had a heart condition, while the 'teacher' had been assured that he would not be held responsible for the experiment.

Here is the really scary bit. How many of the 'teachers' do you think continued raising the shock level to the maximum 450 volts? Milgram had taken a student poll that predicted that 1.2 per cent would be persuaded to obey the orders to that point. In fact, 65 per cent continued to administer the shocks (or so they thought) and inflict a life-threatening amount of electricity on a stranger just because an authority figure told them to.

I remember, when I was at university, being sceptical when I read about these experiments. (You can read all about them online and see the pictures if you don't believe me – just search for 'Stanley Milgram'.) Now I see how easy it would be to replicate them here. We are being trained not to be averse to pain, and we have all agreed to obey instructions. If we had been shown into a room and these Milgram experiments had been set up as part of this course, I guess he might have hit 90 per cent. As far as I can see, I'm the only rebel, the only one missing the odd session, smiling and writing notes. And we all know terrible stories of how young soldiers in Vietnam wiped out entire villages of civilians because they were 'obeying orders'.

My roommate has chosen to extend the 'strong determination' they have asked for in four sessions a day to cover all the rules. The rule to work 'as if in total isolation' she has managed to extend to the point of never glancing up, though we have been sharing a very tiny bedroom all week. She works with such rigidity that she scares me. We have been instructed that when we do resume speaking, on day ten, we are to concentrate on speaking only words of loving kindness. I've been wondering what such words I can bestow on her. I can think only of complimenting her on her strong determination. I wouldn't be concerned if it weren't for the fact that she looks utterly miserable. I know that is her process, not mine, but it's hard to miss.

Those I have ended up admiring here are those who have smiled in spite of the rules – those who I judge have shown greater levels of flexibility and therefore of humanity. But – I keep reminding myself – this is not what it's about. If I kept my head down and just focused on sensation as I'm supposed to be doing, I wouldn't be thinking about Stanley Milgram experiments.

One of Goenka's talks today continued on the theme that when we decide what we like and what we don't like, this leads to craving and aversion, both of which in turn lead to suffering. I realize that I really should speak only for myself when I say that 'we' can tell who we like and who we don't like even without speaking to each other. Maybe others are not doing this. Maybe the other 79 people here are wise enough to give themselves entirely to the process and not be thinking things like, 'I hope Jo will want to be my friend after the course because I think she's fun,' or, 'That person could have been a leading member of the Nazi party coz I can see them committing any kind of atrocity if they thought it was in a noble cause.'

How do I come to be thinking such terrible things? What kind of person am I? If it's true that what we see in others is a mirror of what's in ourselves – am I really this terrible a human being? I found myself wishing today that my roommate would get locked in the loo or something. I just wanted her to be late for once. I suppose at least I am displaying, with my thoughts, all the kind of madness that we are here to root out. Meanwhile it's 11am and I have only done four hours of meditation today. The process goes on.

'Start again. Start again. With a calm and quiet mind, alert and attentive mind, balanced and equanimous mind, move your attention from the crown of your head to the tips of your toes, taking care to notice the most subtle sensations as well as the gross and strong sensations, knowing that they are all changing. This is the law of Dharma. The law of nature. Do not cling to the pleasant sensations or be averse to the unpleasant sensations. Simply observe, knowing that they will pass away.'

It is hard not to cling to the moments when you feel you are successful and to want to repeat them, and hard not to be averse to pain. But each session we are just advised to 'start again, patiently and persistently'. And so, patiently and persistently, I start again.

After lunch, I have ten minutes with Frances. I ask her about preferences, attachments and aversions. I tell her that at lunch I developed a preference for the apple crumble (excellent) and an almost immediate dislike of the pesto sauce (terrible). She explains, with patience and persistence, that there is nothing wrong with preferences as long as you don't develop craving or aversion, 'lose your mind' and go storming into the kitchen if they serve the sauce again, shouting, 'Who is the fool who made this pesto sauce?' Ah, so that is how we know when we have an issue with attachment or aversion – when we lose our minds. Oh dear. I see. And I've been blaming it on my hormones for years. How many times have I unashamedly lost my mind for love? Can we fall in love without losing our minds to an extent? I think not. But here we are brought back to reality by the sensations in our bodies. Goenka forces us to come to our senses.

He reminds us constantly to notice the body the way it is, not the way we think it should be. I recognize this one in relation to my life too. I am so good at seeing how I'd like life to be and where I'd like it to be different, rather than observing it the way that it is. And the lives of others, too: I am upset that this friend is destroying his health as he has put on so much weight and never exercises; another friend rows with her husband all the time, another hasn't given up smoking. Even here I am bothered that my roommate is observing the rules with what I consider to be obsessive rigidity. Is there any hope for me? But this week I am only allowed to focus on the pain in my body – that is my reality and my teacher.

'Is there any evidence that the pains in our bodies will "bubble up and pass away", as Mr Goenka so poetically puts it?' I ask Frances.

'We are making no claims about physical healing, although it can happen.' She smiles equanimously. 'We are training the mind. The evidence is seen when you return home and see whether you react when things happen that would normally throw you off balance. You would previously have reacted in a certain way and now you don't react in anger, fear or whatever your pattern is. You are equanimous.'

'By the way, is that a word?'

'Yes. It's not one that we use very often. But it is a word.'

So this is training in how to have a calm, alert and

equanimous mind. Maybe more pain will help. I get rid of the cushion all together and sit smugly in the single lotus position. This is my ego taking over. No-one is going to be impressed, because firstly they aren't looking, and secondly, even if they do see my impressive lower-limb flexibility, they are wise enough to be working 'diligently' on their own meditation practice.

Cut to a scene in a major feature film. I'm playing the lead, of course. We are all meditating when someone opens her eyes and sees me sitting in the double lotus, humbly, in the back row, levitating about two feet off the ground. Slowly people break the rules, nudge one another to look, and quiet gasps come from around the hall until the whole room is staring, amazed, at my closed-eyed figure hanging silently in the air. Then slowly I descend, open my eyes and allow them the faintest smile. After all, they shouldn't have seen. They shouldn't have had their eyes open.

Back in the real world, without cinematic special effects, I can't sustain the single lotus position for longer than ten minutes. So that doesn't work. It's hard work, this form of meditation. Really. HARD WORK.

For the early-evening 'strong determination' session, I decide that I will not move no matter what happens. It can't kill me. It's only pain. And yes, I do discover that you don't need to scream, even if parts of your body are screaming, and that no matter how much your back hurts, you may still want to scratch your nose. It's good to know that I can keep a calm and equanimous mind in spite of all the self-torture, but I'm sure that there must be less painful ways to learn this.

When is a cult not a cult? Mr Goenka likes to have a go at all the major religions on the grounds that they do not transform people. In his video lecture tonight he tells the story of a man who comes to him and claims to be a follower of Jesus Christ because he believes that Jesus is the son of God. Mr Goenka explains that if God is truth and Jesus is living a life of 100 per cent love and compassion, then of course he is the son of God. But, he goes on, it's no good calling yourself a follower of Jesus and then doing nothing to develop these qualities in yourself. You can't call yourself a follower of Jesus and avoid your next-door neighbour.

His attacks are not limited to Christians, Muslims, Jews, Hindus, or any of the other religions that include a God or Gods. Even the Buddhists come up for attack. 'You can't say "I take refuge in the Buddha" three times and then have the rest of the day off.' But they asked us to repeat this same Buddhist vow three times on day one. They have said, 'This is not a sect,' a hundred times, but he still asked us to say these words, which are usually used only if you wish to become a Buddhist in a formal sense. He says that this path is 'nonsectarian', but I have still heard him say that this is 'the eternal truth', which is funny, as I'm sure a Roman Catholic once told me that Roman Catholicism has the only eternal truth; I distinctly remember a Jehovah's Witness saying the same; and I'm sure there are a few people in the world who believe that only Allah really has it. Sigh.

Fifth Breath (Days 8–9)

I am now reacting to all this with a kind of rage, which itself is ironic as everything he teaches is about not reacting. This morning I am adding to the list of things that make this very much like a sect. Or at least things that anyone with any knowledge of cults would recognize. Goenka says that he is not a cult leader because he doesn't have long hair, flowing robes or garlands round his neck – he just looks like an ordinary house-holder. So what? Being a cult leader is not about the costume.

His videos and audiotapes have obviously not been edited at all. No attempt has been made to make them more suitable for a Western audience. Why not edit the videos? Is this because they see his words as sacred in some way? We have been told all week that the course doesn't demand 'blind faith', but it is impossible to debate or discuss any of his teachings. Questions with his assistant teachers are limited to instructions on the method and seem to receive the universal reply, 'Focus on the sensation.' So, in one sense, blind faith in this method is exactly what they are asking for. You can't disagree with a video.

We have all been bowing at the end of each discourse and each meditation session – not even to him but to a video of him – and even though they have been to great lengths to explain that this is 'purely a mark of respect and gratitude', we have still been bowing. Personally, I don't object to bowing. Firstly it stretches the back after the meditation and feels good after an hour of sitting, and secondly I learned during my travels in Tibetan Buddhism that it's good for our humility. But I don't feel like bowing to him today.

Also, I notice with amusement that although he has said every day that the course is nonreligious, he can't resist blessing us at the end of every discourse. He raises his hand in the gesture that any priest or religious person from any tradition would use – and he blesses us. The intention is pure, but it does rather contradict his claim not to be a cult leader of any kind. If I gave a talk and, at the end, raised my hand, closed my eyes and said to the audience, 'May you be happy,' I would have to be unsurprised if I wasn't booked again and if a rumour went around that I'd been swallowed by my own ego.

Every night in his blessing he wishes us 'REAL happiness and REAL peace' with the emphasis on 'real', as if implying that any happiness and peace that we may have chanced on so far can't quite be the real thing because this path alone offers the true liberation. This, he claims, is because his method is the true version of what Buddha himself taught. Presumably those teachers of Buddhism who do not use pain as a tool, like Thich Nhat Hanh and His Holiness the Dalai Lama, just haven't quite got it?

And yet another thing that got me hopping mad last night was that in order to 'come out of your suffering' you have to 'commit yourself to the path of Dharma'. One way to do that is to come back here as server – in other words, ten days of voluntary work. But not because 'it's good to give service' or 'because it's fun', as Shelter may say to those who volunteer to feed and care for the homeless at Christmastime. No, here you serve because it is the way to 'come out of your misery'. So it follows that if you leave here and you are still miserable you can't be practising right. Based on the sum total of human misery out there and the human tendency to blame ourselves, it's no wonder that his courses are full up months in advance. Am I sounding a little cross this morning?

Amidst all this there is much good here. They give us a bed, feed us and provide an opportunity to meditate all day. This is no small gift. Today we are asked to continue the awareness of sensation when eating and walking and everything else that you do in a normal day. This is a practice that I'm familiar with from Vietnamese Buddhism and it is a blissful experience. So I will practise awareness of sensation all day with joy – but no more forcing myself not to move. My knees are still hurting from yesterday.

I sit relaxed and perfectly still for an entire hour today, completely still like a statue, cross-legged and straight-backed, running my consciousness up and down my body, looking for each sensation, but manage to run my brain through the entire plot of the film *The Shawshank Redemption* at the same time. I remember how Morgan Freeman was prepared to spend two weeks in solitary confinement for the joy of playing three minutes of Mozart's opera *Le Nozze di Figaro* over the loud-speaker system and I feel that I have a whole new understanding of that film now. (You can watch the scene if you type 'Shawshank Redemption – Excerpt' into YouTube.)

I'm less freaked out, however, by my roommate's fanatical adherence to the rules. Now I just feel sorry for her. She seems to have misunderstood the instruction to 'practise continuously', which is supposed to be about the constant awareness of sensation. She woke at 4am and instantly sat up and screwed her face up into the expression it has had on all week. When the hours of 'strong determination' are over and everyone else gets up, she is still sitting there tense and grim. I very much hope, for her sake, that she is having some kind of sublime inner experience. Although even if she is, as our venerable teacher reminds us, she is still in danger. Should she cling to any good sensation she will develop a 'new sankhara' – an attachment stored in the body in some way – and from that will come 'deep misery'. Goenka always repeats this for good measure, elongating the E's: 'Deeeep misery.'

A girl who was crying yesterday still looks very miserable today. I wish I could pass her a message: 'It's OK – out there, chocolate still exists.' But of course she may be 'releasing a sankhara' or getting over an eating disorder, so it's probably a good thing that I can't.

So I'm still unsure about all this. The larger part of me believes that it is these tiny touches of human kindness that can stop us wanting to die if we are in pain. I know myself that when I've been through really bad times, it's some friend showing up, being absurd and making me laugh, that has reminded me that life is, after all, worth living. It is possible that she may be here attempting to get over some major trauma; she could have been attacked or anything. She has been in isolation for a week telling herself that she must not think about her pain with aversion but just observe it. If all this goes wrong for her and she doesn't understand the process correctly, she has two problems: the initial pain and the guilt that she will now feel because she has 'created an aversion' and so is furthering her 'deep misery'. I've always tried to advise people that suffering is bad enough without adding guilt on top of it.

If it doesn't go wrong and she understands what they are teaching correctly (as far as I understand it myself), she will observe and realize that she may be creating an aversion and just let it go 'with a calm, quiet and equanimous mind', not reacting to pain in the past but being fully in the present moment, aware of the impermanent nature of all phenomena. Something like that.

Meanwhile, I am still here, in the meditation, aware of sensation and scanning my body. Sometimes I feel subtle sensations and tingling, sometimes I don't. Sometimes I swear I can feel virtually no sensation from my body at all. Today my attempt to take my attention down my body seems to get wedged somewhere – the scan just can't progress. In these instances we are advised to 'simply observe with a calm and equanimous mind'. Am I being repetitive? If I want to succeed in passing anything from this course on to you, I will have to ask you to copy this on to your fridge door and start every day with it.

'Start again. Start again. Start with a calm and quiet mind, alert and attentive mind, balanced and equanimous mind . . .'

Anyway – I must stop writing and go back to the meditation hall. I am sometimes terrified of being caught and having this little notebook confiscated. Is that a smoke alarm above the loos or a camera? And then I catch myself – this may feel like a prison, but I'm pretty sure that it's a smoke alarm.

Neither Viv's lips, nor my daughter, or even the neighbour's cat seems to be real any more. The only reality seems to be internal. Can't decide if this is good or bad.

Teatime. I spent another hour today, one that could have been used for meditation, sleeping. It feels incredibly wicked and slothful. I am a bad person. Have discovered why I was experiencing heat in my body earlier in the week. Apparently it's the pickle I've been adding to my food at lunchtime. Amusingly, they have hot pickle among the available condiments, presumably as there is always a high percentage of Indians from various groups on these trainings. But then Goenka says in one of his evening discourses that if you are experiencing much heat in the body it's probably due to the pickle. So much for mystical experiences.

The girl who was crying yesterday is now banging chairs down loudly and looking pissed off. There is also a young Indian girl here who is so calm and gracious you'd think she had been meditating for a hundred years. This morning the young Indian girl looked up at the pissed-off girl with such compassion it was truly beautiful. Except the pissed-off girl didn't see this look, as she didn't look up. Only I saw it – because I looked up when I shouldn't have done.

Almost all of the 40 women are making eye contact and smiling now. Only my roommate keeps her eyes firmly down. How ironic for her that she ended up with a person often nicknamed 'Tigger' as a roommate. I know it is bad of me, but

I've even started to find deliberate ways to distract her. Today I washed out two very skimpy thongs and hung them on the washing line outside our room. How bad am I? And I brought a yellow bath duck with me (I had a feeling that the course might be a little lacking in surreal absurdity) and I have put it in our window so she can't help but see it. The yellow bath duck in its incongruity appeals to my sense of the ridiculous. But it may not appeal to hers. I'm bad. I know.

In the evening I do another whole hour without any movement and I'm pleased with myself again, but oh, how our bodies are able to provide pain. I approach Frances and ask, 'How can I not have an aversion to pain? It hurts!' She is very sweet and tells me to observe it neutrally and analyse it a little, asking, 'Is it worse here or here? Where is the centre of this sensation? Where does it seem to end?' And study it, much the way NLP practitioners advise those who are scared of spiders to study the creatures objectively, looking for information. Frances is a good example of the teachings. She's equanimous. But her posture is terrible. See how bad I am?

The evening of day eight and finally the old man is saying some things in his evening discourse that begin to make sense of all this. He has explained again that if you see something out there in the world that you either like or don't like, this can lead you to create a craving or an aversion. That much we know, right? Now the idea is that, not discerning whether it's craving or aversion, the body holds the sensation in the unconscious mind. It's the *sensation* of craving or aversion we become addicted to. But by training the mind to just observe, knowing that 'this too shall pass', we come to really know and, more importantly, FEEL what is. What actually is. In the present moment. We need to liberate ourselves from addiction to the sensations of craving and aversion. We need to know in our bodies, not just in our heads, that both pleasure and pain will pass away. Once you really know this, as soon as anything in the world threatens to rob you of your equanimity – or, more accurately, as soon as you find yourself about to allow any external person or event to rob you of your equanimity – you recognize the sensation. And you're not fooled. I think that's it.

Re-training the unconscious mind, huh? So that's what this course is about. Maybe he deliberately waited until the evening of day eight to start spelling it out because he wanted us to have an experience first.

Day nine and I missed the 4.30–6.30 meditation completely and went back to sleep – till 5.30. I only realized this when I noticed that I was the only person out of the 40 women who was using the showers when we were supposed to be meditating. It does seem that I am the only bad person here.

Brief bit of teaching this morning was again fascinating. We are, as we know, both mind and matter. The body is, at the atomic level, just a collection of high-frequency vibrations. I'm sure that's not explained with scientific accuracy, but you know what I mean. We are made of subatomic particles, right? We are energy. So ...

Imagine a teddy-bear-shaped sponge. If the bear is new and you pour water onto its head, the water will flow freely through from its head to its toes. This is similar to what we are trying to achieve by running our mind through the body. A free flow of subtle energy is created when the mind moves through the body freely.

In case you've never done anything like this, let me try and show you. Put the hand that is not holding this book down on your lap, the table, or whatever. Now become aware, in a focused way, of the sensation of your fingertips touching the surface. Now see if you can pick up any sensation from the part of your fingers between the tips and the finger joints. Then between finger joints and knuckles. Then slowly move your attention through your hand, being aware of any tiny, subtle sensations, until you reach the wrist. OK?

So, to go back to the bear ... if your body, like mine, is not free of complications like a sponge bear's, then when you run energy through your body you get stuck. For example, I can focus on the crown of my head, but as I get lower down I find that my forehead won't allow me to feel any sensations unless I stop to relax the tension in the nasal passages. Here they teach you not to try to change the situation. Not to stop and deliberately relax the muscles but just to observe (repeat with me) 'with a calm and equanimous mind'. We are constantly reminded not to react to any negative sensation with aversion or positive sensation with clinging – 'just observe reality as it is and eventually it will pass.' Everything does, both the good and the bad. So he is teaching us both awareness and equanimity. These two are, he explains, 'like the wings of a bird or the wheels of a cart' and equally important.

The whole process is beginning, finally, to make sense. Now I think I understand a little better what Buddhism is talking about when it teaches that 1) life is suffering and 2) there is a way out of suffering. According to Mr Goenka, this is it.

As to how all this will apply in the real world, I guess we'll find out tomorrow when we get our phones back and find out what has been happening out there – for better or for worse. Will we all be surprisingly calm if we hear that someone has died, someone has been born, or a ban on chocolate has been introduced?

By the way ... apparently when all the 'coarse or blocked sensation' (i.e., pain) and 'blind areas' (i.e., no sensation) are gone and you can experience a free flow of subtle sensation in every part of the body inside and outside – it's an extraordinary experience. Are you thinking, 'That sounds cool, I'd want to try that'? If so, tut tut, I have introduced you to the possible onset of a craving. Or you have introduced yourself to one.

Right – back to my meditation – don't want to waste a second and actually want to get back to it. We are so limited here ... we only have ten hours a day to practise.

Evening. I can sit for an hour with no movement, no sleeping and no aversion to pain. Hooray! When I examine the pain by trying to work out where the centre and the edge of it are, as Frances suggested, it really does seem to lessen and sometimes to go away completely. It's very mysterious. Today I was totally concentrated. Towards the end, my right leg went completely numb and I was thinking, 'Numb? Ah, I notice that this is a sensation that is a mixture of "hot" and "heavy" – how interesting.' I didn't even think of moving.

In his discourse on the last night he tells two stories – one I know and one I don't. They are both worth me re-telling and you remembering. Please highlight down the side of the page so that you'll be able to find them later.

So, ready? In the first story, a group of men comes to see the Buddha. One accuses him of being a charlatan, one tells him that he is a god, a third threatens him and a fourth flatters him and fawns on him. The Buddha smiles at them all (equanimously, we may assume) and thanks them, but says that as he will not accept their gifts, they remain the property of those who brought them. Remember the story of the unaccepted gifts next time someone attacks you with unsolicited abuse or flatters you with unnecessary and unwelcome praise. We know that the gifts belong to the giver because ten people will see us ten different ways. Some believe that we are saints and some see us as sinners. Some consider me a gifted writer, while my ex-husband thinks I'm a crazy woman; many people consider me wise, but my daughter often considers my actions to be examples of great foolishness. So where is the truth? The truth must surely be to remain equanimous and repeat after me: 'Please take your gifts with you when you leave.'

The second story concerns a mad artist. The man paints a picture of a very beautiful woman. He paints her with all the external attributes that he most loves and gives her an expression that shows all the inner qualities that he would most like to be with. Then the man sits down and weeps and wails because he can't be with this woman. And he will not be comforted and told that this is just a picture. Ha ha. We've never done that, have we?

He paints a second picture of an ugly woman. He grossly exaggerates each feature that he most abhors and paints her as angry, unbalanced, and insane. Then he doesn't know what to do because he doesn't want her in his home and can't get away from the painting fast enough. Ha ha. This is completely outside our experience too, right?

Sixth Breath (Day 10)

The last day, at last. I feel strangely anxious about getting my phone back. I'll be relieved to speak to my daughter, to pick up messages and to find out where international current affairs are after ten days. Who may have died? We are reminded here that all things, all people, will pass away. Perhaps I've learned something – I'm at least noticing my attachment to the hope that nothing and no-one has passed away.

But when the silence is finally lifted I ignore my phone and instead step outside with one of the other participants, a tall and beautiful black girl called Helen. I ask, 'So what did you make of all that then?'

She laughs. 'Would you like to go for a walk?'

'Yes.' I want to listen to Helen, who has done the course NINE times. It takes all sorts.

'The thing is that I have lots of objections to the course, lots of objections to his philosophy – I have objections to pretty well all of it.' She's smiling. 'The first time I came I hated it so much that I never dreamed that I would come back. But it's helped me. It continues to help me. So I come back.'

I'm suddenly terrified that, on my return to London, the course will prove to have helped me in some way and I'll end up wanting to come back.

'I object to the lack of joy,' I moan. 'I mean, why does learning about happiness have to be so miserable? No smiling for ten days?'

'If you look around today you'll see everyone smiling. Everyone is happy.'

'Yes. That's because it's over.' Helen chuckles at my indignation. 'Whatever people have come from, they are bound to be happier when they get home. Compared to this level of non-happiness, non-laughter, this level of "deep misery" – everything is better.'

'It's serious inner work, Isabel, and it's only for ten days.'

I am reassured, as we walk around the grounds, to hear how many things one of the 'old' students doesn't agree with. 'I distrust the claim that this is the "true" interpretation of Buddhism,' she says. Free thinking – what a relief.

We pass one girl who has looked utterly furious all week. She's all smiles. 'You've looked so angry all week,' I dare to say to her, quite honestly.

'Yes. I have been. I had some stuff that I was dealing with. But I think I've dealt with it now.'

We wander back to the canteen to find that they are serving

chai tea and homemade cake and everyone is chattering as if to make up for lost time. The sound of laughter fills the hall – wonderful human laughter. And what's magical is that there's nothing but goodwill and friendliness. Just as there must be among the mass murderers and their warders when Goenka is through with them.

One of the girls says, 'Have you heard there is a discussion later? "Brad and Angelina – will it last?"'

There is now a lawn where the men and the women can talk to each other, but no-one has moved. Instead we start to do exactly what we have been advised not to do: compare experiences. It turns out that many of the others seem to have experienced something that I didn't even get close to: the apparent rising and 'passing away' of sankharas, some manifestation of buried memories releasing themselves.

One girl confides in us all, 'I was quite horrified by what I saw in the meditations. I saw snakes and spiders coming up and out of my mouth, my nose, my ears, and I just sat still and remembered to be equanimous.'

'That's a relief to hear,' says another. 'I had a weird image of ants crawling out of my ears, nose and mouth and then disappearing. I thought it must be some kind of dream.'

A third girl reports an experience 'like pus coming up and out of me'. And a fourth actually says, 'I had pus too.' I listen to all this with amazement.

One very thin lady tells her story. 'Towards the end of one of the meditations, I was about to get up when I had the most extraordinary feeling, as if a brick had risen from somewhere deep inside me and was lodged just under my diaphragm. It felt so real I was afraid that I wouldn't be able to breathe. So I just sat and did everything I could to remain equanimous. I breathed very lightly and observed as he had told us to do, but it didn't move. I just went on sitting and observing it. I could hear that nearly everyone else had gone off for the break by then, but I didn't dare to move; I just went on sitting and meditating with all the calm mind that I could find. People started to come back and settle for the next hour of meditation. I told myself not to be scared or excited or anything. I just went on breathing in a shallow way, as I didn't feel that I could take a deep breath with a brick inside me. Another hour went by and eventually I felt this hardness rise up and pass right out of me.'

There's stillness around the table as we listen. 'What do you think all that was about?' I ask eventually.

'I think it was something to do with my marriage. I was in a very unhappy marriage for over twenty years. I stuffed so much down inside me. Every day I stuffed stuff down. I guess it was some of that "stuff" coming out.'

So all these women weren't just 'being' after all, they were sitting 'doing' – releasing sankhara?

I complain that my unconscious has not provided me with ants, snake, pus or anything half as rich in imagery. All I have experienced is pain. 'And some white light, I put that down to my brain suffering withdrawal from caffeine. Oh, and lots of heat a couple of times, but that stopped when I stopped putting the pickle on my lunch.'

The girls seem to find my comments believable enough. I

also announce, 'I'm amazed at how everyone kept the rules.'

'I didn't,' says someone indignantly. 'I climbed a tree yesterday.'

'But there is no rule against climbing trees.'

'Oh, no, I suppose not.'

'Sarah has been texting her boyfriend all week,' says another face.

'Really?' Even I'm shocked at this. 'But that means that you haven't been in isolation, Sarah.'

She's rather crestfallen. 'I know. To be honest, I rather regret it now. At the beginning of the week when they said that we had to hand in our telephones, I thought it was a test or a joke or something, so I kept mine. And once he'd sent a text and said, "How's it going?" and I had stupidly replied, then he wanted a running commentary. I see now that I should have handed it in.'

I admit that I've been taking notes. They ask if I feel that the experience has been less rich than it might have been if I hadn't been chatting to you. 'I don't know. Maybe. Maybe not.'

I want to see Jo, but she left the day before. 'Old' students are allowed to come and just do part of a course. I go up to one of the other girls who had seemed to me to be sane. One I could have dug a tunnel with if this had been *The Shawshank Redemption*.

'I like you,' I declare. 'You seem to me to have been doing the process fully and yet have had a sense of perspective about it all. You even smiled back when I smiled at you.'

'I don't think it's true that I have a sense of perspective. I'm just easily distracted,' she says. And it's true – when she speaks she seems charmingly flaky. The impressions I've formed of who these people are – they are all wrong. They're all just pictures that I've painted.

That night I organize a pyjama party in one of the rooms. Just for the girls, of course. Boys' quarters are still out of bounds. But I meet Justin in the field and ask him to bring me the chocolates that I know are still in his car. So I'm very popular, arriving with chocolate caramels after our week of sugar abstinence.

We tell ridiculous jokes till what seems like the middle of the night. 11pm. Even the simplest absurdity is hysterical.

'Did you hear the one about the magic tractor? It goes down the lane and turns into a field.' We laugh for ten minutes.

I made a point of inviting my roommate. But, even with words, she's very serious. Later, back in our room, we chat till 2am. I admit to having found her 'determination' verging on the scary.

'I was just very, very concentrated,' she says.

'And you were always last to get up after each meditation.'

'I just took ages to come back down to earth.'

'And you haven't made eye contact all week.'

'Yes. But it's been hard. You're really funny. One day I had to rush out of the room suddenly to avoid laughing.'

To avoid laughing?!

'Why wouldn't you want to laugh?'

'We were supposed to be in silence, weren't we?'

So she had liked me all along. All those images I'd had – like the man who painted the picture and then couldn't bear to live with it – they were all inside me. Not a very comforting realization.

The next day we finally leave – and never have I been so glad to get into a car and drive away from anywhere so beautiful. I'm sharing a lift with my same two travel-mates again.

'You're looking thinner, Justin.' I've been looking forward to saying this for days. 'So how was it for you?'

'I once walked to the South Pole. We saw nothing but snow for sixty-one days, apart from one day when we saw a bird. And every day was painful because you were pulling a sledge and every part of you ached. The walk was without mercy. It was like that. I kinda enjoyed it, though. '

'Tom?'

There's a very, very long pause and then Tom says, 'I'm glad I came. You, Isabel?'

I have to time-warp the answer. It's two months later now. I don't think I'm one jot more equanimous, certainly not that I'm aware of anyway. But I've had a taste of meditation's journey inwards. This course has made me into a meditative traveller. I have been sitting, not for an hour in the morning and an hour in the evening as Mr Goenka recommends, but for just 30 minutes every morning. I can sit now and not move. It's a start. This is the beginning of what you need to be able to do to meditate in any tradition.

And Emily has a beautiful Buddha made all of wood who is currently sitting meditating in our kitchen. I look at him and I think that he really does house, in his little wooden soul, everything that the element of wood is supposed to bring to me and to the place where he sits. He doesn't do anything; he just is.

If I can just continue to emulate him and sit early in the

morning, then strategy and good judgement will grow in me, I'm sure. Invisibly, imperceptibly as wood grows, I will gain a sense of direction. I may even remember to be equanimous most of the time. Unless someone I love smokes a cigarette, in which case I make no apologies for losing my mind. Sometimes not to be equanimous is important too, isn't it?

The Buddha, though, goes on sitting, perfectly calmly ... and I do admire him. Next time I take a meditation course I'll choose a different route – a different understanding of the path, a different ticket. There are many meditation courses all over the world. Learning how to just sit, be calm and breathe has to be the most important way to put my religion of kindness into practice. Whatever the weather. Whatever life gives us or takes away. I'm quietly excited that by sitting still I may have made a little progress.

The Fourth Element – Water

*Life journey – expression – tremendous
power and tremendous gentleness –
sustains life just by being itself – prevails
without doing – ears*

'Who Are You, Anyway?'

Then, just at the wrong point in the journey, a spiritual master teacher arrives in my life. I was hoping to be taking Viv and his lips off to indulge in the addictive nature of craving and everything is going in the opposite direction. I'm inviting Viv to go a spiritual meeting? Doesn't that sound like the way to put any man off a potential relationship? Three dates in and I'm looking about as weird, wacky, New Age loopy as it's possible to be. Well, all I can say in my defence is that I didn't go out seeking this alternative refreshment for the soul – it just arrived in my 'in' box. Quite literally – on Facebook.

I had been thinking about the next element – water; about power and gentleness, how something so light can cut through a rock. The ridiculous little 'water feature' that I bought after the Feng Shui consultations reminds me of all these things. It creates the sound of running water all day, prevents the air being too dry, and calls the soul back from doing to just being.

There is a story that Jesus once said to a stormy sea, 'Be still,' and the waves grew calm.

I'm not a great believer in the idea that things happen at the time when you need them to. But sometimes I notice that events seem to suggest a certain synchronicity whether I believe in it or not. I had a Facebook message from a reader. Now, as all those of you familiar with the joys of Facebook will know, it is so called because the messages come to you with an image of the face of the sender. The photo was about an inch across on my screen. On one half of the picture was the smiling reader, Hannah, and on the other half a remarkable-looking man with eyes like oceans – full of infinite love, warmth, pain, playfulness and challenge all at the same time. I stared at this tiny picture. His face was about the size of the tip of my little finger.

'Who,' I wrote to her immediately, 'is that remarkable man? Is that your husband? Your lover? He looks extraordinary.'

She wrote back immediately, 'No, he isn't my husband – he's my guru.'

Guru? Was she for real? People have gurus still?

I've always been completely uninterested in gurus of any kind but something in this man's eyes interested me.

'Can I go and hear him teach?'

'Yes, he's based in London. In Brixton.'

'A guru in Brixton? You're not serious.' Brixton is known for good music and lots of ganja.

'He teaches all over the world – mainly in America, Ireland, Germany, Italy and India – but Brixton is his home. But ...' She hesitated, knowing that I'm a writer and suddenly protective of him. 'May I ask why you want to meet him?'

I thought about it for a second. 'I want to meet him, Hannah, because he looks whole. He looks like an ocean, and I haven't met many people who look like oceans in my lifetime. Whatever he's teaching I want to learn.'

'OK,' she wrote back, 'you've passed my test. Have a look at his website – it's www.mooji.org – there's some audio there and lots of clips on YouTube.'

Hannah told me that the meetings are called Satsangs in his tradition (from a Sanskrit word meaning 'to associate with truth') and they are open to the public, but there was a private session for his closer followers coming up. It was on the day of a friend's birthday party on the same side of London, so I enjoyed the party and then called a cab, but all the cab companies were quoting a 45-minute wait. I left the party, took off my shoes and ran down the road looking for a taxi. I could not and would not arrive late. I was barefoot, dodging the traffic, focused and determined – I was going to find a taxi.

Why was I so determined? I don't believe in gurus. I believe that people can become disempowered by seeing the teacher of the source of wisdom, rather than nurturing it in themselves. But I was running anyway. Maybe I just wanted to be in the presence of a man who looks like an ocean. Maybe some of his wisdom would wash over me.

When I arrive it's 6.57pm and he's due to start at 7. Everyone else is already seated and waiting. There is only one tiny space left in the front room of his home, and that is at his feet, literally. I'm shown to the front and sit down gratefully. They give me water to drink. This is obviously the right place.

The room is painted in bright, pleasing colours with large pictures of Indian spiritual masters on the walls. The people are almost all white, with some Asians; almost all female, plus a few men with what I call 'a very well developed feminine side'.

Then Mooji comes in. Now, I don't know what you think of when you hear the word *guru*. But whatever you are visualizing, I can guarantee that Mooji ain't it. I'd guess he's in his later 50s, Jamaican, beautiful beyond belief, playful and funny – he even has dreadlocks. He says, 'So w'at do you t'ink?' in an accent that makes me laugh and with a deep base timbre that makes me purr.

There is brief silence and then he asks playfully, 'Does anybody have any idea what these meetings are about? Some of you have been coming for a very long time. Some faces are new to me.'

There is a silence from those who have been coming for a long time, and so, not being a shy little bird, I decide to amuse him by telling him. 'Well, I've never been before but I think I can take a guess at what they are about.'

'Oh, yes?' His eyes sparkle with a childish delight.

'I think we may be on the planet to learn unconditional love and I think you know something about that – so that's why your room is full. I've never met you before tonight, but I'd say people are here to learn that from you.'

He listens, pauses for a second or two, and then replies, 'Unconditional love, you say? Then you say something that I'm completely lost about. You say that I know how to do that. And my feeling is that I don't know how to do it.'

'Maybe you know more than some of us?'

'Is love a "knowing" thing? Is it about "knowing" something?' Hmmm. Maybe not. I'm silent. Always a good sign.

'I don't want to make it about a use of words,' he goes on. 'I don't know if it's something that you can do. In some religions it's taught that you must practise love, show love, and all of this is good because mankind needs it. But there is also a point where love flows out of you effortlessly, which requires no practice. You come to a place of recognition – of understanding inside yourself – and thereafter the love just flows effortlessly. Not just love – your being is in effortlessness. Which I think is what we love most. There is no pressure in effortlessness. And why? Because there is no-one who can do effortlessness. Your mind cannot do effortlessness. Your mind can only imitate effortlessness. So something in us is already there which is effortless. And Satsang is an opportunity to recognize and to discover that.'

Now I know why I ran here. Effortless 'being' from which love flows? Yes, please.

He continues. 'Not to create. Not to imagine. But to be in direct – I was going to use the word "contact", but even this word would not be good, because contact means between one thing and another thing, and there is something closer than contact, closer than intimacy – being at one with your original being. Out of that, something flows. And we call it love. Effortlessly and unconditionally.'

'Unconditionally?'

'Yes, because it has no expectation. It's not trading or bargaining. There is no "I will love you if". There are no conditions. All accepting. But how to "do" it, I don't know. And this is where the joy is. Because if you did know, then you could claim to have something special. More than anybody else. My feeling is not like that. My feeling is that we are all that love, fully and completely.'

'But then why is the world in the mess it's in?'

'This love or this being seems eclipsed by some fascination with something external. Some intention, ideal, goal, some thought seems to hide it. And we seem to be investing tremendous energy in thoughts, in efforts and projections. So these have to be recognized and they have to be removed somehow. I don't know if *removed* is the right word – perhaps abandoned or ignored, because there is nothing more powerful that you can offer from yourself than your attention. Your attention is what you have the power to give. And you are giving your attention to many things, so many intentions, and this somehow fragments your power.'

We sit still and try to digest all this.

He smiles at us effortlessly. Then after a while he asks us, 'Who is "I"? How do we "know"?'

I sit silently trying to experience who 'I' is. I'm glad that I haven't come with a question because, instead of giving answers, he's asking more questions. Who is it that knows? Is it our mind that knows? If we lose our memories, are we still ourselves? Who is it that is observing our thoughts? Can you answer any of these questions?

Before long I'm totally lost. The very 'I' that came in begins to disintegrate under these questions and I feel peaceful and weirdly blissed out. It's not even the words, the questions, the tone of voice, the face; it's the presence of the man. It's as if he has spent so much time in meditation in the most profoundly peaceful places of what Christ calls 'the kingdom of God within' that he has somehow brought that kingdom, that state of being, with him. As if he could be both there and with us in the room at the same time.

Somehow in the room there are two Moojis: a cheeky, playful Jamaican man from Brixton who, no doubt, once smoked as much ganja as anyone else in this notoriously drug-filled area of London, and another Mooji, a placeless, timeless presence that has become him, or that he has become. He really is very like the sea. Except he talks and asks the kind of questions that the sea might ask you if it had a voice: 'Who are you?' The answer can't be anything to do with our thoughts, our emotions or our bodies. Who am I? I find I don't know how to answer.

Some people do answer, some ask questions of their own. In a sense I'm not really listening. He could be teaching in Arabic or Chinese for all the difference it would make to me. I'm happy just being here. What on earth does this mean? I certainly don't belong among these spiritual people, but his presence feels like home.

At the end of the two-hour session he reaches out his hand to greet me. Me first, I suppose, because I'm new and spoke first, and secondly, I guess, because I'm seated at his feet. But I feel as if, despite all these other beings in the room, he has still noticed the unique blend of energy and consciousness that is called 'Isabel'. It's not that I want to be special; obviously everyone is special. But I suppose my personality or my ego or someone wants him to notice my specialness amongst all that other specialness that he is more familiar with.

Then everyone gets up and goes forward to greet him. One at a time, some hug him, some just hold his hands for a couple of minutes while they look in his eyes. No words are spoken. I just watch. It's extraordinary watching the level of intimacy of each communication. Not your average Sunday night in Brixton. Not a night at the Ritzy or the Brixton Academy.

All this was about a month ago. This weekend he is holding an intensive course and I'm going back. I want to go back. I want to find out what he is talking about. I want to listen and learn. Christ spoke of the Kingdom of God within us. Mooji seems to be speaking of this, too, but how is it found? Who are we anyway? Mooji knows the answers.

First Wave

I take a friend to the two Satsang sessions on the Saturday of the weekend intensive – Fiona, an old school friend, who says with the natural suspicion that I have come to love in her, 'It's not a religion, is it? He's not going to try and convert me?' I invite Viv, too, but he looks at the pictures on the website and says, 'That's what I call "Primrose Hill people". And there are no black people there.' Condemnation before examination prevents him – and too many of us too often – from exploring new ideas and wonders that may challenge or shift our perspectives. So Fiona and I arrive to find a beautifully decorated community hall in Brixton that's already packed out – all racial groups and, surprisingly, as many men as women.

Mooji comes in, moving slowly and carefully, and takes his place on his seat at the front. In theory he's just an ageing Jamaican with a beautiful face and a beautiful smile, and yet there is something about his presence that I haven't felt since being in the presence of His Holiness the Dalai Lama. And as I feel the similarity I remember that the word *Dalai* actually means 'ocean' in Mongolian. A lama is a spiritual teacher. So Dalai Lama actually means 'spiritual teacher whose understanding is as deep as the ocean'.

The presence of His Holiness was extraordinary, a sense of infinite space from him and in him. As if, as I described it at the time, he were looking at me through binoculars held the wrong way around; he was looking at everything from a perspective that made me feel rather like an ant. His Holiness, in his grace, extended infinite love and compassion towards this curious ant that was asking him ridiculous questions and stumbling over her words, but I felt that I could no more rise to his perspective than I could pull his viewpoint down to mine. He could no more join me than a giraffe could be interviewed adequately by an ant. And I felt this incongruity, even as he shook my hand.

But Mooji is different. The distance is still there – Mooji is also at that height – but somehow he collapses it. This is a different height and a different ocean, but that same feeling of space, of an almost infinitely wide horizon reaching as far as the eye can see. Here, in his presence, is the infinite manifest in this playful man with the dreadlocks. And he's considerably easier to get to see than the Dalai Lama. If you can get to Brixton in South London, you can come and experience him for yourself, or if you look up 'Mooji' on YouTube you can hear him speak on many different subjects.

How has he come to teach like this? Mooji's website explains that in 1987, he had a life-changing encounter with a Christian mystic that brought him, through prayer, 'into direct experience of the Divine within'. The biography on Mooji's website tells us: 'A great peace entered his being and has remained ever since.' Mooji later travelled to India with the intention of visiting Sri Ramakrishna's home in Calcutta but instead met Sri Harilal Poonja, who was known to his many devotees as Papaji. Mooji found Papaji to be 'a living Buddha' – a fully enlightened master. Mooji's biography informs us that 'through the power and grace of his Master's presence, his mind merged irreversibly with its source.'

'Wot?' you may well ask. 'Doesn't our mind only "merge with its source" at death?' Apparently not, as Mooji is very much alive.

Since 1999 Mooji has himself been answering the questions of many types of seekers who come to him in retreats, formalized meetings called Satsangs and even conversations on Skype with questioners all over the world. Papaji and now Mooji are masters of what is known as the Advaita tradition, which is simply knowledge of 'the immutable self'. (Wot's that? Keep reading.) It is conveyed to us mainly by the master asking questions and allowing the seeker to experience the questions rather than seek answers. Does this sound a bit woo-woo? Well, it is. Freedom from anxiety is to be found here – but you're going to have to pay attention.

Mooji bows and greets us with a mixture of 'Namaste' (which means 'I salute the God within you,' for those whose Sanskrit is a little rusty) and a more accessible 'Good morning and welcome to Satsang.' The format is easy: anyone who is 'a seeker after truth' and has a question is invited to come forward and ask it.

'So?' He smiles. 'Anyone for the electric chair?'

A hand goes up immediately and a woman who I'd guess is in her 30s almost races to the front.

'I'd like to ask you about this experience I had about four years ago that has never left me alone. I was reading *I Am That* and the tributes of Stephen Wolinsky to, you know, a guy whose name I can't pronounce.'

'Sri Nisargadatta Maharaj?' suggests Mooji.

'That's the one. I was contemplating his words deeply and I had the most incredible experience. What I had thought to be what I was disintegrated. My mind opened and the world that I had thought was outside of me rushed in as though it was trying to fill a vacuum, and I started to laugh from my belly.'

'Yes.'

'I was laughing because I'd got it so wrong – how I'd been experiencing reality. I knew it wouldn't last and I needed to make the most of it while I was there. I was asking, "Where am I now? Who am I?" There was nothing left where "I" had been. All that was left was compassion. I thought, "I don't have any attributes I didn't have before, I don't have any magical powers, I can't drive a car or do anything that I couldn't do before." Nothing was added, but the sense of who I was had vanished and the world suddenly became right. And then I came back. "I"? I don't even know who is asking you this question, because after that experience ...'

Her voice trails off into confusion.

'OK,' he says, addressing his answer not only to her, but also to us. 'Many people have experiences like dis.' (Love the Jamaican accent.) 'They may vary in detail but in essence it's similar. They say, "This happened to me, six months, six years ago." And in almost every case it's followed by, "And then ..." We thought maybe one day we'd call a book *And Then* because so many people have awakening experiences that may continue for a few hours, minutes, weeks or months. People say, "It was like this ... and then."'

'So?'

'Let's go to "and then" and pick it up there. All experiences pass, they appear in time, have duration and come to an end. So let me ask you: who is having the experience?'

She looks at him blankly. He tries a different tack.

'OK, let's go to "and then ..."?'

'"I" returned.' She seems unsure now even of this.

'You felt that the mind came back and eclipsed the experience? But was there a "me" separate from the experience?'

She looks at him. She's following. I hope you are too. Her look is midway between amused and confused.

'You don't have to reach an answer.' He says, turning to us,

'Some of you have also had these "experiences". When they arose and the little "you" vanished, was there a bigger "you" left?'

He turns back to her. 'What was so different in this experience that it was five years ago and it never left you? Was it that you weren't there?'

'Yes. I was gone and there was just a beautiful feeling left.'

'This "I", do you know what it is?'

'The "I" that I think I am?'

'What went is your idea of yourself. The "me" that is synonymous with mind wasn't there.'

'Yes, my mind wasn't there.'

'And when mind is absent, what remains? Please tell me.' No doctrine, just questions about her experience. I love it.

She sits silently, not knowing what to answer. Mooji answers for her. 'Peace? Joy? Space? Fearlessness? Timelessness? Spontaneous existence. That's what's there, and everyone loves it because it is so effortless.'

'Yes. And then ...'

'How did "and then" rob you of this beautiful "state"? What witnessed the returning of the "I"?'

He watches her carefully as he asks the question. She's still silent. 'Slow down,' he says, although she's not saying anything. He goes on with variations on the same question. 'What witnesses the coming back of mind? Have you considered this?'

She laughs. 'I haven't stopped thinking about this for five years.'

'So? What observes the returning of mind?'

'I would have said, "The mind itself," but ...'

'Mind is thought. Mind is not a thing, brain is a thing – this cauliflower inside our heads. When you say, "Mind returned," you mean, "Thought activity returned," don't you?'

'Yes.'

'Observed by what?'

'I'm lost.'

'You say that ego, time, context, relationship, all left, yet something remained because in the absence of these there was peace. If you get to the button I'm pressing on, everything will become clear to you. There only needs to be recognition.'

'I'd better contemplate this.'

'Who is the perceiver? Contemplate this and "and then" will become insignificant. "And then" is just a thought.'

'I'm still here.' She looks around the room at all the faces looking at her.

'What is?'

'I am. My thoughts. It seems to be a habit.'

'Yes, it's our heritage to constantly measure ourselves by the activity going on in our minds.'

'It feels like that.'

'Yes, and we believe the thought that we need to concentrate in order to find more of who "I" am. But this thought is only powerful if we believe it into existence.'

'Yes. I see that. Thank you.' Finally satisfied, she gets up and bows and sits down again in her place.

So what Mooji seems to be saying is that the 'place' that she had experienced, during what felt like moments of transcending her identification with herself, is always present and available – not only to us but 'as' us. As our own nature. Cool, huh?

Fiona's taking notes. Before I have time to think, or time to not think, about what he's said, the next questioner is up: a thin man with a bald head and beard, looking troubled.

'I experience a duality between the moments of enquiry and the moments of just abiding,' he says.

A rough translation of this by Winnie-the-Pooh would be 'Sometimes I sits and thinks and sometimes I just sits.'

Mooji asks, 'Who is aware of both states?'

The bald-headed man breathes in to answer.

'Careful,' Mooji warns. 'Mind is naughty. Don't use your mind to answer or you'll create a third state.'

We laugh as he struggles not to think.

Mooji smiles. 'If I ask, "Who am 'I'?", what happens in the light of this question?'

We stop to look inside ourselves to experience the question directly. Join in, please.

'It's very subtle,' the man says.

'What observes this subtlety? Do you have race or gender?'

Are you following? This is HUGELY important. This is about your relationship with your very self when you stop thinking. This about who you are beyond your body and your emotions and even your thoughts. That observer – does that part of you have race or gender?

The bald-headed man answers for you. 'No.'

'Who can you be?'

He closes his eyes, trying to answer. But Mooji says, 'I'm not stretching for an answer because an answer is a concept. I'm looking to see what happens to you.'

He opens his eyes, looking decidedly more peaceful.

Mooji's questions continue. 'This place – go there. What's it like? Does *it* change?'

He starts to speak. 'I think there is ...'

Mooji asks, 'Do you want to t'ink now?' I love his accent. Just gives all this a little more gloriousness.

'No. I don't want to think about anything. I just want to stay in this place.'

'You fear losing it but you can't escape it.'

'Yes. Only the mind is the trouble.'

'Mostly the world is suffering from thought.'

The thin man goes back to his place and leaves me thinking about just being. Recently I visited an old friend who has been diagnosed, at a cruelly early age, with MS. As her body is giving up on her against her will, she is feeling increasingly useless. She said to me, 'I can't do anything for my family any more.' I remember feeling at the time that it seems to me that her role is to 'be' for her family, to rest and allow them to enjoy her very presence. Indeed, she has no option but to do this. But I kept quiet. I didn't want to seem not to be listening to her sense of frustration, and I don't know how I would feel if I couldn't walk any more.

Our society seems obsessed with doing. Yet we all know people it's enough just to 'be' with. For all my thoughts of touching Viv's lips with my lips, what I most want is just to be with him. Or to 'be' with him. But Viv has trouble just 'being' with himself. He is the 'doer'. A million important appointments a day ... always busy. Too busy helping everyone to have time for anyone. And he isn't here. He's off doing something genuinely important somewhere, working for justice and keeping the peace. None of this stuff for him that so many people would call 'reflecting on one's own navel'. Yet people here are peaceful. Imagine wanting to create peace and justice in the world outside you before you make time to know it in yourself? None of us have ever done that, have we? Ha ha.

Another thin and bearded man is talking about his identification with the 'I' but, lost in my own thoughts now, I'm not listening. There's something about Mooji's very presence that I'm aware of again. I'd thought, the first time I was in his house, that he could be speaking in Arabic and it would make no difference. I would still want to sit here. Weird.

'There is a knowing so deep that it can't be taught, it can only be recognized,' he says. I reach for my notebook. It can't be taught, it can only be recognized? Mmmm. I'm up the creek on this raft of paper trying to communicate this to you, then, aren't I? How to communicate an altered state of being with words? Pick the easy assignments, Isabel, why don't you?

A woman sitting in front of him is saying, 'I find it hard to let go.'

'So don't let go.'

She smiles.

'Awareness is not waiting for you to let go. You are one hundred per cent awareness – you have no choice.'

'When I try to grasp this, I feel panic.'

She feels panic when she moves into awareness of the universal? Lead people to peace and they feel panic? 'Aghhh, I may have to give up anxiety.' How crazy are we? But Mooji says, 'You are the watcher of the panicking mind. Put your attention on the witness.'

'Hang on a sec,' she says, 'I just have to concentrate.'

'I am,' he says, 'but I'm not aware that I am. That's the blind spot.'

She starts to smile.

'God Himself says, listen, darling – you're home.'

For a second or two she seems to just rest in the being.

'As a contemplative person your journey is towards emptiness.'

'Yes.'

'Just listen, just trust, don't think, "How can I use this?" Pay attention to the witness and be one with that.'

'Yes.'

She sits down looking a little dazed. It's quite funny, really, all these people coming to learn how to be who they already are. Who we already are.

'Let's sit for five minutes in the silence,' Mooji says. We sit and I try to practise five minutes without thinking. It's peaceful. More so even than awareness of the body. Try it.

Thoughts? Who needs them?

Second Wave

After five minutes a girl takes the mike to tell us that the break will be an hour. Mooji won't take questions during the break and we are to keep the silence in the room, 'although talking quietly about practical things is fine.' They have sandwiches on offer, homemade cake and nutty 'energy balls' that some volunteer was obviously up early that morning baking. Some people have extraordinary supernatural powers like that. Fiona and I grab food and water, walk out into the sunshine and sit on the grass. Fiona has not spent a lifetime, as I have, in strange gatherings, so I'm intrigued to hear her impressions.

'So?' I ask tentatively.

'It's weird. I like him. There is something in his demeanour that I really like; he's very ethereal. I don't like the people around him. They seem to be treating him as if he were a god. And I don't like the setup.'

'The setup?'

'All this "Keep your voice down in the room" makes me feel very restricted. I was worried that I might talk too loud when I asked for my carrot cake.'

I laugh at her indignation. 'No, seriously,' she says, 'what's all that about?'

'This is a weekend intensive that is about spirituality, Fiona. They are just trying to ensure that a contemplative atmosphere of respect for the work being done is maintained and people don't start gossiping and talking about last night's TV as soon as the session ends. On the last course I went on, we weren't even allowed to make eye contact.'

'Why on earth not?'

'This is about looking inwards. Surely we spend enough time wrapped up in the mundane cares of the world. A couple of days off and a little silence isn't so bad, is it?'

'I suppose not. But it's too cerebral for me. And it all seems a bit cult-like.'

I have to smile. It's the opposite of cerebral. Cerebral is about using your brain and this is about being beyond thought. But it's true that Mooji has to use words to talk with people. As for it being cult-like – it's a good thing that I didn't invite Fiona on the Vipassana course.

'Why is this cult-like?'

'Again, I don't think it's him. I think it's the people around him. One of the men even got a messianic look about him after Mooji had replied to him. His eyes started to shine.'

I've no idea which person she's talking about.

'He kept asking, "And then?" and I felt it was leading nowhere.'

'It was that first girl who said that she had this spiritual experience "and then" it went away. Mooji just said that from the point of view of the eternal there is no "and then".'

'I'm still not sure where it is all leading.'

'Who is "I"?' I ask, rather provocatively.

'Oh, don't you start.'

'So you're not impressed, then? You seem to be holding his book all the same. Would you come back?'

There's a long pause while Fiona looks at the sky. 'No,' she says, finally. 'Too cult-like for me.' Another long pause while I eat my cult-made carrot cake. 'Unless I change my mind.'

'So you wouldn't come back unless you changed your mind? Well, that's open-minded.'

'Yes, I think so. I'll see how I feel when I've read his book.'

Fiona has been thinking and not just looking inside. What Mooji's offering is not hard, but you have to listen to his questions and go to those places in yourself. It isn't a concept. It's an experience.

So I'm on my own in my undiluted admiration, then. I'm feeling fantastically at peace in his presence. I don't care if I don't have spiritual experiences, feelings of being absorbed into universal oneness or whatever. I'm happy just being here.

I kiss Fiona goodbye and go back in for the second session. Another £10, but this is still only a token donation compared to other work I've done. No-one even thinks that someone like Paul McKenna is an enlightened master ... but try getting to see him for £10.

I want to sit at the front on the carpet. People of more modest desires are happy sitting on the seats. There must be about 100 people at this second session. Everyone looks normal and friendly to me apart from some rather earnest-looking men also sitting on the carpet – one all in white, one in a skirt with a head wrap, the full 'I'm a spiritual person' look. It's 'come as you are' and Mooji has all sorts.

The first questioner up in the afternoon is another thin man with a bald head and a beard. What is this about? Are thin men more inclined to have a spiritual life or do men with a spiritual life become thin? I swear that there is not a single man in the room with a spare ounce of fat on him. Except Mooji – if anything, by our society's current standards, rather like the chubby Buddhas, Mooji is overweight. As he considers the body unimportant, he obviously prefers to feed it want it wants without the mind stepping in to stop him. I don't think he spends money on gym membership.

But the thin man is anxious. 'Everything I thought was outside is in here.' He points earnestly at himself.

'Including out there.' Mooji smiles.

'I experience fear around that.'

So much fear. Why is there so much fear among these thin men?

'I lost an illusion,' the man explains.

'Of what?'

'Of separateness. And then I experienced grief at losing the illusion of separateness.'

Oh, please. I begin to feel irritated. Does he want to know he is part of the infinite or not? Evidently not. Go to the pub and watch the football, then.

Mooji goes on teaching, patiently: 'But is that not also witnessed?'

He struggles to answer. Mooji looks at him. 'It's the questions that are important. Not the answers, the questions are pulling back the curtains.'

He includes the rest of us in what he's saying, speaking to us all.

'What the great sages recognized, they didn't recognize with conventional knowledge but with intuitive knowledge.'

The thin man wriggles in his seat, trying to form an answer. Mooji smiles at him again. 'I don't want an answer.'

I do. I want an answer.

'If you have an answer, you have a concept again. What observes? Look.'

'Something in me wants to run. To resist looking.'

'Where can you go where you are not?'

'I want to answer you.'

'Answers are for infant school. Stay with the questions. What happens in the introspection? You are still here.'

Hello, reader – are you following this? As I said, it's no good just reading this bit. To get full value for your money, you have to do it. So let me do a little process with you, if I may. We'll leave Mooji and the thin man for a minute just to make sure that you really are with me. As you are reading this, I'd like you to take a quick awareness test of your body, like in Vipassana – any aches and pains today? Stiffness in the neck? Shoulders? Tummy-ache, headache, toothache? Any pain or not? If there is or not is immaterial, just notice.

Next, how are you feeling emotionally today? Happy, sad, anxious, angry, peaceful, wot? Which emotions come to you when you look? Again, don't fret about it – just notice. Now let's look at what you are thinking: 'This chapter is really weird,' 'I wish she'd done a sex seminar coz this is difficult,' 'What am I going to have for dinner tonight?' Just notice what thoughts are passing by on that great screen that you could call your mind.

Now, this is the important bit. Notice who is doing the noticing. Where are 'you' in all this? You know that you are not your body, right? Because those who can no longer move from the neck down are still themselves. You know that you are not your emotions, because they rise and fall, and you know that you are not your thoughts as they come and go. Some we follow, some we ignore. Then how about your memory? You can't be that, because, as Mooji says, you can speak of your memory being good or bad. But this *observer* that seems to be unruffled, unchanging, timeless, spaceless, beyond race or gender, who is that? And now – as Mooji says – don't find an answer, just look and let the question stay alive. Where does the question take you?

Now, if you just read that and didn't do it, you may as well skip to the next chapter – but this is crucial. Hundreds of spiritual books have been written about this and I'm trying to get you there in a chapter, so sit up, please. :-)

'How do you live life?' Mooji is asking. 'You are being lived as life. You are an effect of consciousness, not a cause of it. You are being breathed, yet you are also aware of the breath, earlier than the breath. What watches the breath? Is it you?'

These questions make your head spin, don't they? You are being lived as life. You are not the cause. Can you even begin to grasp that one? Keep going, please.

'We are conditioned to feel that we have to force life. Doing, doing, doing ... still pushing the river. Stop and see if your heart will stop. Who is acting and reacting to thoughts? Who is looking through those eyes?'

'I am,' says someone in the front row.

'Behind this seer is a deeper seeing.'

'Why are we here being lived?' asks the man in front of Mooji.

'Well, not just to pay the rent. Who are we? This is the only question for you. Who am I?' He looks at us all again. 'Isn't it worth finding out who "I" is?'

'Don't "I" reside in my memory?' asks the version of 'I' in the front row.

'That which sees is earlier than memory. Who watches memory?'

'Am I my conditioning, then?'

'Something knows you are conditioned.'

'Yes, I see that.' The man is finally smiling now.

'This is your work. This is our opportunity. But it's an inside job. No-one can do it for you. Just ask de right questions.'

'Thank you.' The man bows and vacates the hot seat.

I shift in my place, sitting on the floor cross-legged. Amusingly, I have no problem with the sitting after Vipassana. The mind that Mooji speaks of not paying attention to is grateful to have something to engage with apart from the sensation in my upper lip. People drink water and smile at one another. It is as if, sitting here, listening to Mooji, we all begin to realize that our thoughts, the room, our very selves are all an illusion, and we begin to feel the truth of what the Buddhists say – that reality itself is a projection of the mind. That we are all part of everything, individual waves all part of the same great ocean. You and I. Same thing.

Mooji speaks, not to one person on the hot seat opposite him, but to us all. And, compliments of Microsoft and Watkins Publishing, to you.

'There is not an edge to you. Some of you feel this. You may feel, "Where exactly am I?" and the mind may panic. But be clear that this is not you. You are the watcher of this panicking mind. There is nothing to fix, to heal, to change or to make perfect.' Are you following? Are his words reaching you care of my pages?

He sits and smiles at us. 'I am just pulling the curtains. That's all. You're here. No-one can give you your being. What we are reacting to is just the noise of the mind. But you can only be troubled by what has meaning for you.'

Someone in the audience asks, 'Are you saying that this is all it is? Do you know how long it's taken me to get to this level of problem – and you're saying "It's nothing"?'

It's hardly surprising that she can't get her head around such radical simplicity.

'I just ask you to inspect: are these thoughts or not thoughts? And who is witnessing? Put your attention on the witness and see what you find, what you experience. Right now.'

If you have read Eckhart Tolle's widely admired book *The Power of Now* you will recognize this resting perfectly in the moment. Yet Mooji is going beyond that. He is speaking of effortless being, beyond even your mind.

'Just allow yourself to see. Don't start thinking, "How can I apply this? How can I use it?" Just allow yourself to recognize and this recognition will automatically bless all aspects of you.'

Did you hear that? Recognizing this will bless all aspects of you. Now you weren't expecting that with the cover price, were you?

'This is the existence that we miss because we are so busy. As if it were necessary to push the river. Allow yourself to see that the most powerful thing about you takes place inside you, spontaneously. Change in you will come about where it needs to, spontaneously, and arising out of that is tremendous gratitude and understanding of how beautiful existence is when it plays in the human form.'

Yes, I'm feeling grateful, and I'm in awe of the beauty of the human form. But ... I'm also watching myself vigilantly. I'm not supposed to be grateful to this particular human form, and when Mooji speaks of the beauty of existence he is not speaking of himself. So just how distracted – as usual – am I by an attractive man? And, regardless of the wisdom of his teachings, why am I so touched while Fiona is demonstrably unmoved? Maybe I just fancy him? Can I be that obvious?

Third Wave

OK. Some ruthlessness is called for. Yes, Mooji is exceptional and I feel what I would call the presence of the Divine in him as strongly as I've ever felt it in anyone. But what exactly is Divine? What would some of the sceptics who say that there is no such thing have to say about my intuitive feeling that I am in the presence of a true master?

Come in, Dr Freud.

'Ah, Miss Losada' – Freud sits down in his rather creased suit and adjusts his spectacles – 'it is unsurprising zat you feel attracted to zis man, because at some deep level he represents a fantasy of zat father you have not had and would like to have had. Zis is transference.'

'Yer wot?'

'You have projected on to him all ze feelings zat you imagine a perfect father to have.'

'Oh, God ...'

'Exactly.'

Freud is SO smug. I had a nasty feeling that he'd say all this.

'Can you be sure you are not attracted to him sexually also?'

I knew he'd say that too. I glance back at Mooji. His gorgeous smile, his deep velvet voice.

'Er, no, to be honest, I can't guarantee that the attraction is entirely spiritual.'

'I thought not.' Freud smiles knowingly.

'But, but ... surely this feeling of awe I'm experiencing could be something to do with Mooji? He has a beautiful face. Full of love, joy and compassion.'

'But you do not know zis man, ja?'

'Not really.'

'When we choose lovers, we choose someone who reminds us of ze opposite-sex parent.'

'But I didn't have an opposite-sex parent.'

'Exactly. You do not know what your parent is, so you create an idealized version of him.'

Oh, fuck off, Freud.

He is unconcerned by my irritation. 'So you cannot be sure zis is not transference?'

'I'm fairly sure that these good qualities are in him and not in me.'

'Zat is ze nature of transference, Isabel.'

'So you are saying that what I am experiencing as the presence of the Divine is basically just sexual desire?'

'I think zat is most likely, yes.'

Well, he would say that, wouldn't he? I mean, he's Freud.

For goodness' sake, let's have a therapist who is a little more spiritually enlightened. I call on Carl Gustav Jung.

'Dr Jung, can you help me analyse why I am so attracted to this teacher? I notice that there are many who feel as I do, and yet the friend I brought today is totally unmoved by him. Is it me, then?'

Jung also looks a little dishevelled, it has to be said, and hasn't combed his hair today.

'Vell, many cultures value the archetype of the Wise Man who intercedes for us with the Divine, and he is, for you, that person – the mystic. He speaks to you of the collective unconscious which we seek.'

I think I'm following this.

'Also anima.'

I'm not following this. 'Sorry, you've lost me.'

'The female soul with which the animus, the masculine, wants to unite. The feminine in you wants to unite with the masculine archetype. If this were a dream, then the elements of the dream represent elements of the dreamer, thus Mooji represents a facet of Isabel. Vat facet would that be?'

'My wisdom, I suppose.'

'And the element of the dream represented by Isabel would be?'

'The seeker.'

'And both of these facets are within you and seek to come together. This is why you feel attracted.'

Really? I'm not convinced. Mooji sitting just a few feet away doesn't seem much like a figment of my overactive transference, and I know I'm not dreaming the peace I feel in his presence, no matter what my inner wisdom and my inner seeker may have privately agreed. Who cares if I fancy him too and he represents an archetype? I prefer Mooji's version of events – that Freud and Jung and all they stand for are just belief systems. I dismiss these two seminal figures of Western culture and send them off with a wave of my astral hand to get their trousers pressed. The only reality we really have is the present moment. I'm happy sitting here in said moment – and I may learn something and be able to explain it a bit.

So back to Brixton.

'What about frustration and pain?' a girl is asking Mooji. Maybe she lacked a father figure too? Or maybe I should just shut up the overactive mind, as Mooji suggests, and listen to the teachings? If I'm quiet I can learn what this wise man has to say about suffering. And Mooji is wonderful, no matter how innumerable my own inadequacies may be.

'Suffering is an attitude of how you meet your experience,' he says. 'The pain need not be suffering.'

Only yesterday I read an interview in which Haruki Murakami used the unattributed quote 'Pain is inevitable, suffering optional' to describe long-distance running. It's a clear distinction, but sometimes hard to apply when the pain shows up.

Mooji is not speaking in theory, though; he lost his eldest son to pneumonia. They say there is no greater grief than losing your own child.

'You are not experiencing suffering,' he tells us.

We're not?

'You are suffering your experience. When pain comes, say, "OK, throw your best punch." Maybe pain comes as a friend to help you go beyond yourself. Identification with the "I" is the root of suffering. This "I" is ego: "I like, I dislike." This "I" experience causes itself and the "other" pain. When you try to choose what you should experience, you suffer. When you are constantly interpreting how things should or shouldn't be, what you do or don't deserve, you suffer. Whenever there is pride, attachments, judgements and desires, there is suffering. When we awaken to our true nature, suffering is absent.'

I'm floundering about, trying to decide where I stand on all this. What about physical pain? The woman on the chair in front of him has the question on her lips.

'But great physical pain, Mooji, it throbs!'

'Pain is unavoidable, and where the psychological and physical identification is strong, the suffering is greater. But you are not that body. You are aware of that. When you just let the "I am" be, immediately joy and space prevail.'

'Yes,' she says softly, 'I do understand that.'

'It's not a teaching, you see?'

'Yes.'

'It's an inner experience.'

'Yes.'

'Remain there.'

And we all sit there for about five minutes in the silence, each of us at peace in our own inner solitude. And in those moments, all eternity is present.

At the end of the day, I switch my phone on – no message from Viv, just one from my friend Sarah asking how the day was. And I've made no plans, so I come home to try and ponder all these things deeply. But I am failing, I think, to ponder anything deeply at all. So I switch on Facebook. As one does. As anyone who has joined that site will know. It is absurdly addictive, and, for those that have been foolish enough to succumb to the addiction, it is always the first thing that you do when you switch on your computer. But it is no longer the empire of 14-year-olds who want to chat to their friends at school all evening while their parents sigh wearily, wishing they would switch the ruddy thing off and do some homework. Nope, lots of the grown-ups have got wise to it as well.

I bet, for example, you wouldn't expect me to have a friend on Facebook who is a monk in a Franciscan community in Ireland. He had read my books and joined my mailing list, so when I announced on my website that I was joining Facebook, an invitation to 'become his friend' arrived. The word 'friend' has a very loose definition on Facebook, as it often includes people you have never met. But the friendships can be delightful neverthe-less, as my correspondence with Brother Richard has always been. I sit down and write, 'What are your thoughts on gurus,

Brother Richard? Either speaking personally or on behalf of your community?' Mooji has never claimed to be a guru, but many of the people who go to his meetings consider him one.

Later that evening, when I've had my supper and am still pondering all Mooji's words, the kind of full and thoughtful reply that I have come to know I will receive from Brother Richard arrives faithfully. He touches me immediately, as no other man has ever called me 'sister'.

Dearest Sister Isabel,

In the Hindu tradition (and much of the Buddhist as well) the guru teacher is one in whom the disciple discerns the presence of God-realization. The teacher and God are one and so the disciple can give absolute trust and obedience to the guru so that they themselves may be brought, in turn, to God-realization. However, there are dangers in this which the traditions themselves see. The most obvious difficulty being that of coming into contact with false gurus ... or those who believe that they are enlightened when in fact they are not, or others who use their guru status to prey on their disciples' wealth or sexuality. It is believed that if the guru is for real then the disciple should not enter into judgement of the guru's behaviour, as the normal rules don't apply. I think this is the main difficulty that we, in the West, have with the idea of a guru. The Dalai Lama himself has said that to be sure of one's guru one should spend every moment with them for at least seven years, observing them dispassionately and evaluating their virtue before committing to them. This is a tough teaching but one that would protect both prospective guru and disciple.

In the Christian tradition, the equivalent is a 'gerontas', a Greek term that means 'elder'. This person may be male or female and is usually a monastic although not necessarily a priest. The gerontas is the spiritual father or mother who adopts the disciple. They are seen to be one who has already walked the path of discipleship and reached the beginnings of 'theosis'. This is that state in which our whole being has become one with the divine and there is no longer any obstacle between us and God. We do not become God, but will be as much like God as is possible, journeying into deeper levels of love, wisdom and perfection. The role is to lead the disciple into a more profound relationship with God until the gerontas is no longer needed.

In Christianity, the inner self is only ever surrendered to God directly and never to any other being, so if you are looking at the subject of spiritual guidance for yourself or others, ask yourself whether he's training his disciples to become free so that they don't need him any more or leading them to become dependent on him? A true master seeks only the liberation of his disciples.

In order to live in union with God our selfishness, pride and egoism have to be transformed and healed and a teacher can help us to see these things. But the main thing, my dear, is to pray, and by that I don't mean saying prayers but letting Spirit pray within you. Close your eyes, breathe and – as one of our oldest brothers puts it – get out of God's way.

Any further clarification needed – just let me know.

Peace, Love, Joy always – Brother Richard

Isn't Brother Richard lovely? You can find him on Facebook too. (Look out, Brother Richard – another 100,000 friend requests on the way.) I love it that he is able to see the equivalent of the guru in the Christian tradition rather than just dismissing it outright as some less thoughtful Christians may be tempted to do. 'Get out of God's way' seems very close to Mooji's instruction not to think. What a delightfully thoughtful reply.

My monk seems to have got the impression that I may be looking for a formal guru, whereas I've certainly no intention of turning my life or any part of it over to Mooji. But he still feels like the sea, no matter what Freud and Jung may have to say about my senses. Fiona seemed to think that those who went to him had a look of obedience, but Mooji has never offered any advice – and certainly not advice of a practical kind: 'Leave your husband and follow me.' He teaches by questioning people and his presence is full of love. I find that I am easily touched by love – my heart is easily warmed both by Mooji and by the kindness of a monk in Ireland. My heart is touched, but my mind and my thoughts, which Mooji has spent the day encouraging me to ignore, whirl around in my tired cauliflower brain. 'Who is "I"?'

Fourth Wave

The following morning, on the second day of the intensive, I have a different guest. My lovely friend Chris is one of the wisest young men I know. He has just finished a history degree, but the study of history certainly can't account for the fact that he seems to have acquired the wisdom of several lifetimes. You know how it is when you meet someone you know you could happily sit in a car with and drive from Land's End to John O'Groats and not be bored, even for a second, nor wish that the journey was over? Chris is one of these people in my life. He's 20.

I arrive on Sunday morning to find him already seated, with modesty altogether unknown to your narrator, in the back row of the hall and flicking through Mooji's book.

'Do you want to come down to the front and sit on the carpet? It's sort of a more intense experience if you are right up close to him and can see the faces of the questioners.'

'No, thanks,' he says, totally immune to suggestion from me. 'I'm fine here.'

I take my place cosily on the carpet close to Mooji. I prefer sitting on the floor. If we sit too much on chairs, an Indian lady well over 80 once told me as she crossed her legs to sit on the floor, then a time will come when we will no longer be able to sit on the floor.

Mooji comes forward, bows to everyone in the 'Namaste' that I have grown to love and takes his seat.

A woman raises her hand immediately with a question. She is in her early 30s and looks a little anxious. She wants to know about helping others. 'When you start seeing what is happening inside you, you also start seeing what is happening to other people. It's almost as if people are screaming for help. How can you help them without just giving them a concept?'

'You need to be careful – what you think you're seeing inside them may be just what is going on inside you. There is a saying: "I am not seeing the world as it is – I am seeing the world as I am." So to try and help people is very shaky ground. First you have to understand how your mind works. Out of awareness, something comes to a lovely space of neutrality, and out of this comes ... well, I call it "perceiving life as spontaneous existence".'

'What does that mean?'

'You can meet things spontaneously, without preparation. You meet things as they are. You're just present and empty. Like this, your consciousness finds smooth affinity with others very easily because you are not thinking, "I can see how people are."'

This seems to me to be a beautiful way of saying, 'Don't give unsolicited advice.'

'The next person who you feel is in pain – well, you can never be sure what is there. Each time you have an encounter with someone, you're completely new. You don't have to come from the past. When you are empty, you create together.'

He blows out with a sigh and breathes in – to emphasize this moment. Breathe out. Breathe in. 'Otherwise we are all like energy fields of what we imbibe through our conditioning. What you are attached to, what you project – all of this creates your energy field. Some other people are also energy fields, and you are reacting by either blowing them off or sucking them in, and sometimes you meet beautifully and you think, "Aha!"'

He says this in a flirtatious, 'I like this chemistry' way, and all the women in the room who are seeking an archetype blush a little. He goes on. 'But you've never before been as you are now. You cannot create a genuine state of being through intention. It unfolds in every moment spontaneously.'

In other words, don't try to make them feel better so that you feel better.

'You are like space moving through space. Who is living here? Nothing. Empty. There is still some conditioning but it's not significant. Any time you meet someone and you come from the past, you miss a fresh possibility.'

Oh, my God – can I jump up and down and shout 'Alleluia'? Why can't we do this for each other? It says in the New Testament, in that lovely section in St Paul's First Letter to the Corinthians about love, which people often read at weddings, 'Love does not keep a record of wrongs.' Imagine that. We could just tear up the wrongs again and again for others and for ourselves and just meet what we find and what we are in the present moment. Why don't we do this more? In my experience, even when we meet new people we bring so much of the past with us and want to know what their past is. Even Viv, who I so much admire, wants to know about my past – while I'm doing my best to just deal with what he is presenting me with in the moment.

Mooji looks at us. 'Many people have not arrived at just being present yet. Some are one week behind – some six years behind. In some things you are yesterday and in others you are ten years ago. Where is the point where you are just "now"? When you are empty? The mind does not trust this emptiness; it likes to imagine that when you are empty you are stupid or inert. "How can you function without personality and without past?" the mind asks. And the answer is, "Beautifully, beautifully."'

The woman who asked the question sits and looks at him. This is the most interesting answer to the question 'How can I help others?' that I have ever heard.

Once I was asked a similar question, only in a different form. It was in the context of a talk I gave on my book *For Tibet, With Love: A Beginner's Guide to Changing the World*. A young man stood up at the end to describe the work he was doing on the West Bank among Palestinians. He spoke about the orphans he had met, the appalling poverty he had witnessed, his attempts – sometimes successful, sometimes not – to open schools, to lobby whomever he could to improve their life conditions. He told us of terrible injuries he had seen, the killing and the despair. His question went on for about ten minutes, and when he had finished I don't think there was a dry eye in the audience. At the end he turned to me and asked, 'What can I do?' as if I could add something. But then from somewhere an answer came to me – there was one contribution I could make. 'Ladies and gentlemen,' I said, 'let's give this gentleman a round of applause.' People started to clap, then someone stood, then others stood to clap, till eventually he looked around and the whole room faced him clapping in a generous and warm-hearted standing ovation, with even some cheering to complete the message. He began to smile.

'You got it?' I said to him as he looked at me when they eventually stopped clapping. 'You're doing it,' I said, 'just carry on.' And I thanked him.

So that was my answer. Very different from Mooji's. He in the being – me in the doing. But there is something in Mooji's answer that I love more and more. It's about who we are – just being in the present and listening from a point of neutrality. I can do this with anyone, I think, except my daughter. With her I am too attached. She is my greatest teacher, of course. Perhaps I am also hers.

A woman gets up and tells Mooji that she is falling apart. Again I smile as he encourages her to do so. He reminds her that the fear of 'falling apart' is often, if not always, worse than the falling apart itself. 'If you live alone,' he says, 'you have a wonderful opportunity to fall apart whenever you want, or maybe some of you prefer to fall apart with someone around? I don't know. One woman in New York went home after a Satsang and said, "I feel as if I'm going to fall apart." Her husband went to consult the calendar and said, "No, you can't fall apart this month, because we are too busy – how about next month?"'

Personally, I fell apart years ago, and lately I've noticed that I often fall apart once a month in line with the menstrual cycle. Seemingly random things make me cry for a few days: a piece of music, an interview I hear on the radio. Then, just when I'm convinced that the best thing for me and everyone around me would be for me to go and throw myself in the Thames, the days move on and everything feels good again. Then I laugh and wonder why I was taking all those feelings seriously – I mean, don't I know yet that I have hormones that go up and down? Why do I believe my mind and my feelings? And perspective is restored – until the next month. Some months, if I'm running every day, I can avoid all this, but some months I forget and fall apart. Just as Mooji is allowing – even recommending, it seems. I guess once you have fallen apart a couple of times you learn not to be bothered by it any more. We empower our thoughts, concepts and feelings by believing in them.

Some of the questions are interesting and some I find irritating. Some questions are very general – 'Why are we here?' Some are very emotional – how to stay in 'the being' when it's turbulent at home. And then there's someone who feels totally at peace among the trees but fearful and defensive among people. Mooji answers all the questions with grace and humour, advising the last questioner that people are not, after all, so different from trees.

So many words while he sits and says that it isn't about words.

He looks at us all with great gentleness as he closes the morning session. 'If you feel there is any kind of strain in you to understand these words, don't worry about it. Trust your own listening. Not everything has got to be explained – leave some grasslands inside your own space. Often people come here who don't speak any English and yet somehow a deep seeing has taken place for them.'

Then suddenly we are out of eternity and back into time. Into lunchtime. I make my way to the back of the room to collect sandwiches and Chris and walk out into the sunshine.

'Well, that boy?' I ask as we sit on the grassy bank outside the church hall with our tea.

'The questioners seem troubled.'

'Maybe it's only when people's lives aren't going the way that they want that they question things. I mean, it requires getting up on a Sunday morning to get here.'

'He doesn't seem to give any practical advice. And when he does give advice, how do they know if it's the right advice?'

'How d'you mean?'

'Well, my girlfriend thinks that weird Chinese TV presenter Gok Wan on *How to Look Good Naked* is excellent, but surely to have any lasting impact he has to look at who they are on the inside, not just tell them to wear a tight corset?'

'I absolutely agree with you, Chris.'

'So my point is that Gok is giving bad advice but some women think he's wonderful. So today women and men are looking at Mooji and hanging on his every word, but how do they know that what he says is true?'

'Are you comparing Gok Wan with Mooji?'

'No – it's just that I'm not sure it's a good idea to take advice from anyone, and it's certainly not a good idea to become dependent on advice from anyone.'

'That's just what my monk friend in Ireland was saying. But surely Mooji is just asking people to explore inside their heads, isn't he? He's not giving advice. He's just asking questions.'

'Yes. That's why I'm buying Mooji's book and I have no intention of buying a book ghostwritten for Gok Wan.'

'So you're not staying for the next session, then?'

'No, I'm going to go and see my girlfriend this afternoon. But I am going to read Mooji's book. Are you going to ask him a question?'

'Any question that begins, "I'd like to ask," he's going to reply, "Who is 'I'?"'

'So do you have a question or not?'

I don't answer. Perhaps he'll have one for me.

I go back in, still wondering whether I'm going to speak or just listen. Mooji asks the room, 'Is anything causing you to not be who you are right now?'

A man says, 'Just the odd concern about things that may happen tomorrow.'

Mooji teases him, 'You are thinking about things that may arise tomorrow? Is there anything in the universe capable of removing your being? Not just in this moment but always?'

'No,' the man says.

'The emphasis here is to allow understanding without the mind's intrusion.'

I love that. The idea of doing anything without the mind suits me.

More questions for us all: 'When you are at one with yourself, is that a place of activity or stillness?' he asks. 'Can you look at you? Or are you looking from you?'

Did you get those questions? Have you tried to answer them? When up against them, the mind becomes helpless and has to check out.

A woman gets up who seems to be bursting. 'I read in *I Am That* that the realization is like an explosion.'

'Yes, but it's not what you think. It's not an explosion like "bang!" – it's like the kind of explosion that you'd have if you go to the doctor and they tell you that they have found a tumour. Just those words, would you forget them?'

'No.'

'No, and when you realize that you are not what you took yourself to be, what happens? All your life you have been told that you are just this meat suit, and when you come to a realization – I am not that – the impact can be profound. Maybe what is set light to here will detonate later, when you're on the bus or in the loo.'

He's not precious, is he?

'It's seen in a moment, that none of this is what I am.'

'Can there be many waves?'

'Oh, yes, and this is the version I prefer, because many people wait for a big bang but there may be many little waves. Your mind is like a little piece of ice in a glass of warm water and a gentle melting is taking place.'

I want to get up and take the electric chair. I let a couple of questioners go by, then get nervously to my feet. I gather up some courage – which is needed because I want to not be stupid. Or to be not stupid. I hope that any wisdom I've acquired over the years may be evident. And what am I going to say? This person with whom I am identified, this 'Isabel', really has no question.

'Namaste, Mooji,' I say, bowing.

'Namaste.'

I take my seat on the chair facing him and lift the mike. 'Isabel has no question.'

'Ah?'

'Isabel – that's my name – has no question ...'

He repeats, smiling, 'Has no question.'

'... but is wondering if you have one for her.'

'Who is Isabel?' he asks. Laughter from the audience. So much for my attempt to avoid the 'Who is "I"?' question.

I draw breath to answer, then see the cul-de-sac and laugh self-consciously, momentarily losing myself. 'Oh, I'm not supposed to answer, am I?'

'Who says? The question is asked, no?'

'I'd say that Isabel is that – what was that expression you used? – that meat package with which I identify.' I pat myself affectionately.

'"I" being what?'

'"I" being that which observes.'

'OK. So now just observe.'

'Just observe? Do you mean step out completely from that with which I identify?' asks the Isabel identification.

'Just observe. There is no stepping "out" that you have to do. You are not "in".'

'No,' says the Isabel identification.

'There seems to be a stepping out, but when observed it is clear that nothing has actually taken place. I simply am here.'

'Yes.'

'The power to observe is present. I have not activated that. It's going on by itself.'

I'm silent and move my perspective to that of the observer. You can do the same now, I hope.

Mooji says, 'It seems that I have the power to shift my attention and to point it in a different direction and whatever that attention touches is my experience. But if I don't identify with the experience, it leaves no trace, no record.'

Get it?

'Can you see without picking up? Without collecting?'

Why is he asking me this? Where is this coming from? Am I trying to collect him? I suppose I am – I've certainly noticed him – more than I noticed those people on the train on the way here.

'I don't understand.'

'Some relationships just happen. They come. They move into play. And others are forced into being. They come out of intention, out of desire. And when they come from that place, they struggle, because they are not really a gift.'

I have no idea why he is saying this to me.

'The consciousness can be a bit like that too. For a while it will be a bit aggressive; it will require.'

Good grief – is he experiencing me as requiring? I thought I was just sitting on my seat seeing what he wanted to ask me. Or is my consciousness aggressively requiring an experience of being – even of you?

'It must learn – to just let it happen. That's the opportunity. Just see what happens. There is a movement in life that is just happening. As your breath is happening.'

'So life will unfold by itself?' My experience is that unless I make things happen they do not unfold by themselves. I look at him. He asks another question.

'If you had the power to create exactly the life that you would like to live today, could it compare to the life that unfolds by itself?'

If I had the power to create the life I want? Just as Anthony Robbins tells me that I do have and sets out a path to follow with joy and vigour?

'Yes!' I begin enthusiastically. 'My ego is sufficiently large to think, Yes! I jolly well could work out a life better than the one the universe has provided. I can detail the life that I would create and give lots of examples.'

The audience laughs at my exasperation.

'So why don't you?' asks Mooji.

'Because the universe doesn't do what I want it to.' I laugh at myself, beginning to entertain the audience now. 'I make my requests perfectly clear, I ask, I pray – and the universe gives me the opposite.' More laughter. They obviously haven't seen such absurd arrogance in quite some time.

'So who has got it wrong?' asks Mooji.

'The universe!' I reply with complete conviction.

'Tell me why.'

'In my experience the universe has so often let me down. Done the opposite of what my heart has asked for, seemed without mercy – not only for me but for others I love too.' I stop for a second to re-form my question. 'In your experience, Mooji, the universe, or the consciousness of which we speak – is it a loving consciousness? If we are being guided in some way, if everything that happens to us happens for our greater growth, then presumably this consciousness is a loving consciousness?'

'OK. Yes. You got me on this one. I have to take a little time to tell you 'bout this. Can I?'

'Please do.' I laugh at him asking me permission. 'It's been puzzling me for some years whether, as the Christians and others claim, "the universe" or "God" is really a loving consciousness – when we seem to see evidence to the contrary every day. Any light that you can shed on the subject would be most welcome.'

'In one way I can say that consciousness is not just loving – at the level of humanity looking out. The way we look at it, consciousness sometimes creates complete stink bombs.'

'I noticed,' I interrupt for the pleasure of an easy laugh from the audience.

'It's not just a nice guy; immense cruelty can manifest also. No?'

'Yes.'

'Is it coming from different sources? Is the good coming from one place and the bad coming from another? Or are they from the same shared source? Can you know what is good without having tasted what you feel is bad?'

'I think not.'

'As I said before – human beings are the effect of consciousness and not the cause or the controller of it. I wonder if you follow what this means?'

I'm sure that I don't follow what it means.

'What you are doing as a human being has its origin in consciousness, not in the personal, individual doer. This is why you can't decide – you have the power and the freedom to dream but you don't have the power to make your dream come true.'

'Mmmmm. Realization of dreams is an interesting area.'

'You have the power to dream but not to command the dream into actuality.' Ah – take note, all you readers of *The Secret* or any of those order-what-you-want-from-the-universe books. 'And you're frustrated about it ... because you feel that you could do a better job?'

'Yup!' I insist to yet more laughter.

'But can you isolate your life and change it without altering the totality?'

'No. But I'm not sure I follow you.'

'Have you considered this? Each wave on the ocean has the complete ocean underneath it. A wave cannot decide, "Look, guys, I don't feel like going this way today – I'm going to go that way." How much free will do you have, really? A certain amount – but could you change the picture, which includes me, in a way which satisfies me? Can you change your world – which includes other beings – and satisfy them? Or do you want to isolate yourself and have a sweet life by yourself?'

'No.'

'So you can make plans and when you make things up you can put anyone in your fantasy. But if you want to actualize this fantasy it means that you have to become a dictator. You are saying, "I have this world – hey, guys, it's really beautiful – do you want to come and live in my world? But you have to think as I want you to think and move as I want you to move." This is autonomy – but only for you. Could you live in a world like this?'

Oh, heck. Are you following this? He is basically saying that we can't have what we want – the whole basis of *The Secret* and all that thinking can't work because we can't control others. I have noticed this. Viv's absence being a reminder of it. One person meets another and invites him to play. Sometimes they are on the same frequency and sometimes they are not. I look at Mooji. 'I don't want anyone to do what I want them to do. I want them to do what they want to do. But there are some people I particularly don't want to suffer, I suppose.'

'Presently all the beings are being fed precisely what they need to be fed, even if it looks horrible and disgusting. You need to taste this, for the next step that you need to take.'

'I'm glad this is being recorded, because I'm going to have to listen to this again later.'

More laughter – and now I find that I do have questions, although I'm so overwhelmed that I'm only half following his words. My mind finds itself and I ask him, 'Can you honestly tell me that, in your experience, all that which we experience is for our growth?'

'Yes,' he says, without a moment's hesitation. And then, lest I'm tempted to doubt him, 'I don't feel that this universe is vindictive, it is corrective. If offers you innumerable opportunities to step up to higher ground. If there seems to be punishment, then even that is an action of grace, which, at the time, we don't appreciate. Often you are saying thank you to the wrong guy. Often you say thank you to what makes you feel sweet in the moment. You say thank you for your chocolate-flavoured moments. But some things rub and grate. You don't say thank you – but they alter your being in such a way that it brings wisdom. We are rarely thankful for that.'

I'm unusually quiet. Emily says later when she sees this on videotape, 'All hail Mooji! Mother is not talking.' No – I'm listening.

Mooji looks at me. 'When I was in Spain just now, one man came up and asked, "Can you give me a mantra, Mooji?"'

'Why did he want a mantra? I don't want a mantra.'

'No, no, wait, wait,' he laughs. 'I said to him, I will tell you the best mantra – the universal mantra which any being can say, not just Indians but a mantra for every being. Your mantra is ...'

And he allows himself to pause a little for effect.

'Thank you. Just keep saying thank you. Don't explain, don't complain, just say thank you. Say thank you to existence.'

'OK.' Actually, I'm unconvinced by this mantra, but I'll try it.

'Just say thank you. Thank you, thank you, thank you. Every being – everyone who comes into your life. If you don't understand what they bring – you still say thank you. You don't have to justify it – and somehow you come alive. They kick you. You may not say thank you immediately, but somewhere inside you – you say thank you. Just like this. See what happens.'

'Thank you, Mooji.' The audience laughs. I bow and return to my place on the floor. I try to remember who I am without thinking.

Then another woman sits on the chair. She says, 'I am that which fear is arising in ...'

Even Mooji looks confused. 'I am that in which fear arises? Is that what you're saying?'

'I am, and fear is arising,' she says. I think she is trying to avoid saying, 'I'm scared.'

So much fear. I don't want to listen any more.

'Fear along with every other thing?' he says. 'Maybe in sequence they come? Now fear, now joy, now promise, now rest, now this, now that ...'

And this is how it is, isn't it? Yet something in us is steady beneath all this passing experience. Mooji is inviting us to look there. I want to remain a do-er. I always have been someone who likes to make things happen, to change the world, or at any rate to do everything in my power to make the world a better place. His 'thank you' mantra is a wise one – obviously it makes sense to feel like this about life; on the other hand, there is Darfur, there is Tibet, there is the Middle East, there is the tobacco industry and, as Viv would remind me, there is gun and knife crime on our streets. It's important not to just feel grateful for our own lives and the joys in them while ignoring the realities and suffering around us. It's easy to be guilty of the selective vision that Viv accuses so many of my middle-class friends of – being blind to the suffering of children in our own towns who are led into crime because they know nothing but abuse from their unhappy, substance-addicted parents, who, in their turn, live without hope.

I feel inspired by the whole Anthony Robbins approach to life: making plans and then 'stepping up' your own standards so that you can make them happen. This is an exciting way to live even if, as Mooji says, it is impossible to include other people in your plans. I had hoped that Viv would come and hear Mooji, as

I had thought that listening to this perspective would be a comfort for Viv in the difficult work that he does fighting street crime. I felt sure that Mooji would have enjoyed Viv ... but, as Mooji reminds me, I can't make anything happen that includes others. All we can do is have our dreams and hope that sometimes people will share them. Of course, setting goals and having dreams can come with a heavy price: failure and disappointment are part of this path as well as the satisfaction of successful outcomes. But I remain one of those who would rather make plans and take risks. Even if this optimistic strategy keeps me humble with regular disappointments to remind me that I'm not in charge.

Yet Mooji seems to be speaking of a peace in a place beyond all this, accessible to us all; of our own relation to the place that many call 'God' and of how we get there. Or, no – he has been saying, hasn't he, that we don't need to do anything to get there except realize that we are already there? From this perspective everything is viewed more clearly. From where Mooji speaks there seems to be a clear knowledge of what is illusory and what is really important. There is no fear of death and yet there is a keen, vivid, appreciation of life. Anything that creates a fountain of appreciation for life – I'm there. I'm listening.

Except I'm tempted to try and cheat. Instead of meditating and contemplating the questions deeply as Mooji recommends, I'm tempted to take a shortcut for a little more experience of the observer of my mind. There is a tried and tested way to learn about consciousness: shamans have been using it for centuries. They take what they consider to be a sacred medicine. What it does, I'm told, is provide a little help in the process that Brother Richard speaks of when he says that you need to 'get out of your own way' or what Mooji speaks of when he tells you not to pay attention to your thoughts. In wishing to show people that the spiritual world is a reality, the shamans don't mess about; they say, 'Drink this,' and they sit back and take care of your body while you experience observing your mind in 3D.

This may be taking the idea a bit far, and it's very wicked, I know. I would never normally consider taking a drug. The closest I have ever got to consuming a mind-altering substance is drinking too much coffee. Even alcohol I only take in moderation. I've always seen taking any and all drugs as unnecessary and stupid. But in a spiritual context, with a shaman who has spent a lifetime doing this work? I think that's different.

I am very much at peace after my time with Mooji. I feel refreshed, as if I've been bathing in this great ocean and that has restored my perspective. I've put the picture of the great wave that was on the wall in my bedroom back up again in a place that feels right to me. When I see it I remember Mooji pointing out that when we get the mind out of the way, we can live with effortless awareness that we are not just a wave but the ocean itself.

So I feel ready now to put all this to the test; to go into nature, to explore earth. I want to find a real shaman, and to find one I have to go into the jungle. To do this I have to find a Westerner who has permission to visit tribes that have little or no contact with the outside world. I would like to find an anthropologist with a reputation for going into the jungle but not exploiting or disturbing the people. It would have to be someone who was seeking to protect the tribal way of life. It would have to be someone working with a charity or approved by Survival International. It would have to someone knowledgeable about shamanism and respectful of the shamanic tradition. It would have to be someone who was making a genuine contribution and whose work, if I went, I could support in some way.

As it happens, I know someone who knows someone who knows someone.

The Fifth Element – Earth

*The womb – the mother –
transformation – stomach – harmony –
focus – nourishment for the body –
the mouth*

The Amazonian Jungle, Shamans and Hallucinogenics

How I love to wake up somewhere else – somewhere a long way from my own street. It's necessary sometimes, if there is any way that you can, to muster your courage and just go. And this isn't just any old trip, this is a spiritual adventure.

I am sitting in a tiny café drinking coffee as usual. But, you may be pleased to know, Starbucks has not yet reached Satipo, a tiny town on the edge of the Amazonian jungle in Peru, so it's filter coffee and I'm drinking it black. It's so strong there is no way I'll make it to the bottom of the cup. Today my three companions – Dilwyn the anthropologist (who wrote *The Rough Guide to Peru*, amongst other books), Alex the student world traveller, Jeremy the retired botanist – and I are setting off into the jungle. Dilwyn is taking us to meet an old friend of his, Noemi; she is 70 years old, a member of the Ashaninka tribe, and a shaman.

I was invited to meet a shaman once before, at the Mind, Body, Spirit Festival in London. There are many people in Europe who have studied various aspects of the shamanic tradition; some have spent time with the tribes and learnt some of the wonders of this ancient spirituality. Some of these Westerners may even have lived up to everything that they feel is demanded to call themselves 'shaman' – but they are not for me. If they are speaking on the shamanic circuit and have a slot at the International Shamanic Conference, then, even if they are knowledgeable and erudite, they are a different kind of shaman.

As I understand it, a shaman, both in Tibet and in South America, is at the centre of the community. He (or, rarely, she) is counsellor, doctor and priest, and is needed for any birth, marriage, death, or misfortune. A shaman true to his or her calling, I believe, could not conceive of abandoning the community to pop off for a conference. So while I may admire the commitment of the Western shaman to bringing this knowledge to the modern world, I want to go to the source. In order to avoid comment from Drs Freud and Jung on this meeting, I have found a woman. Noemi (she is Ashaninka but they have all Spanish names) and her sister are the two women around whom the tribal village revolves. Thirty-five years ago they were both married to the same man when he died. They both remarried different men and their children and grandchildren make up the village. Noemi had over 50 grandchildren before she lost count. She owns nothing but sees almost all of her children and grandchildren every day, a kind of wealth that is beyond the imagination of most grandparents in our own fractured society.

Four of us are setting off. Following my usual pattern, Dilwyn the anthropologist is married, Alex is young enough to be my son and Jeremy is old enough to be my father. So much for the chances of a little romantic narrative to distract me from Viv. Short of catching a tribal Amazonian in a net and bringing him back to London, once again my experiences are to be of a purely spiritual kind. This is evidently my destiny. I'm glad that the shaman is a woman. True to the nature of the element earth, which I'm considering, I'm going to experience two mothers: The jungle is as close to what they call 'Mother Earth' as you can live, and then Noemi herself is mother to the village and will be mother to us all while we are there.

We leave for the earth womb of the jungle in about four hours and I'm ... well, I'm scared shitless. It seemed like a good idea when I was in London to shortcut to the experience of 'getting the mind out of the way'. But now I'm wondering what was wrong with the idea of just sitting and pondering as the Advaita tradition suggests. Now I am removing my mind, there is just the teeniest part of me that is wondering whether I will ever get it back again.

'Now, Isabel,' says the conversation currently going on in my head, 'shamans have been using plants of various kinds to kick people's minds along the spiritual path for generations. Even children are given weird potions to teach them about other realities. In native tribes, what you're going to experience is as commonplace as teenagers in our cities popping pills.'

The thing is that I'm a coward, a drug virgin. I've never taken anything. I did try smoking cannabis a bit but had a number of problems with it. Firstly, I'm not a smoker. The option to fill my lungs with the fresh, clean air that my nose prefers is not a choice that wafts in the window on a regular basis in London – so the thought of deliberately filling my lungs with smoke has always seemed to me to be a dubious choice. Secondly, when I have smoked cannabis it has always just made me feel I want to go to sleep. That's not it, is it? That wasn't the experience I was supposed to have. So to keep to the drug virgin comparison, I suppose I once had a brief grope in a fully lit room, found it not to my taste and never went further.

So you can see why I might be a little terrified. I found myself today remembering the woman who sat in front of Mooji and said, 'I am that in which fear is arising.' I mocked her in my mind, thinking, 'Oh, fear, fear ... why is there so much fear everywhere? What is everyone so afraid of?' Dammit. Well, I can tell you what I'm afraid of now.

I'm marginally afraid of malaria, yellow fever, hepatitis B, typhoid and so many other potential horror diseases that I was advised in London not even to bother inoculating myself against them all. I have some fear, not of bugs themselves, but of those that bite: mosquitoes, wasps, bees and ants with bites worse than a spider bite. Spiders? Not scared of spiders, happy to stroke their cute, furry little legs, but would very much appreciate them not biting me. And – get this – I've discovered that vampire bats are not mythical. I thought that bats that land on you and suck your blood were the stuff of gothic novels – but no, apparently they are real and, I'm told, 'If they land on you it hurts.' But even the vampire bats are less scary than swallowing a brew that is going to separate me from my own mind. I have asked several times, 'Has anyone ever died drinking this stuff?' but no-one has given me a straight answer – not even a 'Don't be silly, Isabel, of course not.' Just no reply.

A friend in London said, 'Aren't you afraid that you'll lose your marbles?' I replied, rather glibly, 'I have very few marbles anyway, and those that I have are responsible for the way my life is, so the shaman's welcome to them.' But now I'm here, I find that I'm strangely attached to my marbles – even visualizing them as quite shiny and of different colours – and I fully understand why I never wanted to endanger my limited supply.

Last night, while Dilwyn discussed practicalities with one of our local helpers at dinner, I quizzed Jeremy and Alex on how they felt about taking the shaman's potion – a drug called ayahuasca. Alex, at 24, is the old boy in the field of mind-altering substances.

'So what exactly have you taken, Alex?'

'Weed, ecstasy, MDMA ...'

'What's that?'

'A purer form of ecstasy. And magic mushrooms.'

'Lots?'

'No, say, three times. Then philosopher's stone.'

'I thought that was a book by J K Rowling?'

'It's also a truffle.'

'Isn't that a chocolate that you eat at Christmastime?'

'No, it's a plant that grows in the ground and is a natural

hallucinogenic. Oh, and cocaine, of course.'

'Of course?'

'Cocaine is a stupid drug.'

'Why do you say that?'

'It makes you feel powerful, invincible and infinitely more confident, but, as you know full well that these are the effects of the drug, you can easily identify these qualities as only reachable while you're on the drug, and end up pushing these qualities away from yourself. Actually, it's not a stupid drug. It's a really stupid drug.'

'OK.'

'Then *Salvia divinorum.*'

'Again?'

'A species of sage,' chips in Jeremy the botanist, 'of the family *Salvia officinalis.*'

'You smoked sage, Alex?'

'It's an extract that you smoke concentrated.'

'Sage is also used by North American Indians in sweat lodges,' says Jeremy.

Obviously I'm the only one who doesn't know these things.

'Is that it, Alex?' I'm beginning to think that his mother may read this and I am worried on her behalf.

'Well, speed.'

'Do you do all this often?'

'No, not often. Nothing stronger. No heroin, of course. I'm not stupid.'

'So are you both going to take the ayahuasca if the opportunity arises?'

'I don't know,' says Alex. 'I'll see how I feel at the time.'

'What about you, Jeremy?'

'Yes, I may – unless something unexpected happens to put me off.'

'The thing is,' says Alex, 'normally, when you take any kind of mind-altering substance, you do it with your best friend in the whole world. It's something different to take a substance that you don't know, in a community that you don't know or feel safe in, with people you don't know.'

'Jeremy, have you ever done anything like this before?'

'No. I once tried marijuana but I didn't like it and I've never tried anything since.' Ah, another virgin. By this analogy we have just turned Alex into Don Juan, which I'm sure he'd like a lot.

'So you are both here mainly to experience being with the people?'

'Yes. I learnt so much in Africa being with people who are close to the earth.' Jeremy is an old-fashioned 'good man' – I'm so glad that he is joining us. 'One of my dreams has always been to experience living with a community that lives completely off the earth and doesn't depend on technology. This is an indigenous tribe that lives entirely from nature, a culture that has remained unchanged for five thousand years.'

'Rather boggles the mind,' Alex responds for both of us.

'When the very first Britons came to colonize the British Isles after the Ice Age, these people were living in the jungle in much the same way as they are now, eating manioc as their staple food, growing cotton, spinning and weaving it to make clothes, using bows and arrows to hunt.'

'Are there any differences now?' We turn to Dilwyn.

'They have some clothes that Westerners have brought in. Apart from that, they have guns that they use to hunt instead of bows and arrows, and sometimes doctors come in from outside. Some tribes are voluntarily not in contact with the outside world at all. But this tribe is, and their children are learning to speak Spanish at the local school. Other than that, the way that they live is unchanged. You'll see for yourself.'

So both the 'boys' are here to experience the people. I hope I can learn from Noemi's presence, just as I felt that I learnt from Mooji's. Maybe I can just do that – just 'be' there – and skip swallowing the brew altogether. But then again, shamans have been using ayahuasca to separate people from their minds for centuries. It would be foolishness of a different kind to come all this way, put myself in the care of a living shaman and then not trust her to teach me in the way that she thinks best.

I'm digressing, aren't I? You know why that is? It's because when I stop writing it'll be time to go. When I leave here, it will be to meet the others and set out for the jungle. And I like writing to you. It's less scary than leaving. You know what one friend said to me in London? Well, obviously I'm about to tell you.

'I really don't understand why you haven't done any research into shamanism and ayahuasca before you set off.'

'I didn't want to read about anyone else's experience. I figured that my mind would experience that as suggestion and try to replicate it in some way. Better, I thought, to go as a clean slate, with no expectation, knowing nothing. Then any experience I know is mine.'

'That's all well and good. But this is serious stuff. It's con-sciousness-altering.'

'What? You mean permanently? You mean that I could be permanently altered by taking this stuff?'

'Yes.'

What I'd forgotten is that sometimes when you force yourself outside your 'comfort zone' the rewards can be extraordinary. I got to fly over the Amazonian jungle today. The plane was so small that Alex commented, 'I've never flown in a car before.'

We then had a very hot three-hour walk through the jungle. I was carrying four young chickens that Dilwyn had bought for Noemi and, with one or more of them making regular attempts to liberate themselves from the torn cardboard box that was their prison, it was a journey requiring all my attention. The beauty of the canopy above constantly invited me to risk a twisted ankle by not watching my step but, filled with awe and wonder, gazing upwards instead. I succeeded, during that walk, at arriving perfectly in the present moment, trained by chickens.

Finally, with some very hot and cross birds, we turned a corner and there among the trees was a little village. Well, 'village' probably brings a different image to mind, of a church and a little green and a pub – so maybe 'clearing' would be better. Some wooden huts, mostly without walls – just roofs made of palm leaves supported by wooden poles at each corner. One of the huts had palm walls and a floor that was raised a couple of feet above the ground, and next to it an open fire on the ground built with sticks. There also stood, smiling at us, a little group of short and evidently very friendly people with red markings all over their faces. They are Dilwyn's friends and our hosts for the week.

Dilwyn's company, Ecotribal, which I'm travelling with, has put a lot of thought into how this way of life can be supported without being disturbed or destroyed by outsiders. This kind of 'low-impact' tourism is an easy solution. Only a few people at a time, hand-picked by Dilwyn; four tents go up, we bring cloth, beads – simple things the community likes – and then we pack our tents and leave them in peace. Ecotribal only brings in one small group a year.

The head man of the village, Jaime (pronounced Hy-me), speaks Spanish and has even travelled to Britain. He wisely considers that since encroachment on their way of life is inevitable, best to work with the outsiders and find out which have the best interests of his community at heart and which don't. The Ashaninka are constantly under threat from oil companies or illegal loggers who want to use their land or cocaine smugglers who want to use their little airstrip for clandestine business deals. Sometimes there is the danger of one tribe member being persuaded to sign away land that belongs to an entire tribe. Only recently a disaster of this kind was averted when illegal loggers were offering someone in the community a pittance for access to thousands of hectares of Ashaninka forest. The charity that Ecotribal work with, Cool Earth, has just paid £15,000 more than the loggers were offering. Now, for the first time, a group of 2,000 Ashaninka tribes (within a total tribe population of

45,000) have a community organization and meet to decide how to protect the forest (entrusted straight back to them by Cool Earth) and discuss how the money should be spent.

So far, they have bought a community canoe so that they can sell coca beans farther down the river and take people out of the jungle for emergency medical treatment if necessary. Ecotribal and Cool Earth are also working with the Ashaninka to put together a sustainable development programme, and where the development works well, it's good to see. When Channel 4 came here briefly, Jaime used the payment to have a solar panel fitted to the roof of his hut. Now a single energy-efficient bulb hangs in the porch of Jaime's hut and gives them a gentle light at dusk. The best of what our world can offer theirs.

Arriving here, one small solar panel aside, it's extraordinary to think that an almost identical sight would have greeted us if we had arrived here 5,000 years ago. Each family has one area for sleeping, one for cooking and one for visitors – and that's it. Exceptionally, in the case of this family who know the Western people's inexplicable inability to sit on the floor, a table and benches have been specially made for us. We have also brought in, for our visit this week, forks and food familiar to us. This may seem as though it will take away from the authentic experience ... but I am so very glad not to be eating insects or monkey meat. Jaime is drying out a tarantula by standing it on a metal plate on the fire. As he does a gentle dry-roasting job on it, various tiny worms that had lived inside it start to feel hot. As they emerge from the spider's body, he picks them off with a stick and puts them in the fire. They're going to eat the tarantula with a little banana, or so he tells us, but he's just entertaining himself with the gullibility of the visitors. He later admits he's drying it to give to the local preschool for them to put on display.

I'm crestfallen that I don't speak Spanish. Not that it would help me speak to any of the women or children – they speak only Ashaninka – but I would at least be able to talk with Jaime without depending on Dilwyn to translate. The women and I can only look at each other and smile shyly. It's like stepping into a history book and coming face to face with women who make and use every day the sorts of combs that you see on display in museums. The life you imagine prehistoric people living has always been reported to us as 'primitive', but here it seems to be more the way we imagine life in paradise to be. They live in harmony with nature and in harmony with each other.

To cool off in the afternoon, we go swimming in the Mamiri river, a crystalline Amazon headwater – naked, of course. I smile to myself about the pointlessness of feeling at all self-conscious in front of three men I barely know. The banks of this part of the river have perfect beaches of light-coloured stone, the current not too strong and the trees high around us. I feel as though I have dived into one of those perfect places that you normally see only on a Lonely Planet calendar.

Dilwyn tells us, once we are swimming, that it's actually a bad idea to swim naked, as they have those creatures that swim up inside women and enter men via the little hole in the tip of the penis. (Apparently it does have a posh name – 'external urethral orifice' – but is more commonly known as 'the little hole in the tip of the penis'.) Dilwyn, swimming in his trunks, casually mentions this and then watches as the rest of us leave the water with varying degrees of rapidity. As we three stand on the beach searching for swimwear, he starts to laugh. 'Not really – only kidding you.'

No, it turns out that this really is paradise. We have no such horrors to fear. Not even any piranhas to eat us alive. The water is clean and clear and the gravest danger in swimming turns out to be the possibility of stubbing a toe on a rock. Dilwyn has organized vegetarian spaghetti and a large salad to be served for supper, before it gets dark. By about 8pm we all head off to our tents to sleep on the sweet-smelling earth with the sounds of the jungle in the background, and everything feels just about as perfect as it can be.

First Dawn

After a night in my little tent, I wake before dawn to find the women and children already tending the fire. They are beginning the daily task of making the only liquid they drink, which is a kind of mild beer made from manioc tubers, the local staple carbohydrate. They chew it and then spit it into the bowl before boiling it. Little tiny children help with the chopping and grating as well as the chewing and spitting.

As I sit in the dawn light and watch, more women and children arrive with wood in baskets on their heads. They have been carrying wood like this for 5,000 years. I have not heard a mother raise her voice or reprimand a child in any way. I see a little boy of about two fall. He cries for about two seconds, none of the adults look round, and he stops. Sounds simple, doesn't it? Yet our children will cry in supermarkets for a full half-hour before a mother gives in and buys sweets.

When Dilwyn, Jeremy and Alex emerge from their tents, we are all served a mouth-watering breakfast of papaya, bananas and manioc. The bananas and manioc have been picked five minutes before and freshly baked. We sit and eat and watch their morning.

The peace seeps in. So many things that I don't understand – the harmony of it all seems impossible. Even the simple things – there are dogs and cats, chickens and chicks. None of the animals have had operations to stop them producing offspring, so, as food seems plentiful, why isn't the little village overrun with cats and dogs? The balance here seems so perfect – it's as if I feel mankind must interfere in some way to maintain it. Have I been conditioned to believe that real harmony and balance must be an illusion?

'Do they kill the puppies and kittens at birth to keep the numbers down?' I ask. No, apparently not.

'Last year there was a dog that was ill and started to foam at the mouth, so it could have been rabid.' Dilwyn tells this story in explanation for my confusion on the dog and cat population. 'So they dug a big hole, put the dog in and covered it with earth.'

'I hope they killed it first?'

'No – that was their way of killing it.'

'Oh, God. Wouldn't a machete be kinder?'

'That's what I thought,' says Dilwyn. 'But apparently it's hard to kill a dog with a machete in one blow, and if it's two or three blows then it's worse. They consider it the kindest way. We heard a whimper or two and that was it.'

'I'd rather not think about that.'

'Injecting dogs with chemicals as we do isn't that nice either. I've heard that some dogs howl when they are injected.'

'So no vets, then? If an animal gets ill, it dies or they kill it.'

'That's life and death in the real world, Isabel. That's where we'll all end up, in the earth.'

Well, there is the answer to my question about keeping the numbers down.

'What about the children?'

'They have a natural form of family planning – herbs that they can take if they don't want to have children. Jaime has only four children – that's a very small family. The family we passed on the way here has twelve children – that's a large family. They like large families because so many Ashaninka have been killed that they want to increase their numbers again to look after the jungle. Jaime's wife lost one – a little boy of two who was "taken by the river" one day. He got too far out in the current in the season when the current is strong.'

The river has also taken a girl from the village who was epileptic. The villagers had appealed to visitors from our world for medicine that could help her, but were told that the medicine is 'very expensive and doesn't work', that she would 'probably grow out of it' and just to keep an eye on her. But one day she went swimming with her friends, had a fit and was too far out for the other children to help her. So it's not as if the village doesn't know sadness. There is one woman in the village not able to have children. But there seems to be no sadness in her and she wears a very large smile. Obviously, even here, not to have children can be seen as a blessing, just as it sometimes is a choice among women in London town.

Dilwyn explains as we sit and absorb the beauty around us that the Ashaninka have been through hard times. Fifteen years ago, a Communist group called the Shining Path wanted the land and seized it by going into villages, killing everyone and burning the huts to the ground. Jaime's family had to leave their homes and gardens and flee into the mountains. They would have starved except, having heard rumours of this crisis approaching, they had planted other gardens in random places in the jungle. During the two years or so before they were able to return, they had to hunt monkeys with bows and arrows as their fathers had done (guns would have given away their hiding places) and search out the hidden gardens at night to return to feed the women and children. One man became trapped when a rock fell on his arm. He took out a knife, cut off the arm and walked to safety. I am told this story before I meet the smiling face of the one-armed man, who, this morning, greets me politely with a shake of his remaining hand – a greeting that they have learnt the visitors expect.

But this horror is due to outsiders. When they are left to themselves, the life here breathes with a miraculous peace. The women and children do the cooking, the men the hunting. The women collect wood for the fire and the men chop the larger pieces of wood and build the homes. Everyone digs the earth, works the ground and plants the gardens. Everything comes from the earth and returns to the earth, all the food is organic, there is nothing artificial anywhere and everything recycles. Most of the objects around seem to be made from the coconut palm leaves that the women weave: baskets, floor mats, little cupboards on stilts for storing eggs, fans for the fire, thatching for the roof. If you have a coconut palm you can live – without ever having seen a shop or a unit of money. They harvest cotton from the trees, spin it and dye it, and weave remarkably fine and beautiful cloth. The adult men like to wear the traditional caftan-like robe, known as a cushma, that is woven for them by their wives.

'They want to be beautiful, as the jungle is beautiful, so they aim to be as beautiful as nature and also please the ancestors,' Dilwyn says proudly of his friends.

'So, what's the plan for today?' asks Alex. Plan? My plan had been occasional standing but mostly sitting, with optional watching and learning and possibly even some swimming. All is perfect peace except possibly my shiny new insect bites that no-one else is troubled with. (I am covered in insect repellent; it smells horrible and seems to attract the insects.)

'Tonight Noemi is preparing an ayahuasca session,' Dilwyn says nonchalantly. 'We are all invited to participate.'

'I'm in,' says Alex.

'Jeremy?'

'Er, yes, I think it might be an interesting experience.' Jeremy amazes me constantly. 'I hadn't planned to do anything like this. But as the opportunity is here, I think I'd like to.'

'Isabel?' Dilwyn looks at me. It seems that as well as being the being that is looking out of my eyes that Mooji is trying to draw my attention to, I am also someone with eyes being directed at me. And a decision is called for. In theory this is what I am here for.

'Tell me, Dilwyn, is this stuff dangerous?'

'It needs to be approached with caution. I've heard it described before as "wielding a chainsaw inside your head".'

'Er ...'

'What I mean by that is that, in the wrong hands and without respect for the power of the tool, yes, it's dangerous.'

'But are you recommending it?'

'I'm not recommending it. No. But they are offering it.'

'A chainsaw can be used with the precision of a surgeon's knife in the right hands,' Jeremy suggests diplomatically.

'Noemi is like a mother for me. I've taken it with her for over thirty years.' Dilwyn seems to be offering this information as proof that we are all likely to survive.

'Has anyone ever died?'

'Not as far as I know.'

I sit and stare at a huge turkey that is strutting around the plot, perfectly in his own present moment. Why does anyone here take this stuff when everything is so perfect?

'Why are they using it here anyway?'

'The Ashaninka people have always taken ayahuasca to communicate with the spirit world, the spirit of plants, the river and the trees. Noemi has been taking it once or twice a week all her life and she's seventy.'

'So what can we expect?' Jeremy asks.

'Visions.' Dilwyn smiles. 'Of one kind or another.'

'A little more information perhaps, Dilwyn?' I get out my pen.

'The experience depends entirely on what you bring to it. It's primarily a visionary vine and it's different every time. You'll be talking to yourself a lot inside your head and the visions tend to reach back quite deeply into your unconscious. That's the first stage. After that you start to feel sick and may be sick. In the second phase you may feel things churning in your stomach and you need to try and shift your focus from your stomach to the pineal gland in the middle of your forehead, which is the centre of the visual consciousness. Trying to shift the focus involves trying to let go of the internal dialogue along with the churning in your stomach. Then the third stage, when you are through all that and everything seems just right.'

'Funny, this "Let go of the internal dialogue" is similar to the meditative aim, isn't it?'

'Yes.'

We sit and eat our baked banana.

'I'd like to add ...' Dilwyn goes on. 'This isn't part of the Ecotribal tour. It has just happened. If we'd been heading up to waterfalls and canoeing back down, which is what I normally do, then we wouldn't have been including an ayahuasca session. It is not for me to recommend or not recommend anyone joining in, but I do want to say, on the record, that this is a powerful drug. It should only ever be taken with a highly experienced shaman and it could be very dangerous for anyone with an unstable mind. I do know people who, using other plants, have been unable to function in the world afterwards, so this does need to be taken with respect and caution.'

I become a little more scared than I was earlier.

'Is the dose adjusted for us as people from outside?'

'She gives us all individual doses.'

'And vomiting and opening the bowels is guaranteed?' Cringe.

'Well, it builds up pressure in your gut and it tends to come out somehow. To be crude,' – Dilwyn is now providing the 'more information' that I asked for – 'I've taken it fifty or sixty times. I've been sick ten times or so, but I always end up having a shit at some point.'

I suppose I wanted an earth experience.

'Is it addictive?'

'No. Not at all – you'll see why. It demands a lot of respect. I went into all this much more lightly when I was Alex's age but now I tend to be more in awe and far more fearful of the experience.'

Jaime wanders over to ask if anyone wants coffee, but it isn't recommended before an ayahuasca session. He sits and drinks some.

'Will Jaime not be joining us tonight?'

'No. He only takes it about once or twice a year.'

'On special occasions?'

Dilwyn translates my question.

'No – he says that he takes it when he feels like it.'

'Does the community use it for special occasions? Is it part of any preparation for births, marriages or deaths?'

'No.'

'Not even for the dead? To pray or help them "pass over to the next world" in some way?'

Dilwyn translates patiently.

'No. Not for the dead. In fact, he's somewhat bemused by the question. If someone dies, then they dig a shallow grave in the earth and bury them. He says that if someone is ill they might use it to help understand why they are ill. At one period in his life Jaime was working in Cutivireni as a bilingual teacher and seems to have had some kind of brain haemorrhage. He was taken to a hospital and they wanted to operate on him but his family didn't want them to cut his head open. We had to help them to get him out of the hospital and back here. Anyway, once he got here they gave him a concentrated form of ayahuasca and he was able to cure himself. He says that the ayahuasca gave him visions of his ancestors coming to him, all with different faces and wearing different-coloured cushmas. One told him that he would be OK, and by the following day he was.'

'Does he meet the same ancestors and spirits in his various visions, or different ones?'

'Different ones – different ancestors.'

'And the spirits?'

'It's difficult, Isabel. If I push him with questions like this he'll close up.'

'Oh, that's OK then, just stop. I don't want to push at all.'

'No, I'll ask him in a slightly different way. I'm just saying that it's tricky.'

They chat for a while. God – how absurd of me not to speak Spanish.

Dilwyn turns back to me. 'Last year I had a very strong vision and I have been trying to understand what it was about. I asked him as a way of asking your question and he tells me that the images that I saw were certainly the spirit of ayahuasca, which takes many forms.'

'Would he be interested in knowing that in Tibetan Buddhism they have a person known as a medium who allows a spirit to enter him to communicate messages from the spirit world?'

'No. I think he'd be spooked. That's one of the main differences with shamanism. In other traditions the spirits are asked to come to our world in channelling or via possession of various kinds, but in shamanism they use ayahuasca to go to theirs.'

Alex has wandered off by this time to do an hour of yoga.

'You have no questions, Jeremy?'

'No. I want to keep an open mind.'

Mind ... ah, yes. I remember mind. According to Mooji, I'd be better off not to use my mind at all. I'm banking on ayahuasca forcing me to step out of my mind completely and experience the observer. I think. No, I don't. I don't think.

'One final question, Dilwyn. Will I be able to write at all while this is happening? It's kinda what I do – write.'

'You won't want to. Writing is part of the internal dialogue and that's what you want to be rid of in order for the visions to flow freely.'

I won't want to write? Well, that will be a first-time experience.

The turkey ruffles his feathers at the passing lady turkey. I look around, still incredulous of the village, the people, and the way that we are about to enter, in the fullest way possible, into the spiritual life of the community.

'It's incredibly gracious of Noemi and these people to be prepared to share their most sacred ceremony with us. After all, we could be any old Toms, Dicks or Harrys. They don't know anything about us.'

'They will by the morning.'

I take a breath and walk away from the table, grab swimwear for the sake of modesty and set off for the bathroom/Amazon.

Lying on my back in the water, looking at the clear blue sky and the canopy of the trees, I contemplate my insanity. This is a class A drug that I'm about to take. That puts it with heroin, LSD, cocaine, crack and a couple of others. If the local police popped in and found me doing this on the Battersea Park Road I could get seven years in prison, and if I shared it and let people pay me for the experience I could get life. Perhaps I've already taken leave of my wits. How do I know that this won't have some seriously damaging effect on me? The phrase 'unable to function in the world' resonates with alarming clarity. It's certainly what one of my old seminar teachers would call a 'red flag': a warning, drawing my attention to my responsibility in making what could be an idiotic choice.

But, if I choose to focus completely on the positive, I need to bear in mind the Buddhist teaching that everything that I will see in the visions – or hallucinations, or whatever I want to see them as – can be nothing more than projections of my own mind. No visions can occur that I am not the source of. But does that mean that I don't believe in spirits? The Ashaninka don't believe, as some Tibetan Buddhists do, that everything comes from the mind. They believe that the plants and the spirits of nature around them speak to them through the trance state. These are all concepts and theories anyway. Could I really come up with a theory for you about floating in the Amazon and looking at the sky? Will you really believe how peacefully these people live unless you come here and see for yourself? There is an idiom, isn't there? 'Suck it and see.' I guess this is one further on from that – 'Swallow it and see.'

It is evening and we have been brought to the place where Noemi lives. She has a fire and on it a large pot looking very like a cauldron. She is singing, stirring the pot, occasionally adding things and spitting into it. To complete the image, she even has a cat. A long bamboo-leaf floor mat has been laid out and we are invited to put our sleeping bags down on top of it. We will swallow our potion and then lie down and close our eyes. We have been told where to walk to in order to avoid being sick on her ground. I'm writing this as the moon goes down.

I don't believe that there is anything ayahuasca can reveal to me about myself that I don't already know. What's the difference between a vision and a dream, anyway? Isn't this just having a dream while you are still awake?

While we lie here someone is playing a flute to summon the spirits. Alex isn't in the least scared, and when Dilwyn says tonight's brew will probably be milder as it's our first time, Alex says, 'I may come back for further doses, then.' I'm very, very glad that it's going to be mild for us. Earlier this evening there was a rainbow in the sky. In the style of the Tibetans I decided to interpret this as an auspicious sign. Now there is a ring around the moon and I'm peering at it trying to remember if it's supposed to be a harbinger of anything more than bad weather: impending madness, for example.

I don't feel scared now, only curious. It's just dreaming while awake, I'm telling myself. My mind isn't going to explode even if my bowels do. I'm lying happily on the ground with the sounds of the jungle all around us: the river in the background, the waterfall, the crickets. There is a wonderful smell of wood smoke, and I can see the red embers under Noemi's pot. I can't smell her brew, thank God. Dilwyn says that one of the reasons this plant isn't addictive is that it's so horrible to drink – rather like acrid grapefruit juice, apparently – and that he'd rather eat a dog turd. A tasteful way of describing how bad it is. Noemi looks so much like a witch, bent over her pot ...

Bats! Oh, please let them be fruit bats. I am writing now unable to see the words on the page – just black on white and I have to trust that the scrawl of my beloved Lamy fountain pen will be comprehensible to me later. Outside the white ring around the moon there is now a brown ring. They have given the flute to two young children and it turns out that it is a plastic descant recorder that some visitor brought in. Suddenly a wonderful touch of the absurd is added to all this: far from the eerie music to welcome the spirits that someone was playing earlier, now we have the same dreadful noise that children all over the world make blowing a recorder, and listening to that and looking at the serious expression on Alex's face I start to laugh.

And then, oh God, the brew is ready. Pray for me please Santa Maria (I'm not Roman Catholic so why Mary? I've no idea). Pray for me whoever is reading this ... Dilwyn is drinking it. Should I have prepared in some way? Too late. Alex is drinking it now. He's still drinking it and it seems like five minutes later. Oh God, the dog-poo tasting ... Now me.

OK, I've swallowed it. Not too horrible. Just very acrid and strong. I pretended it was some medicine and swigged it down bravely. I said, 'Well done,' to myself as it went down. I have to lie down now and see what happens.

Nothing so far. Lots of burping from Dilwyn. Actually, it does taste horrible. Acrid aftertaste too. I'm starting to feel strangely warm. Alex says, 'Good journey, everyone,' and lies down to close his eyes. Oh my goodness, the little kids are taking it too. One of them must be about five. No-one said how long this takes to kick in and now I can't ask. No talking to anyone, they said. It's an inner experience. Everyone else is lying down still as I sit up writing to you. It's so dark I can barely see the paper to write to you. No torches allowed either. The bats are swooping low over us. Fruit bats, I tell myself again. Not vampire bats. I still feel fine. No getting out of it now – I've swallowed it.

It feels wonderful here under the sky. I don't feel at all sleepy.

There are some clouds in the sky. Just feel very relaxed. Not at all fearful, just a weird feeling of sinking. Oh – a shooting star. I just feel unusually and completely awake, but woozy. Completely in nature. The only man-made things around here are the sleeping bags, my notebook and this pen. People lying under the stars. Maybe it's the job of one of the plants to keep you awake? I don't understand why I'm awake. God, it's beautiful here. Am I supposed to be lying down and focusing on sensations and pictures inside my head? I guess I am. So far I just feel good. Noemi is spitting in her pot a lot.

I guess I'd better lie down and switch off the mind.

– Now I'm just feeling weird – don't know what to think –

– Don't think. Just watch the sensations –

– OK –

– Stop writing –

– Oh, shut up –

I put down my pen and lie down, then sit up to write again.

– Must now finally stop and have this experience – there is a pulling to do so –

– Lie down –

– Weird pictures in my mind – chess pieces – each one turning into Buddha statues – moving pictures that vanish when I open my eyes –

– So don't open your eyes, idiot –

– If I go with them they are bizarre and extraordinary – ever-changing –

– That's good, isn't it? Fun?

– Weird – but I don't feel afraid of any of them. Why should

I? Weird patterns, weird faces – it's huge fun – dreaming while awake – warm –

– People spinning Tibetan prayer wheels – maybe it's the suggestion of the shaman's strange song – it sounds a bit like the monks chanting. She is spinning prayer wheels in my head. It doesn't feel as if I'm doing it. I'm just observing it. A show inside my head –

It's like those moments just before you fall asleep when you see weird things or people. You know that you're still awake and starting to dream and if you open your eyes they go away. It's like that.

– Just saw a huge church, a nave that went on for ever and an obviously very gay man in a cowboy hat dancing! What the fuck? A gay man in a cowboy hat? And then everyone was dancing –

Then Dilwyn's voice from another reality: 'Isabel, it's very mild – Noemi is asking if we'd like more? I've had some more.'

'OK, why not?' I seem to be enjoying this.

Have to stop writing. Have to get back to it. Next instalment in full technicolour.

– Lie down – close your eyes –

– Dancing shaman! – tribal people all dressed up – some weird dance – they are forming a circle – they want me to hold hands and join in. Suddenly Emily is here. She takes my left hand very firmly with her right hand as if to give me something that I know to protect me and then reaches out her left hand to take that of a tribal dancing native in a mask. 'THIS IS WEIRD,' she says – in a voice clearer and louder than Dilwyn's voice. It's as if she has had to turn up in her astral body – wrenched from a perfectly normal dream in Battersea to have to arrive in the jungle to take care of her feral mother. But she looks round, interested all the same, in the proceedings –

Next I see Emily in a dark black place, polluted with soot, dirt, and tar – an obvious projection of my fears for her well-being – weird.

I watch in amazement, four golden dorjes pointing in the four directions of the compass with light pouring out in all directions – so bright. Then more confused images.

Then, lurching back to consciousness feeling more ill than when I drank too much lemonade liqueur once, I stagger off in the direction of the bare earth, grateful for my body's knowledge that it wants to remove the witch's brew the quick way.

I stand in the woods feeling miserable and very ill when Dilwyn appears like a shepherd in search of one of his lost sheep, with his white hair in the moonlight completing the image. He has come to lead me home, or back to my sleeping bag, at any rate.

'Thank you,' I think I manage to say. 'I'm fine.' I sway back to my sleeping bag to fall asleep instantly. An hour later, a rerun. More staggering, more sickness, but as I lie back down I have a fantastic feeling of warmth all through my body. I begin chatting to this feeling of warmth about some minor health problems I have – asking if it can fix them while it's around – when I guess I fall asleep again.

– I feel sick. Get up and walk to the woods. Water the trees with ayahuasca and wish them a good trip as it soaks into their roots –

I have no idea what time it is. My head is spinning. More visions? Very little that our mind makes up while we are asleep or awake matters all that much. Why do we identify so much with the dream that is our life? Why do we take everything so seriously?

The sky is so clear. I can see into infinity.

Second Dawn

The following day now. We wake to the sound of cockerels. They seem peculiarly anxious that we should be aware of the dawn, as they start to announce it while it is still dark and continue without shirking their duties for at least two hours. I lie there, completely awake again, listening to their bombastic absurdity and enjoying the subtle arrival of the light. Strangely, after such a night, I feel none of the usual grogginess that I feel when I wake in Battersea. I suppose I've done one version of Tony Robbins' detox.

The night did not end where my writing ended. I had felt fine until the second gourd full of brew. Now I think back, I don't know which visions came when. I remember more Tibetan imagery ... golden dorjes! Why golden dorjes? I don't even know what the dorje is a symbol of – must look it up!

Now, permitting a slight cheat in time here – you may imagine my surprise when, weeks later, I read this:

> The Dorje, as a thunderbolt, is represented in the hands of some of the Tibetan gods, especially the Dragshed – deities who protect human beings.

And Noemi tells us that thunder and lightning are the owners of ayahuasca. I also read that the dorje is a symbol of the nature of reality and a symbol of power over invisible evil influences:

> One aspect of its use by the gods is the purification that ensues. It purifies the human constitution as the thunderstorm does the earth's atmosphere.

The dorje (or *vajra* in Sanskrit) has layers upon layers of meaning, none of which were known to me as I was seeing them. Some say that the two ends represent the seen world and the unseen world. Some say one end represents the 'poisons' of the mind while the other represents the enlightened mind.

Now, in the morning, as the cocks crow and crow, I am glad to have travelled on this weird inner journey. Glad to have felt the fear and done it anyway. And where does that leave me now? Supremely happy to be in the present moment and joyful at finding myself alive in the jungle with my sixteen pus-filled insect bites. All spiritual work, no matter what we do, leads us to the present moment, doesn't it?

And to simplicity. All spiritual work seems to lead to simplicity. Years ago I read the diaries of Brother Roger, the monk who founded the Taizé Community in the South of France. He wrote often about his desire to simplify everything and the daily choices he made in order to achieve that. 'Simplify, simplify, simplify,' he wrote, quoting Thoreau.

He'd have liked it here. A hut for sleeping with nothing in it but a palm mat under you and a woven cloth on top, a fire on the ground to cook and the river to wash your clothes in. And what do you do all day? There is no rush or busyness here, but no idleness either. They work the gardens to grow, gather cotton and weave, cook, make necklaces, hunt, have parties, have babies. They never seem to be in a hurry and I've not seen anyone look grumpy or bad-tempered. No-one ever need be lonely, as they sleep in family huts and everyone they know lives around them or in the next village.

The simplicity extends beyond the lifestyle to the beliefs – or lack of them. They have no religious ceremonies apart from taking the ayahuasca, and even that is done without ceremony. Lie down, drink, lie down again; someone sings while others take it. That's it. They have zero religious imagery, no depictions of deities of any kinds. And there are no hierarchies here. It's matrilocal, which means that when there is a marriage, the man moves to the woman's village. Every family in every hut does the same job as every other family in every other hut. There are a few specialists, like the shaman or a leader like Jaime to take charge in times of crisis. Some men may be better at fishing and others at hunting but there is no competition.

This sounds, doesn't it, as if I'm seeing them all through ayahuasca-enhanced spectacles? But Dilwyn says that sharing everything is fundamental to their coexistence. They share all the food and everything else that they have between them. They seem to have no 'better than' or 'worse than' in their minds and seem to be, therefore, without ego.

Don't you find that in our Western society we use the word *ego* as loosely as we use the word *love*? In that 100 people have

100 different definitions? If I hear someone comment that someone else has 'a big ego', I always ask them what exactly they mean, and I've never had the same answer twice. I asked Viv once what he thought it meant and he said that he thought of it as someone who was an attention seeker and always wanted or needed to be in the limelight. I have always thought of someone who has a big ego as someone who thinks he or she is important in some way, even, perhaps, more important than anyone else. Surely to believe that you are more important than the next person you have to have a sense of yourself that is quite illogical. How can anyone be more important than anyone else? Unless of course you are Barack Obama and have the potential to make a real difference to the world. Or you're a doctor and could be put in the lifeboat if the ship were going down because of your ability to save others. But even then it's a superficial difference. Mooji would say, I think, that too much ego comes from 'over-identification with the self'. In other words, you really do believe that you are that 'I' person and haven't understood (even on a mind level) that we are both nothing and everything.

Anyway, whatever definition of ego you want to pick, these people don't have it. The implications of this are surprisingly huge. Is anyone here unfaithful? No. Does anyone leave their partners? No. Does anyone shout at their kids or row or fight or in any way assert themselves over others? No. I know it sounds as though I'm making this up – but think about it for a moment: If they don't think that they are any more important than anyone else or think that things 'should' be different, what's to row about? They are not 'pushing the river', to use Mooji's wonderful phrase, or wanting things to be different, as I often am. As far as I can see, they are simply enjoying being and celebrating what is.

I crawl out of my tent and see Dilwyn emerging from his tent, closely followed by the other two appearing out of theirs. I stumble over to the outdoor breakfast table. It really does feel like the morning after the night before. We sit and chat about nothing much: to drink coffee or not to drink coffee? It seems that no-one wants to ask, 'So ... how was it for you?' Jaime comes over and sits down amused, looking at us all. We are none of us virgins any more.

Wishing to start the day's conversations on a lighter note, I ask about marriage. Surely there must be some kind of ceremony? I thought that ceremony on occasions of this kind was universal to humankind. Apparently not.

'If two young people want to be together – they are usually about fourteen – then they build a hut and move in together.'

'No ceremony at all?'

'No.'

'What happens if two men want the same woman or two women want the same man?'

Dilwyn translates patiently.

'Jaime says that it has never happened. Or he has never seen it. He says that all over the animal kingdom animals mate for life.'

'But it's extraordinary. Would you tell him that in our society, all the way since Shakespeare, since Anthony and Cleopatra –

well, maybe just that for thousands of years men have been killing each other for women?'

Dilwyn starts to speak and then says, 'No ... no, I don't want to tell him that. They have harmony here. Why do I want to tell him something negative?'

'You're right, of course.' I should always have someone to vet my words before they come out of my mouth. It would be so useful. Maybe we should be studying what their harmony is based on instead. 'Are they required to be faithful? Do they take vows of any kind?'

'No vows. They like faithfulness to each other in the same way that we do, and I suppose adultery must happen, but I've never heard of it in the thirty years that I've been coming here.'

The major aim of this community is to live in harmony with nature and with each other. Doesn't that do your heart good to read? Want to come here yet? I go on listening.

'Sex isn't an issue here the way that it is in the West. We are not constantly bombarded with sexual imagery here, so it's not something that you tend to think about much. You do occasionally see a breast, but it always has a baby attached to it.'

'Maybe ...' I speculate, 'maybe one of the reasons for our society's obsession with sex is that we are all so stressed all the time and sex is a natural release. So perhaps without the constant build-up of stress the need for sex isn't so great?'

'Definitely that's so for me,' says Alex, the young stud. 'When I get stressed it definitely makes me horny.'

As we sit and chat, a woman comes to visit with a mass of children around her. I ask Dilwyn to ask her how many children she has. His Ashaninka isn't fluent, but it's good enough for this job.

'She says that she has eight.'

And then, although I already guess the answer, I ask him to ask her how many husbands she has. She laughs and points at the smiling man now appearing behind her. She holds up one finger. 'One.'

'Dilwyn, please tell her that I have visited a country called Tibet where women often have more than one husband.'

Dilwyn translates and she and her husband laugh, as we might after considering it for a bit.

'She says that one is enough for her.' I watch her with her one husband and eight children, not without a certain envy. Although I wouldn't like to do as much cooking as she has to do. I look at her and wonder if anyone here ever leaves a husband or a wife? But then why would they leave anyone? With no sense of competition drilled into them, no sense of 'better than' or 'worse than' and a natural tendency to share and take care of others, it wouldn't make sense. Anyway, as everyone you know lives here, you'd see your old husband or wife every day. I consider asking more about adultery, but then think better of it. It all seems less important here. If sex is for making babies and you already have seven, why would you want one by another man? Also, you don't do it in your hut where the whole family sleeps; you go off into the woods. And you don't want to lie down as there are ants and spiders. Apparently that's why Westerners are famous for preferring the 'missionary position'; it was only the missionaries who liked to do it in that weird position, lying on the ground.

Even animals don't do it like that. The laugh is on us.

I think that sex on beds where we can be comfortable is a good idea (radical, huh?), but how did it all become so excessively important? Sex is often so complicated in our crazy, mixed-up world. Here, like everything else, it seems simple. I see no reason why it should be any the worse for that.

Of course I'm longing to go off and talk with the women. Women talk about sex in a different way when we are away from men. The women are all sitting together, chopping vegetables, making the beer and laughing regularly. I imagine them saying, 'And it was how big?' But it's more likely that they are laughing at us: 'Have you heard they lie down to do it? Ha ha ha.' Or maybe this is just how my mind works. For a while I do sit with them and chop vegetables, but Ashaninka isn't like Spanish where you can pick up the odd word, and we can only go on looking at each other shyly. They seem a bit self-conscious with me sitting there, so, after a while, I drift back again. They are confused by me. I'm wearing trousers, I'm here with a group of men and none of them is my husband. Dilwyn tells me that several of them have asked where my husband is. There are no women of my age in this community who are not married, so I guess I must seem very strange.

Among our lot, the talk has now turned to the experiences of last night. I run for my pen. They are discussing how ayahuasca affects you differently depending on whether you have your eyes open or closed.

'With your eyes open it's more like acid.' Alex kept his eyes open and is launching into telling us about his experience. 'It amazed me how all the logic is totally intact. At first, everything seemed to get wider, the sounds of the jungle crisper, more clearly defined, more powerful. Then the clouds all became faces and I was hearing strange sounds. I looked at a cloud and it seemed I was being told a story by an old woman ... a lion came to a pond, he found a leaf and was playing there and then ... damn. That's all I remember of the story now. But there were lots of stories – images of the human race – abstract images. And it was if the clouds became different spirits and they were laughing at the belief systems of the West.'

He hesitates for a moment.

'Yes, they were laughing at us and our silly belief systems. It was intense but not scary. They seemed to show me things from their past and say, "Does that make sense?" and I said, "Yes." Also they seemed to be asking how the West can mock other belief systems when theirs is just another belief system and it is such a limited one. It was mocking, but not malicious. And I found that the singing came at just the right times. They were good, weren't they?'

'A father and son came to help with the singing,' Dilwyn tells us.

Goodness, I hadn't even noticed them. I'd assumed it was Noemi doing all the singing.

I look at Jeremy. 'Good time?'

'Good wouldn't be the first adjective that would come to mind, no. I had little pictures at first of all sorts of imaginary plants and animals.'

'Not animals that you recognize from this world?'

'No. None that I recognize. And then the images became bigger and more varied. The most memorable was a sort of forest version of a big tent I went into once where people could experience being fully surrounded by different colours. It was like that except it was all the colours of the forest. I was moving through it. The images only came when I closed my eyes; when I opened them everything was normal. Then there was a second phase when I seemed to be in a Japanese garden. I wondered if I could control the images in any way or choose what images to create, and I found that I could but that they were not as strong as the images that came by themselves. Then things got wilder and more intense – so much so that I felt I needed to break the images by opening my eyes. The intensity was too great for me. I thought – is this like wielding a chainsaw inside my mind? And I concluded that it was, so I opened my eyes.'

'Dilwyn?' There's a long and impressive pause while Dilwyn ponders.

'Well, a lot of things went on.'

'Yes?'

'I haven't fully digested it.'

We sit and wait patiently. I rub more anti-itch cream into my bites. Then he says, 'I had a good communication with my father. Who died a couple of years ago. And I saw my children in Wales. Which was good. They all seemed very well. It was mild what she gave us last night. Some things happened that I wasn't expecting or looking for. A lot of children's faces – very smiley and clear, mostly Peruvian children. The landscape was from here but inside my head became a giant spider. It took me a while to work it out – first I saw the feet and then I realized it was a spider. There were lots of really positive images. Images of abundance.'

Oh, dear. How am I going to admit to seeing a gay man in a cowboy hat? Perhaps I can just admit to the rich and wonderful symbolism of the golden dorjes and leave him out? But of course when it's my turn I admit to all of it.

'Why a church, do you think?' asks Alex.

'For me a church is spiritually a very safe place. A cathedral building is often compared to an ark, and it did feel a bit like a huge, safe ship.'

'And what about the gay man in the cowboy hat?'

'It was weird. I felt almost angry when I saw him. He was almost naked and behaving as if he were in the middle of a gay pride march or something – in the middle of this awe-inspiring cathedral he was dancing, in a cowboy hat!'

'Maybe he represents a part of you that wants to be free?' suggests Dilwyn.

'Mmmm.' I consider this. 'Well, he certainly looked free himself. The cowboy hat was almost an "up yours" to all convention and he was dancing in a very "I don't give a fuck" kind of way. I was thinking, "What is he doing here?"'

'How do you feel about gay men in cowboy hats?'

'Well, I'd be happy to dance with them if I was passing a gay pride march, but not in a church and not like that. I'm pretty sure that I'm not being told I'm gay. Fancy men too much and don't fancy women.' I ponder. 'Maybe the ship of the church is big enough and wide enough to contain all spiritual pursuits of whatever kind. Maybe it's OK to dance, to take ayahuasca. Maybe he's an expression of my inner rebel – who I'd like to think of as always dancing. As to the cowboy hat – well, maybe my sub-conscious is just a little playful.'

I go on guessing. 'Maybe I've just been living in southwest London for too long?' I wanted visions of snakes and spirits from the jungle. Am I to be held responsible for the absurdity of my visions?

The interpreters give up on me.

'Anyone for a swim?' I offer in a gay, celebratory kind of way.

Later that afternoon Noemi comes to visit and sits and paints my face with the red markings that they all wear. I feel happy with her and in her presence. None of the strange awareness of what I have called 'the Divine' that I feel with Mooji – more just a feeling of strangeness, of other-world-ness, as if she is only half in this world, but it's a different 'other world' from the one in which Mooji rests. I don't mean that she is sleepy at all or 'out of her head' in the way that you might expect of someone who had taken hallucinogens every week since her early childhood. With Noemi, it feels more as if she looks at us, realizing how unim-portant we are, as if we are all passing figures in a dream. She offers kindness and shows interest, but in a detached way, as we might if we met an old woman in a dream. With her I really feel as if 'I' am nothing more than a passing wisp of a presence in a vision that she is having.

Alex gets out his digital camera and the children gather around, curious to see the captured images of themselves. They have no mirrors here, so the young children seem to have very little concept of what they look like. Very spiritually healthy, of course – little concept of 'I' and no importance attached to it anyway. Little girls look at images of themselves and laugh shyly. Little boys peer at their faces curiously. I remember a Tibetan monk in Nepal once saying to me that too much 'me' leads to too much 'mine'. And in turn, I suppose too much 'mine' leads to too much 'me'. But here they have neither. I was warned in London by a friend who travelled here years ago, 'Don't be surprised if you give something to one person and a day later see someone else with it.' I gave Noemi a peace mala bracelet when we arrived, and, just as my friend predicted, today I see one of the other village women wearing it. Pieces begin to fall into place. The less we identify with the 'I', the happier we can be.

'Why can't we live more like this?' I say out loud.

'This is why I'm here,' says Jeremy. 'This is what we are trying to move to, slowly, in our little town in the South of France. There is a movement, you know, for local and sustainable living.'

'Do you mean that you are creating a different kind of people or just that you are getting rid of competition?'

'We are working on creating more cooperation.'

I think about where I live in Battersea. It has taken me years to lobby successfully for a recycling bin. I am the only one of 18 flats that composts my food. I can imagine what my neighbours would say if I suggested that it might be a good idea to grow some food in our communal garden. One person actually built a shed, on communal land, and only she has the key to it.

Seriously. The idea of sharing anything is anathema to them.

'All you need to start, Isabel, is a small group of like-minded people.'

Makes it sound easy, doesn't he? Does anyone who lives in a major city have around them 'a small group of like-minded people'? I have wanted this for so long, to live in a community of people who care about the planet. Londoners have most of their focus on just paying the bills; none of those I know are growing their own tomatoes.

We then have two days to ponder the wonder of all this and get our hands in the earth planting manioc and picking cotton. The earth, the earth – how subtly it restores us. When Buddha achieved enlightenment, he pointed at the earth, but many of the Buddhists I know meditate only on cushions and don't ever get their hands dirty. My hands rarely leave my laptop. I amaze the women by having no clue how to spin cotton. I imagine that they must wonder how I manage to clothe myself. Jeremy asks about all the plants and takes endless photographs. Alex volunteers to help carry wood and join in general physical tasks to demonstrate that the Westerners are not totally useless. One day it's announced that we will go on 'a walk'.

After three hours of walking I've gone beyond being in the present moment and arrived in the present microsecond. I imagine that perhaps Jaime mentioned to Dilwyn that there was a little trek that we could go on. I'm not sure if even Dilwyn knew quite what he had agreed on our behalf. The jungle isn't flat. At times we climb up or slide down almost vertical banks. You reach out for support to avoid falling and see that the tree that your hand is about to grab on to is covered in huge ants ready to bite you or spikes ready to lacerate your skin. Every footfall has to be watched, as there is always a piece of root ready to hook itself around your foot or a rock ready to help you twist your ankle. And there are other tricks the jungle wants to play to make sure you give nothing less than 100 per cent of your attention to the walk: a branch that pretends to be offering support to pull your body weight up turns to powder when you touch it and comes away in your hands. At the same time bugs of all kinds are intent on devouring the maximum amount of my anti-insect cream for their breakfast, lunch and dinner.

At one point, after I've fallen three times and sworn rather a lot, I look down at the impossibly long and vertical descent we are about to make, and – knowing that we are to be climbing it again later on what is, well, an absurdly hot day with a humidity that feels just as you'd expect the Amazonian jungle to feel – I turn to Dilwyn.

'What are we doing here, Dilwyn? Are we walking in the jungle just to walk in the jungle?'

'Well, that's part of it,' he wheezes. At least I'm not a smoker. I hope he isn't about to have a heart attack; it wouldn't be a good place to choose and my cardiopulmonary resuscitation techniques are a little rusty since I earned my Girl Guide qualifications. 'It's important to experience the terrain.' Bathed in sweat, hearts thumping and panting just to keep moving, we are certainly 'experiencing the terrain'.

'But are we going anywhere? Or is this just an exercise?' I make myself laugh. There has to be a reason. I have to feel I'm doing something other than just being.

'We're going to visit a waterfall.'

'Oh, that's all right, then.' Now I know that we are heading somewhere and a nude shower will make the descent worthwhile. And it is beautiful when we finally arrive. I've never before stood under a natural waterfall until I am well and truly cooled off. The local women who have come with us are very amused by my thong, which I've kept on for the sake of a little modesty.

Dilwyn looks at the minuscule amount of material I've kept around me. 'We brought some of those in once, but they didn't wear them, they made slings out of them.'

The locals are probably wondering why I'm wearing a sling over my butt. I pull on clothes to eat some bananas and manioc root. Again I'm weird – I'm not eating meat. They watch me and chuckle. All the monkeys aren't in the zoo. Every day you meet quite a few.

For the four-hour walk back I'm assigned the assistance of a tiny Ashaninka man who takes my hand so that he can pull me up the banks and prevent me falling. I really don't know how I would make it back without him. 'Pasonki (thank you), Benito,' I say about 100 times. He looks bemused as to why I seem unable to climb a vertical bank unaided. The Ashaninka language didn't have a word for 'thank you' until the missionaries came. The well-meaning missionaries considered it so necessary to say 'thank you' and for themselves to be thanked that they had to introduce a new word into the language to make it possible. Meanwhile, it is yet another experience to keep me humble – having my hand gripped by the hand of a man who, I later discover, came to the village that we are staying in from one of the voluntarily isolated tribes. His face is painted with crushed berries and we have not a word of common language beyond my 'thank you'. On the flat sections of the walk I sing and try to get him to sing songs he knows. He won't sing but obviously enjoys listening to me. For two hours of the walk he hears, unknown to him, the complete Ella Fitzgerald repertoire, a range of silly songs from musicals, rounds in which I am forced to sing all the parts myself, and even Girl Guide songs designed for marching. When I sing the old Australian song 'Kookaburra sits in the old gum tree' and get to the bit that goes, 'Ha – ha – ha,' he laughs out loud every time.

Dilwyn says later that listening to me singing will have been the most cross-cultural contact that he has ever had. This should help him maintain a commitment to a happy and simple life in the jungle.

Third Dawn

Another day. Another perfect morning. We have escaped to a place that is outside time. I have no idea what day of the week it is or what the hour of the day is. I don't care to know.

This morning I sit and watch a little girl of about eight peeling, chopping up and grating a huge pile of a root something like a sweet potato. She works for about two hours and as she works she sings. She's completely concentrating on her task and completely happy. I read an amazing book years ago called *The Continuum Concept* by Jean Liedloff, who spent time living with native tribes and compares the way they raise their children with the way we do. She points out that one of the many ways we ruin our children is by occupying their attention and assuaging their boredom with toys. Children learn by watching their parents and by imitation; they naturally want to copy and do what the adults do. So here they prepare food, cook and garden and all the time can understand the relevance of what they are learning because they are making a genuine contribution. They are participating members of the community from the time they can stand up. Little children cook and carry wood and you never hear that dreadful whining voice that our young people make so often when asked to work.

There was a TV series, I recall – I saw a trailer – in which the producers took a group of overweight British teenagers to live with tribal people. In the trailer, one of the local women said, 'Whenever we give them a job to do, they cry.' These teenagers had seemingly never lifted a finger to help their parents, nor in all likelihood been asked to do so. The job of spending two hours preparing vegetables would obviously have been a form of torture. Yet this morning this little girl sings a wonderful high-pitched song all the time she works and it seems that there is nothing in the world, in that moment, that she would rather be doing. And if there is, then she certainly isn't thinking about it.

It may be a different kind of 'effortless being' from that which

Mooji is pointing to, but in some senses perhaps it is close. No 'I' with which she identifies, no 'better than' or 'worse than' in her head, no judgements as far as I can tell, and possibly even, having taken ayahuasca all her young life, some kind of knowledge that this life is a passing vision anyway. She is certainly residing effortlessly in her being-ness in a way that I've not seen in Western children, and certainly not when they have in front of them a couple of hours of vegetable peeling and chopping to do.

So to get back to the subject of toys. I'm not advocating that we get rid of toys altogether, just pointing out that we undoubtedly have too many of them. When Emily was little, she came home full of envy one day after visiting the house of a girl who had about 27 versions of My Little Pony, a shelf full of Barbie dolls, the Barbie house, the Barbie car, another doll's house, three stables for the ponies – 'And so many other dolls I couldn't count them all.'

'Did you feel sorry for her?' I asked.

'No! She's so lucky to have all those dolls!'

'Mmmm,' I said. 'Do you think so? Do you think that she really loves those dolls the way that you love yours? Who do you think loves her doll more? A little girl who has a hundred dolls or a little girl who lives in a country that is poorer than we are and only has one doll?'

She thought about it. I think she was about seven at the time. 'The little girl who has one doll,' she said.

Here they don't have dolls at all. Often the young children are passing around a real baby, so they don't need dolls. They do play, though. Today they are playing high jump. They have two sticks in the ground with nails banged in at different heights. A third stick rests on the nails horizontally to make a crossbar. Tiny children rush at it and hurl themselves into the air to fly over the stick. This game seems to have kept them happy for over an hour today.

Now just in case you are a parent and want to make this clear to your own children – let me list what they don't have. No computers, obviously; no TVs, no radios, no recorded music, nothing that plugs in, no taps, no mirrors. There is the odd flute and pipes made of hollow sticks tied together. If you want music you play it. They own nothing apart from a few items of clothing and, when they start school, schoolbooks. Now here is a question for your little ones ... who is happier?

Here, there is none of the 'coo-cooing' of children that we do. Why do adults put on baby voices when talking to children and coo, 'Isn't he cute?' No, he's not cute; he's a young person and is to be treated with the same level of respect as everyone else. Why is this cooing and talking down to kids so endemic in our society? It's so intensely patronizing to children. There is no bossing of them either here. They go to bed when they want to and yet are always up helping to prepare the fire before it gets light. I suppose it helps that, the solar-panel light aside, everyone goes to sleep when it gets dark, which is at about 8pm. I still haven't heard either children or adults raise their voices in all the time we have been here.

As I write this, the really little sister in this family, who is only three, is looking after the open fire. She's poking in sticks and fanning the fire to keep the flames up under the cooking pot. She's not tending the fire to win her mother's approval. Her mother is not even watching. She's busy because the fire needs fanning to keep it alight so that they can all eat. Liedloff says that we have blunted our children's instincts because we don't let them go near anything that may harm them. We rush to prevent them from falling. Here, children sit with huge knives or tend the fire but no-one seems to get cut or burnt. I suppose they must do sometimes, and that's one way they learn. Or maybe that three-year-old won't get burnt or shouted at because she has got close enough to the heat to feel it herself.

We are too busy, it seems, telling our children what to do and what not to do to allow them to learn firsthand. This is doubly damaging. Firstly, the kids resent the adults, and secondly, they don't learn. When Liedloff studied all this, she noted how bizarre a concept a 'play group' is. Children are in the middle of the room, literally the centre of attention, while the adults sit, bored out of their minds, around the edge. Kids climb in and out of plastic cars or on and off climbing frames and an adult leaps up to make cooing noises as soon as one of the supposedly helpless little creatures lets out a wail.

It would be more logical, Liedloff writes, to have the parents in the middle doing a range of activities that were important and interesting to them – cooking, sewing, gardening, working with clay – and the children learning these activities by imitation. Yet as I write this I realize that the concentration abilities of some of our kids have become so poor that they would get bored and sit and cry. I blame the passive nature of watching a TV. But then I blame TV for most of the world's evils. Coca Cola, the tobacco industry and TV.

'It's been talked about many times, usually by North American Indians, who say that we need to allow our children to learn by direct experience,' Dilwyn says as he joins me to watch the vegetable chopping and fire fanning and I raise some of these thoughts.

'And yet,' I reply, 'our society is so lost that many parents are afraid ever to let their children out of the door. Somehow we have to turn all this around. We have to simplify our lives, get rid of stuff, liberate ourselves from our dependence on so much technology.'

'Grow our own food, as Jeremy says.'

'Learn to live in harmony with nature. Realize that "I" am not important.'

'Yes. And create genuine community.'

'I'm convinced that it all begins with switching off the TV.'

Fourth Dawn

The second to last day has come, I'm told. This morning, words that I had feared were uttered, with infinite gentleness.

'Noemi has offered to make some more ayahuasca tonight.'

It's not obligatory, of course – but Alex, Jeremy and Dilwyn are all instantly up for another go. It's the nausea that I remember more than the interesting images in my mind's eye. So easy to understand why taking this stuff is not addictive. It's a shame that they can't include something in cocaine that induces nausea and vomiting. That would put the trendy media crowd off. 'Darling, we had such a marvellous evening before we were all sick over the carpet.'

But of course this isn't the same. This is their medicine. So I have to decide. It would be so easy to say, 'Been there, done that.' And curl up happily, not feeling the least bit sick, in my little sleeping bag and doze the night away.

On the other hand, I know a little better what to do now – how to handle the experience. The sickness is unpleasant but won't kill me ... and as I'm not planning on taking anything that counts as a hallucinogenic again for the rest of my life ...

I really, really wish that she hadn't offered this second act of kindness to us strangers. It will take her all day to prepare, but now that she has offered – oh, dear. I'd be more willing if I could believe, as they do, that any issues that the visions may represent are purged along with the vomiting. In their ceremonies, Central and North American shamans apparently call the vomiting 'getting well', and welcome it. I can see how this could work, as I think the power of our beliefs is huge. If you believed fully that, after a session with a therapist, you could be sick and this would release all your problems, it might be more effective than our current method, which is often to explain why our problems belong to us and how they are 'deeply ingrained' (or whatever) and that you take all your problems home with you after the session: £200, please. And if, as more and more of us believe, our physical problems are caused first by mental ones, this would work to keep us both mentally and physically healthy. But, sadly for me, I don't believe that I can pollute the earth by leaving any issues that I may have all over the plants. I'm not expecting to be contacted by local spirits, although I do remember some curious dancing characters from last time. So why would I do it again?

It's something to do with understanding the nature and power of our own minds – and, as Mooji says, what we are beyond our minds. With looking at our self-created fears and our self-created freedom. It's all there, isn't it? It's all in our heads. As the Buddhists say, 'Your mind creates this world.'

And here I am, with a shaman offering to make me a potion to give me insight into that strange place. How could I say no?

Not fear this time. This time it's dread. Noemi comes over to peer at my writing, to watch the black ink appearing on the white paper. I draw a cat to amuse her. She smiles; obviously I have succeeded in drawing something that looks like some kind of animal. Then she wanders back to her cauldron and the dread magnifies itself and sits on my head. And my stomach.

'Why am I focusing on the impending nausea rather than the interest of the experience?' I ask the guys as we sit on our palm-leaf mats in our sleeping bags.

'You must be focusing on the interest at some level or you wouldn't be here,' says Dilwyn generously.

Focus on the positive. Focus on the positive.

It's getting dark now. 'That's a very big bat swooping down at us,' says Jeremy.

'It's a fruit bat, Jeremy. A fruit bat,' I announce with more conviction than I'm feeling.

She's making it stronger tonight. I guess 'making it mild' last time was just to lower us into this world gently. Oh, help.

'As soon as you get the smell and the taste, your body may react to the memory of it, which it associates with being sick. But just ignore that and drink it all down anyway,' Dilwyn says.

'OK, boss.'

Right now I should probably be focusing on the fact that this is sacred medicine and being far more respectful and prayerful in my approach. But the total lack of ceremony here means that I feel no particular preparation is necessary. I am experiencing the ayahuasca here just as they have taken it for thousands of years themselves, right here, in the tribe. There is a clear simplicity to this.

Apparently when ayahuasca is taken on the psychedelic tourist trail they put you on a strict eight-day diet beforehand, and they throw in lots of ceremony in order to make the Westerner feel more comfortable. But here we have a bit of recorder playing and singing through the night and that's it. In the morning we are given warm water to put into our mouths and then spit onto our hands. But this is hardly ceremony; it is more because, as Dilwyn so delicately puts it, 'A lot of vomiting and shitting has gone on through the night.'

I'm going to have to leave writing tonight and just hope that I remember the key images in the morning. There is only so far in this process that I can take you.

We are sitting listening to the river in the distance, the crickets, the crackle of the fire and the recorders. Around us people with gentle faces are sleeping in their huts. Above us there is not a cloud in the black sky, lit up by a full moon and billions of shining stars. Alex doesn't want me to put on my little hand torch at all to write, and he's asked us all not to speak to him, as he's determined to commit himself totally to his experience. And we're off ... Alex is drinking, oh, fuck, I'm next. (Actually, now I'm typing this out from my notebook, I didn't copy that honestly. What I'd actually written was OH FUCK I'M NEXT.)

It's MEDICINE, Isabel, I tell myself – swallow it like medicine. But oh, God, it's strong. OK, I have to lie down and close my eyes now. Santa Maria ... here goes ... come with me, please.

When I came around I couldn't write about it. Not that morning, not that day, not the following day or the day after. I am back in a hotel in Satipo before I write this. But I remember it so vividly that it falls naturally in the present tense. In fact, this could only be written in the present – as it is so intensely and utterly present. As if someone has taken your experience and hit 'magnify' and then turned it up to 500 per cent just for good measure. Thanks for living through it with me.

At first nothing – just looking at the stars and listening to voices in the background somewhere, talking in Ashaninka.

– What's the strange hum inside my head? What's with the swirly pictures?

A visitor or two walks by and says hello; one even wants to

shake my hand. I raise my arm, as if from inside a dream to outside it, and say, 'Tai-terry,' which makes a sound vaguely like the word they use for hello. I have no idea whose hand I am shaking.

– I feel warm all over. Very warm. Ah, the healing medicine. 'This is healing you of everything, body.' I give my body instructions –

– Oh my God, how weird. Suddenly, fast, intense spinning images in my head, spinning out from that bit that I think is called my temporal lobe – all colours, incredibly strong psychedelics. Someone has kidnapped my brain and my visual field. How is this possible? –

– This is terrifying –

– No, it's not. It's not you. You're here –

I go to the place of the observer that Mooji speaks of, or as close as I can get to it. It's like standing back to watch my own mind.

– It is standing back to watch your own mind. It's not 'like' anything –

– OK. So what's the observer like then? –

– Totally at peace, thank you –

– This spinning is intense. It's like ... like nothing on this earth ...

It's being inside the psychedelics that you may have seen on film when people have tried to recreate the drug experience with graphics. Only then you look at it on a screen, and this is inside my head. Spinning images forever outwards, whirling tubes of light.

– Is it trying to pull me out of myself or into myself? I'm being pulled –

There is a pull to take me along, down some kind of tube.

– Sure, OK. Let's go. Take me. Anywhere. I'm on board. Go –
Down, down a long tube.

– Who do you think you are? Alice down a rabbit hole?

– Shut up –

– A woman dancing naked –

No ... I look again and see her better. She's not naked. She's
wearing some kind of shorts. How odd, I think, that she's not
naked here.

– Hold on, she's taking her clothes off –

– That's because you just asked her to –

– No I didn't. Hey, she's an amazing dancer. Who are all
these other people dancing with her?

– You're asking me? I've no idea –

Displays like fireworks.

– Fireworks don't spin –

Catherine wheels, then.

– Thousands of coloured dots and patterns. Hang on – where
have the figures gone? Who are these children?

Human children so clear I could be watching a video. They
are chasing a truck that is moving out of my area of vision stage
right. Are they chasing it because they are hungry?

– Is there food in the truck? No, the children are young and
barefoot but they seem happy enough –

I feel sick. Nausea is rising through me, more and more
putrid.

– Ignore it. Concentrate on the visions. Enjoy the show –

The whirling is more and more high-pitched, out of control.

My head is screaming.

– Little dots everywhere and then those multicoloured necklaces where each bead is made of sugar and a different colouring. Then healthy food boxes for children – what on earth is this? Brightly and coarsely packaged like McDonald's kids' meals, but containing only healthy things. Dried cranberries in little sections ... how many different kinds of nut to put in? Three, I think, two wouldn't be enough; four and the children may not eat them. What do I call these boxes? Izzy Pop Boxes ... no, don't need my name ... Pop Boxes, something ... or necklaces that you can eat, strings like the sugar beads, only dried fruit and stuff. Buy them, wear them and eat them. Sell them in health-food stores –

What on earth? I don't want to be coming up with ideas for food products for kids. Weird beings applaud the boxes and display them to me.

– Look, peoples, I'm really not interested –

– Sugar necklaces. Why is my head full of sugar necklaces? They are so clear –

I have to be sick now. Can't ignore this nausea any longer.

– Open your eyes, get up, walk to the bushes –

– Oh, God, I can't move, the nausea is too intense –

What is this inner dialogue? Who is talking to who?

– STAND UP, WALK. OK. OK. Oh, God, I'm swaying. I can't stand straight. I want to be sick. It's up there. The earth is up that way. Move your legs. OK. But I feel so awful –

I walk about ten paces to the place where we were told to be sick. I'm sick several times.

– Oh, thank you, body, thank you for getting me out of this – But none of the sensations are dimming.

– Spinning colours. Intense. The nausea feels as putrid as ever. Go back. Lie down. Watch the pictures. That's what you're here for. I can't lie down again. I can't get back that far. I feel too sick. I can't walk –

Dilwyn appears, his white hair outlined against the night sky. 'You need to go back and lie down.'

'I know. I know that's the idea, Dilwyn, but I'm not sure that I can move.'

'Take my arm.' He leads me back.

'Sit down on your bag. Well done. Listen to Noemi's singing.'

The high-pitched sound that she is making – it's the same as the psychedelia inside my head. It's a map she's singing, a guide for this other world.

I lie down and try to work out what is me and what is her. That sound that I thought was in my head – she's making it. The sound of the spinning psychedelics, the whirling – she's singing it. She is singing the sound inside my head. No, she can't be.

– Do the zip of your sleeping bag up so that you can lie down. I can't. I can't lie down. I feel putrid –

I turn and retch just close to where the others are lying. But I know that there is nothing to retch up. My body goes on retching anyway.

– Get away from them. But where do I go? I don't know. So go back, then. Lie down. Do I feel better now?

No, I don't. Part of me is quite lucid. No. No. I don't feel better.

My body is burning up now. I am throbbing all over with my fingers vibrating.

– Isabel, this is poison that you have inside you. You have poisoned yourself. This isn't medicine. This is poison. Where are the images? I see no images – just crazy psychedelic fire-crackers and my body struggling to keep me alive. Lie down. Breathe calmly. You aren't going to die –

– Are you sure? Does my body know that? Where is the part of me that is at peace beyond all this?

– Here. All the time here. Untouched. Still. Calm. Eternal and perfect –

– Yes. Lie down and try to sleep –

I lie down, maybe sleep for a very short time, and then am lurched back to consciousness by my body.

– You have to be sick again –

– I can't move. I have to move. Oh, God, Isabel what did you do this to yourself for? Why have you filled your body with acrid poison? Move. Stand up. No way –

– OK, crawl then. Hands and knees. OK. You can crawl away. Right, left, right, left, that way, up there, you can make ten paces. Go on. Can I be sick here? No. Ten paces, go on ... 7, 8, 9 and 10 –

I reach a tree and am sick again and again and again until my body is just retching with incredible violence but there is no more to vomit into the receiving earth.

– Do you feel better now? No. No. I don't feel better. I feel worse. I'm shaking. I'm sweating. I can't see any visions. Just the swaying ground –

I fall back from my hands and knees into the yoga 'recovery position'. I put my forehead on the earth, breathing heavily. I lie in the mud panting.

– Just stay here a bit. THIS TOO WILL PASS – Anicha.

– Change your focus. Think. Think of home. The kitchen floor. Yes, very soon you'll be sweeping the kitchen floor. There is that bit of wood that needs fixing under the kitchen cabinet. Keep breathing. The oxygen will help. The oxygen isn't poisonous –

Dilwyn's voice from nowhere. 'Let me help you back.'

'I can't stand up.'

'Yes, you can. Give me your hand.'

I reach out and he pulls me up. I grab on to him with both hands and he leads me back, my body still retching. 'Lie down,' he says.

'I can't lie down. I feel so sick.'

'I don't think your body has any more to throw out, Isabel. Just sit on your sleeping bag for a while, then.'

I can do that. I can sit here.

– Oh, God, this is worse than I've felt in my whole life. This is some version of hell –

What are those whimpering noises?

– It's you –

I am lucid enough to make sure that they aren't loud enough to disturb Alex or Jeremy on either side of me. Perhaps they are just loud enough for me to understand what I've done to myself.

– Lie down. But every time I try to lie back down I just feel worse –

– Lie on your back, shut up, breathe normally and watch the pictures –

– Fuck the pictures –

I try to lie down and it makes me retch again. I see Jeremy nervously moving away from me. I speak to him quite lucidly. 'Don't worry, Jeremy, I'm not going to be sick over you.' I lie down and close my eyes. Still whizzing circles, disassociated voices.

Then there is Emily sitting watching me rather despairingly. She seems to be saying, 'Oh, Mother! What are you doing now? Look at this mess you've got yourself into.' Last time she seemed surprised to be there herself, taking my hand in a circle of dancing Incas. But now she looks positively uninterested, as if she has better things to do than to come and take care of me all night. But then she says loud and clear, 'Of course I'm here. Of course I love you.'

– Why did she say that? I didn't ask. But is anyone else here to help me?

I look around in my head and see Jaime, our host, quite clearly. That's nice. Obviously he feels that his duties as host extend to this realm too. He looks at me. A steady, calm, kind presence.

– Who else is here? What about Viv? Hello? Viv? Nope – can't see him. Can't hear him ... but strangely I feel that he may be here in some sense, just not showing himself. And there is another man I love, who was once called Harry, he's here too – but hiding. Not speaking, not showing his face, yet it feels as if he's here. And then there are other faces, strangers, people I don't recognize. How strange. Who are these people?

– I feel so ill. Oh, God, everything in my stomach feels putrid –

– Go and shit!

Oh, God, where did that voice in my head come from?

– Do you have to be so vulgar?

– MOVE. I can't walk. Crawl, then –

So once again I crawl, like a sick dog, stopping every three paces to rest and pant.

– Up to the tree. Can't get that far. Over there by the bushes. It's OK by the bushes. Jeremy says it's good for the plants –

I pull off some clothes. Now it's coming out both ends. All dignity is gone.

Dilwyn's voice. 'Not there. You have to go into the undergrowth.'

'I can't get that far.'

He takes my hand, even as it's all in process.

'Behind that tree, then.'

I'm on my knees now, trying to ensure I at least stay clean. Crawling forwards all the time and then kneeling back in the recovery position to breathe. Breathe slowly. The air is your friend.

All the time the observer watches. Unconcerned.

Dilwyn's voice. 'Get up now. You can't stay here in the earth.' I pull at my clothes. He pulls me up and leads me back. I have to hold on to him with both hands. Part of me feels like crying, but I don't have the energy. I feel so awful.

'Can I have a hug?' I say, although Dilwyn and I had never

met before this trip and there is no element of touch in our new friendship.

'Of course you can.' And he lets me hold on to him for a little human warmth and contact, even though I am still retching violently as he hugs me. Then I realize he's laughing.

'Why are you laughing?'

'Well, you're not afraid at all, are you?'

'Afraid? No. Half dead? Yes.'

'It's just when I'm that ill it always scares me. You're amazing.' Am I scared? Of the inside of my head? No. I feel quite safe with him and with Noemi. It wasn't their intention that I should have such a bad time.

'I just feel so ill. So, so, so ill. I never knew that it was possible to feel this bad.'

'Lie down now. Listen to the singing.' I crawl into the sleeping bag and close my eyes. I promise you, Isabel, I will never do this again. I will never never ever do this again. It will pass. I will pass. I want to promise, here and now – to all of you, to you, Emily, to me, to everyone here – people are here that I don't know – and you out there – anyway – whoever you are – I will never do this to myself again.

never,

never,

never. OK, got it.

Why aren't I scared? I am experiencing, in full technicolour, one aspect of what Mooji teaches. This is not happening to 'me'. Or the 'me' that this is happening to is observed and there is another 'I' in that place, untouchably beyond all this. It's only my body that is poisoned. I'm neither of these, so how can I be afraid? My body has to rescue itself. I'm not in control.

– My hands feel as though they are going to explode. I'm so hot. Sweating so much. What's that whimpering noise? It's you – you're still making whimpering noises. Stop it. I really want to howl like a sick dog. No. Not a good idea. Don't do that. I will never do this again. Yes, you said. What's that weird high-pitched noise? That's Noemi singing. That's what you are supposed to be listening to. I don't want to listen to it any more. It brings me back to the psychedelics inside my head and how sick I feel. Is it inside my head, that noise, or outside? Oh, God, when will this pass?

I open my eyes. Alex seems to be lying beside me, quite still, with a blissful smile on his face. Jeremy, on the other side, is curled up with his back to me.

– I think I'm going to be sick again. I don't care. It won't hurt anyone. Lie down again. Do I have to move? It can't feel worse than this. Breathe deeply. I'm so hot. I'm burning up –

Then suddenly Noemi is beside me. She lifts up my top and sprays something from her mouth all over my heart chakra – that's the little bit between your breasts that hurts when someone you love goes away.

– Oh, God, she's spitting on me. What's the witch doing now? She's cooling you down, Isabel –

She does it again, spraying liquid from her lips, lower down over my diaphragm. She seems to have a way of spitting that sprays all over my stomach. She rubs it all over the front of me, up and down.

284

Suddenly I start to shiver. I'm freezing.

– Pull up the sleeping bag, Isabel –

She's still spraying me. A fourth and fifth time. I pull the sleeves of my top down. It feels wet under my top. I feel like a petulant child. I don't want her cold spit on me. I wipe it off with my sleeve.

– Get into the sleeping bag. Keep still. Breathe. When am I going to stop feeling so awful? Try and go to sleep now. THIS TOO WILL PASS. I'm never going to put anything bad inside my body ever again –

Somewhere a quiet whimpering sound is still going on. Lightning starts to flash across the sky. Thunder in the distance. More streaks of white until I don't know whether my eyes are open or closed. But then I feel one tear that falls onto the outside of my eyelid. Rain.

Dilwyn's voice: 'We'll have to go back to the tents.'

– Get up. Good God, my legs are working again. I feel sick. Yes – but my legs are working –

– Pick up your sleeping bag. Pick up the mat. Follow Jeremy now. One foot, now the other. Well done –

God, I'm glad to walk away from that. Dogs bark as we pass other huts in the middle of the night. Bats fly above us. Drops of rain fall.

The tent. Somehow I unzip the tent, crawl in and get into my sleeping bag. Close the door. Keep the bugs out. I look around in my mind for a man I can summon up to come and put an arm round me. 'Are you here?' I ask. He's here.

'I wouldn't normally do this,' he says, 'but I'll make an

exception tonight. Someone has to take care of you.'

And I smile to see that a man I have no right to call on has showed up in spite of himself. Who knows what is real and what isn't? What dimension is which? What reality is anyway? Or who I'm not?

'I'm never, never doing that again,' I tell him, and, with a smile on my face, finally, I fall asleep.

Fifth Dawn

The following morning someone awakens and – writing nothing about the night before – starts writing from that moment.

I feel as if I want to turn into a vicious snake today. I want to bite and snap and hiss at everyone. I want to allow myself appalling behaviour that I never indulge in and never normally want to. I want to be rude and aggressive and upset people. I want to walk out of the tent and say, 'What the fuck?'

Part of me feels like a dog that was promised a special meal and gobbled it down trustingly only to find that it had been horribly poisoned. That's not so much what I feel like – that's what happened.

But of course I do not allow a vicious snake to crawl out of the tent. Just a battered Isabel.

'How are you this morning?' asks Dilwyn, looking full of the joys of spring, as if he's just heard that he had a large win on the lottery.

'I'm glad to be alive, Dilwyn,' I say, quite calmly.

He misses, or ignores, the strong undercurrent of hissing.

'Glad to be alive is good.' He pauses and looks at me. 'It's good – to be glad to be alive.'

'Yes.'

Alex is up chatting about what an amazingly good experience he's had, the wonderful clarity of the visions. First of all, he tells a story that seems to have the quality of cinema shot on very good quality film. He is being led away by three beautiful women who he later realizes are sirens. 'Noemi came to me in that world to warn me and rescue me.' Then his vision moves into an experience of the eternal – teaching him that he doesn't need to fear eternity. He's exhilarated, excited; I peer at him through my snake-like consciousness with a mixture of irritation, indignation, envy and admiration. He has certainly had a different experience from my all-night puking session. His enthusiasm is 100 per cent and he's hardly experienced any sickness at all. If I were a rattlesnake, I'd rattle at him.

Then Noemi turns up and I think, 'Ah, the old witch is here,' but I can't maintain this level of venom. She doesn't look like a witch anyway, she doesn't even look like a shaman, she looks like a tiny little Ashaninka woman of about 70. She has come to see how I am. It turns out that what she sprayed onto me was a tobacco mixture.

'That shamanic healing she did on you – I've taken ayahuasca about sixty times and I've never seen her do that with anyone before,' says Dilwyn. Fantastic. I have so many outstanding skills. Being sicker than anyone in 30 years is a new one, but fairly typical of me. I was the only one of our party to nearly die of altitude sickness in Tibet. It's good to know that you have talents and abilities.

'It worked, whatever she did. I was so hot I was sweating all over. I felt as if I was burning up. She sprayed that tobacco mixture over me and I was shivering in about two seconds. I don't understand. How did it cool me down so completely and so effectively? It was only on the surface of my skin.'

'You don't end where your skin ends, Isabel.'

'So she was treating what the New Agers call my astral body?'

'That as well, yes.'

I'm not angry with her, or with Dilwyn, or with anyone anymore. I've survived. They had all wanted me to have a good experience.

'It was so awful, Dilwyn. So bad that if you offered me a billion pounds to do it again, I'd still say no. No ... no ... no ... never. It wasn't the mind stuff. That was fascinating and, as you said, I wasn't afraid of that internal chainsaw at all. Actually,' I smile, interrupting myself, 'that's a really good description of the experience. But I never realized that nausea could be so ... SO intense that I honestly wouldn't take a billion pounds to go through it again. It was beyond my awareness of how awful I could feel.'

Jeremy's sitting listening with his head buried in his hands. He had a lot of sickness too, but was just more of a man about it all.

'Funny thing, I took the same as you in the same amount and I wasn't sick at all,' says Dilwyn.

'You're joking. You were so lucid last night I thought you hadn't taken anything.'

'No, I took plenty, and had some amazing visions too.'

I sigh. But we go down to swim in the Rio Mamiri: a true paradise on earth, clear running river water under lush overhanging trees, bright red and peacock-blue butterflies and the perpetual summer sound of sunbathing crickets. And as I splash about naked in the deep, cool water, I start to calm down and be happy again. It's not during Vipassana or under ayahuasca, but here, that the snake leaves me.

That day, a family that lives in another part of the village invites us for a farewell lunch. They serve the homemade beer that they chew and spit into to prepare, and some poor chicken has been killed in our honour, although its sacrifice is pointless in my case; I pretend to eat it, sneak the meat back onto the platter and wickedly throw a bone, unseen, to a passing dog while it still has some meat on it.

As it turns out, I'm the entertainment again. At one point a group of women are looking at me and laughing unashamedly. I'm not even trying to be funny.

'What is it?' I insist that Dilwyn find out. 'What exactly are they laughing at?'

He speaks to them amid more laughter.

'They are laughing at all your insect bites. They say that the insects must be biting you because they have never seen anything like you before.'

They evidently think this hysterical. Although I must admit that my bites are good entertainment ... about 63 of them and a fair percentage oozing with yellow pus.

'And they are laughing that you will go back and say that they have biting insects in this part of the jungle, although this area is famous for not having any.'

'It's a personality defect, Dilwyn.' I can't help laughing with them as their laughter is so infectious.

'And they were wondering,' laughs Dilwyn, 'how you got on with the ayahuasca?'

I oblige them with puking and farting noises. More laughter.

'They would like to see more of your experience.'

OK, I can perform if called on to do so. I get to my feet and move to an area where they can all see me. With full sound effects I do the puking performance for them, re-creating with some enthusiasm the retching noises before the puking. Then I fall to my knees and do a grand imitation of a mammoth shitting, rocking backwards on my knees. I lean forwards again with more varied puking sounds, backwards to more shitting sounds, before staggering back to my place as if I have lost the use of my legs.

They have clearly never been treated to a performance of this kind before. Presumably previous Western visitors maintained some dignity. Anyway, I have won approval from them and maybe even a little sympathy. And I'm laughing, too, at this absurd Western woman covered in bites who couldn't even keep down one gourd full of ayahuasca without nearly killing herself.

Then Noemi comes around and, as they finish off the

remains of the poor dead chicken and I eat up the manioc and bananas, she paints my face anew with a wonderful red pattern. Maybe, just maybe, she feels bad that I had such an awful night. They say that everyone on ayahuasca has just the experience that they need – the perfect experience for them. So maybe I had the experience I needed to be able to say to you – with 100 per cent conviction – do come here, come to the jungle and learn how to live off the land. Do not, if you want my unsolicited advice, swallow or consume in any way, for any reason or on any occasion, class A drugs. Maybe those classifications, so hated by the young and trendy who wish to experience these things, are also put there as a warning and as a protection? Maybe if people have decided, 'This stuff is dangerous,' they are not just small-minded officials wanting the populace to conform? Maybe they are experientially inexperienced lawmakers and it may still be a good idea to listen to them.

That afternoon we do the three-hour walk back to the bone-shaking car-sized plane. Children four foot high and with bare feet carry all our bags while I clamber up and down hills and, at one point, through a river, without removing my boots. I am quietly determined to get out without twisting or breaking an ankle. When we arrive at the home of the chief who looks after the airport, in a moment of true magic, Noemi is there. It seems that she insisted on being brought down the river by canoe to see us off. We all sit down and share a meal, and there are one or two people at the table who speak both Ashaninka and Spanish. There is a brief opportunity for some limited and indirect conversation, and she seems to be trying to take it.

'Noemi is asking what you saw in the visions.' Maybe I won't try and explain about the gay man in the cowboy hat, the pop boxes of healthy food and the sugar necklaces. 'Mainly just spinning pictures, psychedelics, images that made no sense to me. It was all very confused.'

'She says that it was only when the thunder and lightning came that you started to get better. The thunder and lightning are the owners of ayahuasca. We thought it was going to rain more but it just danced around us in a circle and rained just a little. It wasn't necessary to rain, it seems.'

Ah, dancing in circles like the mythological figures in my first visions. I look at the deep mystery in this old lady's eyes. What can I say to this figure in my life's dream? She is trying, in some way, to talk with me, her world to mine, two languages, two cultures, a continent and about 5,000 years apart.

They have set up a generator that Sky TV left in this village. Once or twice a year they put it on to cool down beer for visitors. Now it's shining a bright light in my face, so, although my every expression is fully lit for her, to me she appears just as a dark and mysterious silhouette emerging from the jungle behind.

'Could you please ask them to translate, Dilwyn? Could you please tell her that I am very glad to have met her in this lifetime?'

They translate and she takes my hands and speaks to me.

'She says that you are very welcome to return.'

I smile, shake her hands and thank her. I am thinking – that's lovely but not for all the tea in China and all the coffee in Brazil, not for all the spiritual riches of the universe could I be persuaded to taste her brew again. But later, as I sit in the tiny plane, looking down at the incredible beauty of the jungle and the Amazon, I realize that in the rush to sort the bags out and load the plane, I left without saying good-bye to her. I feel an almost overwhelming sense of loss.

'Dilwyn,' I shout over the noise of the engine. 'Noemi – I didn't say good-bye.'

'Don't worry. They don't really do good-byes.'

It makes sense. If they place no importance on the 'I', who do you say good-bye to?

So here is my body back in Satipo. I found an Internet café today and Facebooked Emily to thank her for showing up in her astral body to look after me when I needed support and reassurance.

'You said, "Of course I love you."'

'Glad I was able to help. Incidentally, in my astral body – did I have a good outfit?'

Epilogue

S o now I'm back in London, on the Battersea Park Road sorting all this out. The first thing I've noticed is the reaction of friends when I tell them what I've done. Typically it is something like, 'Oh, my God! I could never take anything like that. I would never dare. I'd be far too terrified.' But of course it isn't the thought of the extreme nausea that horrifies them.

What they are afraid of is losing control of their own minds, or of having control of their minds taken from them; of demons that they fear live outside or inside them coming, as they sometimes do in nightmares, and trying to devour them, or scaring them to hell – or to what feels like hell.

In listening to my friends, I am beginning to understand what I have learnt, and it all fits together perfectly. What fascinates me when I look back is the different inner voices I experienced that seem to belong to different levels of consciousness. Some of them are obviously superficial – the chatter as if from two sides of my own head: 'Get up. I can't, I feel too sick.' They seem to be the mind playing with itself. There are different levels of consciousness, perhaps: a voice more like the child, a voice with greater wisdom; still different aspects of what we call ourselves. But there is a deeper place – there really is – that just observes all this, and it is unchanging, ever steady and ever secure. The experience of being that observer meant that I was never really scared. Superficially, yes, but I knew that 'I' couldn't be reached by nausea. And, just as Mooji says, peace comes from knowing that we are each that observer. Even if my mind had been damaged by an internal chainsaw, there would still be an observer within, observing the damaged mind, who is at peace – who is the ocean – really there is. One trick is not to mistake our thoughts for who we are.

Once upon a time, I ran a leadership course for teenagers. It was a residential course at St Donat's Castle in Llantwit Major, on the coast, in Wales. The teenagers were full of concerned responsibility for their lives – a conscientious group that wanted to make good decisions, and unbelievably stressed for that reason. So, having done some simple work on goals, I gave them some homework one day that boggled some of their hectic, overloaded inner-city minds. 'Take your goals and dreams,' I instructed, 'and I'd like you to go to the beach with them, sit down somewhere and discuss them with the sea.'

I had already won their trust earlier in the week, so they were ready to try out my crazy suggestions. They came back the following day and I smiled at them. 'So? How was the homework?'

'The sea didn't listen,' said one, 'it just went on being the sea.'

I laughed. 'Yes, it does that, doesn't it? Anyone else?'

'I found that the sea did listen – but it was just like talking to myself,' said another.

My daughter was there and, being conscious that she was my daughter and not wanting to stand out too much for that reason, she had been atypically quiet. Now she raised her hand.

'Yes, Emily?'

'I agree that it was like talking to myself. But it was the best and the wisest part of myself.'

Perhaps it is this unchanging state of peacefulness within that Feng Shui is gently trying to point us towards. It uses the elements that I have been considering to enable us to create an environment around ourselves that brings us back to this awareness. As if, in the very placement of objects around us in our home, we are whispered back to 'Be at peace,' 'Be balanced,' 'Do not be too distracted by the cares of the mind – the thoughts that come and go.' This is the energy of the element of metal, to protect, and is representative of the exterior, our skin, our boundaries and the breath we take. Can we breathe – take in and let go – in the place where we live? Well, it's vital, innit?

And then there is the role of fire. All that 'You can create the life you want' school of thought – from the most basic, 'write a list of goals and then go and do them', to the more mystical 'you create your reality based on your beliefs' – all these ideas have great value. If you want to change the world, sort out knife crime in the inner city, then the law of action is what you need. I love Anthony Robbins and all that he advocates. I love all those teachers who encourage us to take complete responsibility for our lives, never blame others, never blame external circumstances or make excuses for ourselves – to set clear targets, get our exercise, jolly well drink our wheat grass and then go after them. Make no excuses – just do it! That school of thought has helped me achieve great things in my own life. It is full of heart, of energy, of impetuousness. I adore all that fire energy, all that is red and vibrant – go, Anthony!

But it has limits that Mr Robbins doesn't mention. You cannot – however much you want it, visualize it, work for it and pray for it – create everything that you want in your life. Lots of people read *The Secret* and decided that they would like to be millionaires but are still broke. And even those of us who may have more achievable goals still don't always get what we want. Some women can't conceive, and no matter how much they visualize babies, it just doesn't happen. Some people have legs that don't work and can't walk, no matter how much they want to.

There is a school of thought (and I don't think Anthony is part of it, but I believe the first Feng Shui man who came to see me was) that claims we create our experience to learn lessons from it. I do not subscribe to this. Some of us get cancer, but I don't believe that we create it because we 'need the lesson', even if many who have suffered in this way can see how they have learnt and grown as a result of the experience. That's not the same. Learning from something that just shows up is not the same as believing ourselves responsible for having created it. Some things we're not responsible for.

Last night I had a phone call from someone who asked me if I'd 'met anyone significant' in the jungle. By which she meant, of course, had I had sex with someone and, if so, was it with someone I was now going to be spending the rest of my life with? A tall order, I think, for a week or so in the jungle. I explained that it had been a very small trip, the organizer was very happily married and my other two companions were aged 24 and 64. Now – listen carefully! She told me that if this was so, then, 'You created it like that because you don't want a relationship.' Now, this was not someone pulling my leg. This is the now amazingly widespread belief (the same one that the first

Feng Shui man was using to blame me for odd corners in my house) that each of us creates everything in our lives.

This, I think, is an absurd, dangerous and egotistical corruption of the ancient Buddhist teaching, 'It is your mind that creates this world.' 'Mind' may create the world, but to say 'my' mind creates it all has led to gross misunderstanding.

Yes, my beliefs influence my experience. If I expect the world to be good to me, it often will be. It's the vibe, or as the New Agers would say, the 'vibration' that I give off. If I expect the world to attack me and be against me, then I will interpret the world in that way. Someone will make a careless comment and I will take it personally, interpret it negatively and build my consciousness accordingly. Yes, of course our beliefs influence the way we see and the way that we are seen.

But! Am I really egotistical enough to believe that Alex had not been planning his trip around the world for a year before I even thought of going to the jungle? That Jeremy's desire to experience people living from nature was, in any way, my creation? It's utterly ludicrous to take it that far. All those of us who take an interest in alternative ways of perceiving our lives must be aware of this. Surely?

I have learnt this at my cost by losing much of what I had worked hard for, prayed for, and believed with all my heart would be good for me and good for the universe and everyone and everything in it. But still the universe did not listen to Isabel. Can you imagine?! I ended up feeling hurt and let down, not by any human being, but by a universe that had not given me my heart's greatest desires nor even allowed me to complete the hugely worthwhile projects that I had striven to create.

So, while all this creating what we want in our lives and taking action is fantastic, there is also the law of inaction. We are told that the journey, for a contemplative person, is towards nothing. And that is the balance for all of us who try to live a spiritual life. The element of wood represents this strategy. I read once, 'This element houses the soul': it's about how to get the balance right, when to swim like fuck against the tide and when to let the river carry you along in the direction the river wants to go in. There is the law of not pushing the river – just resting, splashing your feet a bit and seeing what happens. The law of just being. That wonderful old teaching, 'Don't just do something, sit there.'

This is what Vipassana points to. By making you just sit there and not move. And, no, I didn't like the course – but after ten days of sitting, I was still, and yes, I'd learned as an experience and not just as a concept that I am not my body. I am not my thoughts. I knew this intellectually before, but Vipassana shows you this experientially (for no charge), and in spite of all the things I didn't like, it did teach me to be still. It put my mind into overdrive – and sleep and rebellion – but also taught me how much that part of us which we call 'the mind' will fight when we tell ourselves to just sit down and shut up. Wood grows slowly but knows its direction. It is energetic but gently powerful, unlike the fire energy that says, 'I think I'll rush here and see what happens.' Wood just sits ... and slowly and imperceptibly grows.

Then suddenly water. Suddenly Mooji – like a clear, fresh

drink from a mountain stream. Water is powerful and gentle, gives life, sustains and prevails. Somehow I get to meet this remarkable loving energy and he laughs at my complaints that the universe is not complying with my wishes. An incarnation of an ocean laughing at my resistance to the whole concept of doing nothing, as if I were a wave that wants to rush off by itself without being aware that it is part of the ocean. Or that it is the ocean.

I wrote to one friend, 'Mooji seems to be suggesting that the world can turn without me providing the energy. Can you imagine?'

'He is clearly a charlatan,' she replied.

Ha ha. I guess the laugh is on me.

And then finally to consider earth in the womb of the jungle. Earth represents the mother and transformation. I feel as if I went to meet the mother. Or at any rate 'a' mother. And it was certainly a transformative experience, albeit not quite what I had anticipated. 'Let's just lie Isabel down and show her that we can kidnap her mind and body and she's still there.' So that now when people talk to me about not feeling safe in themselves, I wonder that they don't seem to have an awareness of this place within that already seems so familiar to me, this silent and confident observer that is unchanging despite all the madness of the mind.

From that place, anything that happens tomorrow seems irrelevant. This doesn't discount planning and dreaming, but none of our tomorrows exist until they arrive, do they? Most people are wiser than I am and they know, if they make a plan, that some unforeseen event may come up and scupper it.

Viv is coming to spend the day with me tomorrow and I'm so free of any expectation, either positive or negative, that I'm amusing myself. It will be wonderful to see him. And, yes, it will be lovely to see his lips too. But I genuinely feel that I can just enjoy the present moment. If I choose to, I can imagine good or bad outcomes to either dating him or not dating him. So I will meet him again just in the present. All new.

And as for being here, in London's Battersea, in a hole ... what hole? I wonder why I fretted so much about a hole that I'd made up in the first place. It's true that if we want to achieve something we need a clear idea of what it is and then to take action. The law of taking action still does get results – just not always the results that we want, dammit.

And what if Mooji's question, 'Who are you anyway?' really is the most important one? Who are we beyond our mind, our memory, our conditioning, desires and attachments? Who is the one that watches? What if we are indeed 'being lived' rather than being right in our egotistical view that we have control over anything at all? What if we are all being lived by the same consciousness and so really are all one? What if we don't have the control over ourselves that we think that we have? If you think you are in control of your body – try having a baby. If you think you are in control of your mind – go to Peru and swallow some ayahuasca. Sure, it made me sick, but it was worth it for the lesson. I am not in charge. Whoever 'I' is.

And once we have sorted out our relationship with ourselves and experienced that we are eternal and unchanging (that sounds hard but it isn't – if I can do it then anyone can), then there is getting our feet back on the ground. And once we are standing there firmly, we have to build community again.

Isn't it ironic that the Ashaninka tribe are, in so many ways, living more happily from the land than most of us are living in our boxes in our towns and cities? They live simply and with the people they love around them. We have to learn to love and cherish one another. We have to bring people together. We have to hold parties – not the kind where people drink, but the kind where people listen to each other, where real friendships are made. And it's no good waiting for someone else to build community. As the great teachers say – find one or two like-minded people and do it yourself. And don't hang about. Life is short.

I did not set out to change who I am in the hole. In fact, if you had told me when I set out that the change would be in me, I would have screamed with rage. I just wanted to get out of the hole. But now I look around and the hole that I was in has quite simply ceased to be. I have got myself back on the road again simply by changing my relationship with this 'Isabel' thing. Whoever she is – your narrator.

And if the part of the ocean that is me has, at any point, made the part that is you smile, then the Isabel wave splashes extra foam in the sunshiny air for joy. And if you are clever enough to have learnt anything useful from being here, then I bow with gratitude. Namaste. Write to me. I'm found easily, virtually, on the www.

I have 30 people coming to my home next month to sing

African songs together. Very few of them will have met before –
should be interesting. Everything is changing at the house and
I haven't done anything to bring this about. Emily is earning
enough money that she's giving me the large bedroom back
and moving in with some friends. Simon the lodger is leaving
and instead I have two amazing women moving in. I'm afraid
that, being a nonfiction writer, I can't give you the romantic
'tie-up' so sought after by publishers. I am not walking along the
sand at dusk with Viv. Real life rarely has neat endings.

One New York literary agent said, on reading a draft of this
book, 'But what about the romantic narrative? What about Viv?
Or, I thought I sensed the beginning of a possibility with Mooji?'
Ha ha. She wants me to date the guru? Along with the other
million women and men in the world who love him, I assume?
Or am I to bend Viv to fit the needs of my story? It would be
useful sometimes if, like writers of fiction, we could 'develop the
characters' in our lives along lines that suit us. I could have
written, 'And now we have decided to take up the study of erotic
massage.' But, wonderful as some of my choices would be, no,
thank you – I'll take nonfiction and a life in which I am not in
control. We can't develop the storyline of the characters in our
lives; our job is more demanding. It is simply to love them.

As to the events and vicissitudes of life, all the things that
happen to us or don't happen to us – happy is the person who
can celebrate and love all of them.

I have to stop writing now because I have a lunch invitation.
I met a man last week who has been kind enough to invite me
out to a local restaurant. He is 92.

'I was born in 1918, Isabel. Ask me what I have learnt.'

'What have you learnt, Jack?'

'I have learnt that we are nothing.' He smiles at me. It is a positive statement. I smile back.

'And everything?'

'Yes. And everything.'

'Anything else you've learnt?'

'Yes. It's important to be kind. But you know that, don't you?'

'Yes, Jack.'

FURTHER READING/
RESEARCH/INVOLVEMENT

Isabel Losada has a website and current links to everything in this book can be found there at www.isabellosada.com. Isabel has a strange tendency to reply to many of the e-mails she receives.

If you would like to experience anything in this book, details of how you can do that is all in the section of the website that relates to *Battersea Park Road to Paradise*.

Links to the books in this section can also be found there.

If you have enjoyed this book or any of Isabel's other books, she invites you to place your review on Amazon or on Waterstones.com. She reads every review and considers all feedback.

Isabel also has a fan page on Facebook (www.facebook.com/authorisabellosada) where she is often found chatting to readers about the subjects in her books. Readers also talk to each other. Extraordinary friendships have been formed, across the UK and across the world.

Life really is stranger than fiction.

FURTHER READING

The First Element

The Feng Shui Doctor: Ancient Skills for Modern Living, by Paul
Darby (Duncan Baird Publishers, 2007).

*The Feng Shui Bible: The Definitive Guide to Improving Your
Life, Health, Home and Finances*, by Simon Brown
(Godsfield Press, 2005).

Feng Shui in a Weekend, by Simon Brown (Hamlyn, 2002).

Lillian Too's Little Book of Feng Shui, by Lillian Too (Konsep
Lagenda, 1998).

*Feng Shui Made Easy: Designing Your Life with the Ancient Art
of Placement*, by William Spear (North Atlantic Books,
2010).

Feng Shui for Dummies, by Grandmaster Lin Yun and David
Daniel Kennedy (John Wiley and Sons, 2011).

The Second Element

Unlimited Power: The New Science of Personal Achievement, by
Anthony Robbins (Pocket Books, 2001).

*Awaken the Giant Within: How to Take Immediate Control of
your Mental, Emotional, Physical and Financial Life*, by
Anthony Robbins (Pocket Books, 2001).

Giant Steps: Small Changes to Make a Big Difference, by
Anthony Robbins (Pocket Books, 2001).

Tony rarely comes to the UK any more to do live work. But if
he is anywhere in Europe it will say so on his website:

www.tonyrobbins.com. On this site you can also get a
sense of the general Anthony Robbins energy. Love him or
hate him (I do both), he leaves you with no excuses.
Similar seminars in the UK are now being done by the big-
hearted Joseph McClendon.

The Third Element

I wouldn't recommend these books unless you also do the
course – which, on reflection, I do recommend! It's hard – but
worth it.

*The Art of Living: Vipassana Meditation as Taught by S. N.
Goenka*, by William Hart (HarperSanFrancisco, 1987).

Beyond the Breath, by Mark Glickman (Tuttle Publishing,
2002).

*Discourse Summaries: Talks from a Ten-Day Course in Vipassana
Meditation*, by S N Goenka and William Hart (Pariyatti
Press, 2001).

The brief story about the Karmapa that I remember in this
chapter can also be found in *The Power of Compassion:
Stories that Open the Heart, Heal the Soul, and Change the
World*, by Pamela Bloom (Hampton Roads, 2010).

Teach Us to Sit Still, by Tim Parks (Harvill Secker, Random
House, 2010).

The Fourth Element

*Before I Am: The Direct Recognition of Our Original Self –
Dialogues with Mooji* (Stone Hill Foundation Publishing
2008).

*Breath of the Absolute: The Manifest and Unmanifest Are One –
Dialogues with Mooji*, edited by Zenji and Manjusri (Yogi
Impressions, 2010).

The above two books can be most easily bought via
www.mooji.org/shop.

I Am That: Talks with Sri Nisargadatta Maharaj, by Sri
Nisargadatta Maharaj, translated by Maurice Frydman
(Acorn Press, 1990).

I Am That I Am: A Tribute to Sri Nisargadatta Maharaj, by
Stephen Wolinsky (Quantum Institute, 2006).

A New Earth: Awakening to Your Life's Purpose, by Eckhart Tolle
(Penguin, 2006).

Some music: Omkara writes her own music and often sings
at Mooji's Satsangs. Utterly wonderful and you can hear
short clips from each track on this site too –
www.cdbaby.com/artist/omkara2.

The Fifth Element

The Continuum Concept, by Jean Liedloff (Penguin, 2004).

The Cosmic Serpent: DNA and the Origins of Knowledge, by
Jeremy Narby (Tarcher, 2000).

*Salt of the Mountain: Campa Ashaninka History and Resistance
in the Peruvian Jungle*, by Stefano Varese, translated by
Susan Rascon (University of Oklahoma Press, 2004).

*The Transition Handbook: From Oil Dependency to Local
Resilience*, by Rob Hopkins (Green Books, 2008).

Ayahuasca Reader: Encounters with Amazon's Sacred Vine,
edited by Luis Eduardo Luna and Steven F White

(Synergetic Press Inc., 2000). Lots of firsthand reports
from shamans

*Vine of the Soul: Medicine Men, Their Plants and Rituals in the
Colombian Amazonia*, by Richard Evans Schultes
(Synergetic Press Inc., 2004). A medium-format book with
great photos from the world's top ethnobotanical specialist
on this plant.

Breaking Open the Head, by Daniel Pinchbeck (Flamingo,
2010). The best general overview of modern and ancient
use of consciousness-expanding plants and chemicals.

The Rough Guide to Peru, by Dilwyn Jenkins (Rough Guides,
2009).

Travel and/or Supporting the Ashaninka

If you would like to be considered as a candidate to go and live
with the Ashaninka yourself or would like to buy simple
products that they have made, look here: www.ecotribal.com.

If you want to protect a tree or save an acre of rainforest,
look here: www.coolearth.org. Cool Earth don't just say that they
protect the rainforest – they are out there doing it. I know, as I've
seen the trees planted by donors and seen areas that have been
protected from loggers with my own eyes.

If you are interested in learning more about the protection of
tribal peoples, please look here: www.survivalinternational.org.